THE FUTURE
OF
HUMAN
EXPERIENCE

"Zohara interweaves the conscious and subconscious, rational and intuitive; she combines science and art to blaze a trail from the past, through the present, into the future . . . a must read for anyone interested in the destiny of our planet."

JOHN PERKINS, *NEW YORK TIMES* BESTSELLING AUTHOR

"*The Future of Human Experience* provides a concise introduction to current out-of-the-box thinking on the fundamental and timeless topics of the nature of consciousness and humanity's relationship to the Earth and Cosmos. The innovative, controversial, and penetrating ideas presented in this book should surely make you think and react!"

ROBERT M. SCHOCH, PH.D., AUTHOR OF *FORGOTTEN CIVILIZATION: THE ROLE OF SOLAR OUTBURSTS IN OUR PAST AND FUTURE*

"*The Future of Human Experience* brings readers a message of wisdom and hope for the 21st century and beyond. Zohara has interviewed several thinkers and writers who are on the cutting edge of human knowledge. She has pulled together their comments into a carefully crafted blueprint for a balanced world that combines science and spirit, technological advances, and traditional wisdom."

STANLEY KRIPPNER, PH.D., COAUTHOR OF *THE VOICE OF ROLLING THUNDER*

WHAT OTHERS HAVE SAID ABOUT AUTHOR AND BROADCASTER ZOHARA HIEROINMUS, D.H.L.

"Zohara is always in front of the curve of innovation. She identifies and deciphers trends so the rest of us better understand the future."

DR. MEHMET OZ

"Zohara is a true futurist and a visionary like Alvin Toffler, the author of *Future Shock*. Zohara was years ahead of her time in the past century, and she predicted exactly what we face today in the 21st century. I consider her work a must for anyone who wants to understand what's happening today and what is in store for us tomorrow. Zohara is the source of information if you want to know where our brave new world is heading and, more importantly, why."

CHARLES R. SMITH, JOURNALIST, AND PRESIDENT
AND CEO OF SOFTWAR

". . . No one surpasses Zohara's keen intellect and penetrating insight. Zohara is a treasure."

LARRY DOSSEY, M.D., AUTHOR OF
HEALING WORDS AND *ONE MIND*

"Zohara is a natural talent. I am delighted to support Zohara's creative endeavors."

CAROLINE MYSS, AUTHOR OF *SACRED CONTRACTS*

"Zohara is exceptionally talented, intelligent, compassionate and wise."

DIANA VON WELANETZ WENTWORTH,
AUTHOR, PUBLIC SPEAKER, TELEVISION HOST

"A Renaissance woman."

JUDY COLLINS

"A visionary."

INGO SWANN, PSYCHIC

THE FUTURE OF HUMAN EXPERIENCE

VISIONARY THINKERS ON THE SCIENCE OF CONSCIOUSNESS

J. ZOHARA MEYERHOFF HIERONIMUS, D.H.L.

Destiny Books
Rochester, Vermont • Toronto, Canada

Destiny Books
One Park Street
Rochester, Vermont 05767
www.DestinyBooks.com

The text stock is SFI certified.

Destiny Books is a division of Inner Traditions International

Library of Congress Cataloging-in-Publication Data

Hieronimus, J. Zohara Meyerhoff.
  The future of human experience : visionary thinkers on the science of
consciousness / J. Zohara Meyerhoff Hieronimus, D.H.L.
    pages cm
  Includes bibliographical references and index.
  Summary: "Explores the future predictions of cutting-edge scientists, spiritual
teachers, and other visionaries and how we can affect the future"— Provided by
publisher.
  ISBN 978-1-62055-087-8(pk.) — ISBN 978-1-62055-136-3 (e-book)
1. Technology—Social aspects. 2. Science—Social aspects. 3. Technological
forecasting. 4. Consciousness. I. Title.
  T14.5.H545 2013
  303.48'3—dc23
                                                              2012045856

Printed and bound in the United States by Lake Book Manufacturing, Inc.
The text stock is SFI certified. The Sustainable Forestry Initiative® program
promotes sustainable forest management.

10 9 8 7 6 5 4 3 2 1

Text design and layout by Brian Boynton
This book was typeset in Garamond Premier Pro with Avant Garde and
Copperplate Gothic as display typefaces

To send correspondence to the author of this book, mail a first-class letter to the
author c/o Inner Traditions • Bear & Company, One Park Street, Rochester, VT
05767, and we will forward the communication, or contact the author directly at
www.zoharaonline.com.

The Future of Human Experience is dedicated to my husband, Bob Hieronimus, whose companionship, loving support, and devotion to finding truth and serving the planet has inspired me from the first day we met (in this lifetime) in 1975 when, after visiting him in his library study, I thought, "Now that is the most unusual man I have ever met."

I also dedicate this book to our shared family of humanity, to all the Earth's species, and to the natural world we are called to love.

CONTENTS

ACKNOWLEDGMENTS

All of the perspectives presented in *The Future of Human Experience* derive from interviews that were conducted on my regional and nationally syndicated radio programs. The first one, *The Zoh Show* (1992–2002), is the longest aired whistle-blower program in broadcast history. The second is a program called *Future Talk* (2002–2008) and the third is *21stCentury Radio* (1985–present), which my husband and I cofounded many years ago and which airs each week in Maryland, Pennsylvania, and Virginia on WCBM Radio 680 AM. It is also heard online worldwide at www.21stcenturyradio.com.

This book is the result of thousands of hours of interviews, with only a small portion represented here specifically. I want to thank Amy Ford for her help with this book's illustrations; John Vinson, John Ford, Nate Thompson, Mike Healy, Sally O'Hara, Alden Briggin, and Megan Bowen each of whom took part in producing either *The Zoh Show* or *Future Talk*. I especially want to thank Laura Cortner, executive producer of *21stCentury Radio* for insuring Bob and I host well-crafted programs with amazing guests on what is the oldest "new paradigm" radio program in the United States and perhaps the world. I also want to thank Laura for editing the initial manuscript of this book.

After a year and half of my writing, followed by Laura's swift and excellent editing, we celebrated our collaboration on January 13, 2003: my forty-ninth birthday. On this day the final product was sent to the printers and then mailed to over twenty publishers. It was rejected by every publisher I sent it to, most saying it required too much intelligence to read and should be published by a university press. My hunch is that it was just a bit ahead of the curve.

After some time had passed, I sent out another round. It was just after another birthday of mine, this time in 2012, that I heard from Jon Graham, acquisitions editor at Inner Traditions International. They were interested in publishing this book. (Inner Traditions published two of my other books: *Kabbalistic Teachings of the Female Prophets* in 2008 and *Sanctuary of the Divine Presence* in 2012.) In addition to this wonderful news, Jon told me that *The Future of Human Experience* would be published in, you guessed it, 2013. (When I got a score of thirteen on a math test on my thirteenth birthday on a Friday the thirteenth in 1967—the year preceding my first public environmental activism—it was reinforced to me that thirteen, although not a good math score, was a good number.) Interpreting these birthday dates and the year of 2013 as being significant to this book, one might say that I was born to write it!

Ten years after I penned the original manuscript, *The Future of Human Experience* is being published (it is fitting for a book about the future to wait *for* the future in order to manifest publicly). Additions have been made to it, including interviews conducted between 2003 and 2013.

Given the nature of its topics and the information first assembled by interviewing extraordinary researchers, inventors, physicians, psychics, activists, historians, astronauts, astronomers, geologists, physicists, creative thinkers, and so many others, I realized that my interests tend to run about twenty-five years or more in advance of the collective culture and, judging by the people whose work is presented in this book, I am not alone. There are always front-runners in society, in every field of human endeavor, who point to where we are going and how we are going to get there long before the dominant culture endorses the new way of seeing the world. Often it is in retrospect that those in the vanguard are understood and appreciated. It is my hope, and the purpose of this book, that the ideas and solutions presented here inspire others to make their own significant contributions to our culture and to our planet.

I want to thank all of the people I have interviewed for the intelligent discussions and their consideration of things outside the box. Bless you for having the courage to stand against academic and societal bias and to often undergo personal economic peril in order to tell others what you have discovered, what you know, and what questions you are currently asking. Most of all, thank you for enhancing my heart and conscious awareness and that of our shared audiences worldwide, declaring that we are *one humanity, of the one Divinity within all of us, in the shared cosmic body we inhabit together.*

Knowing that others will now benefit from the collective service of all whose work is showcased here, words cannot adequately express my gratitude to Inner Traditions and their wonderful staff, especially Anne Dillon who edited the final manuscript of this book with me. I can only close by saying to everyone: enjoy the adventure and love of the world that we all share.

PREFACE

As a lifelong student of the mystery traditions of the East and the West, and as a nature lover since childhood whose mother insisted we play outside no matter what the weather was, I have always believed in the divinity of humanity and the holiness of nature. Among numerous nature-oriented activities, I have been a leader in holistic medicine. In 1985 I founded one of the oldest outpatient holistic health centers in America, the Ruscombe Mansion Community Health Center (www.Ruscombe.org) in Baltimore, Maryland. I am very delighted to say that it is still in operation today, offering numerous services that promote health and well-being, including services that feature homeopathy, acupuncture, herbalism, rolfing, yoga, massage, meditation, and more.

In addition to participating in the performing arts as a singer-songwriter, dancer, and mime, as well as in the photographic and other fine arts (painting and sculpture), I have been and remain an animal communicator and an environmental and social activist. At the age of fourteen I handed out flyers in Southeast Baltimore for a talk by Ralph Nader on acid rain and I was hooked. Since then I have led and participated in numerous environmental and social actions—locally, nationally, and globally—concerning the impacts of the nuclear, oil, and gas industries, the electromagnetic fields from high power lines, and the health impacts of underground geomagnetics, among others. I spent many years involved in trying to stop the misuse of pesticides and insecticides on crops and golf courses and in homes, schools, and hospitals. I took part in national campaigns exposing the dangers of nuclear food irradiation and years later participated in campaigns against genetically modified organisms (GMOs). I also participated in campaigns focusing on weather engineering, underground nuclear and oceanic tests, other water related issues, and the issue of nuclear materials in space and their obvious danger to human and all other forms of life.

The work of Gary Whiteford, Ph.D., professor of geography at the University of New Brunswick, Canada, who has shown a correlation between man-made detonations underground and the subsequent earthquakes and ocean quakes they cause, allowed me to predict—on my radio broadcasts—when to expect registered earthquakes. These and other types of geoengineering and weapons testing are a violation of our shared and inherited natural world.

My voice, together with the voices of millions of others worldwide, has been actively engaged since the 1960s. Many of my generational peers and elders are lifelong activists of one sort or another. All of us are trying to improve the world and create more inclusive philosophies, methodologies, and solutions. In short, the paradigm of greed, cover-up, corruption, separation, prejudice, limitation, scarcity, war, inequality of all kinds, domination, and exploitation in many institutional frameworks is about to change. Every person on Earth will become part of this change. Whether humanity goes kicking and screaming under the footprint of Earth changes or some other human-made calamity, or whether we work to improve and safeguard the world will in part determine what kind of future we will have.

The old paradigm of what I call the *death economy,* which exhibits a pattern of abuse globally—of people and the exploitation and ruination of nature and life in general—seems to me to be less the result of a conspiracy, as some would argue, and more the outcome of a conformity in education, in worldviews, and hence in thinking and feeling. The death economy is an overarching description of the destructive side of the industrial and material age that has ignored the natural world's needs as well as the spiritual nature of the human being, life's formative forces, and what we call consciousness as well.

It seems to me, and no doubt millions of others, that it would be an easy step to change to a life economy on Earth, which is most simply stated as choices that support life—and in so doing, move away from destroying the Earth through domination and exploitation toward sustainable collaboration and elevation. To countless others, however, this might be undesirable, impossible to imagine, or too grand to hope for. However, it is our mandate about which we have no choice. It is our natural next step in conscious evolution; many human beings have begun to make this shift.

The Future of Human Experience invites the reader into the world of discoveries already at hand. It brings ancient wisdom traditions to the forefront of our awareness and reexamines our Earth history, exploring a cyclical rather than a linear view of evolution and how civilizations rise and fall. We aren't the first nor will we be the last civilization to stand on the verge of its own self-destruction. We'll explore the tools we have for restoring balance on Earth in the ecosystem, in the arena of human health, and in our hearts and minds. Each person will learn that reverence is the cornerstone for consciously engaging the world and will see why it is so vital to develop our intuition and other farseeing and innate powers by developing our nonlocal consciousness. The intuition of each and every person can help to find answers to serious issues that the rational mind cannot grasp.

The Future of Human Experience explores the body of the world, the mind of the world, and the soul of the world through the human experience and suggests ways to engage each aspect of the manifest and not yet manifest realms, becoming their equal and respectful partners. Each human being is the co-creator of the world's formation. *The Future of Human Experience* shows how this takes place. Whether taking action to preserve the honeybees on Earth or reciting a holy prayer; whether enhancing life expectancy planetwide with sustainable agriculture or creating policies that make space a weapons-free zone, *The Future of Human Experience* and the wonderful visionaries presented here show us the way to create peace and bounty locally and globally, in our hearts and in our journey beyond our home planet, during this century and in the centuries to come.

INTRODUCTION

THE REFLEXIVE UNIVERSE

We project ourselves into the future every day of our lives. We all think about tomorrow, today. This book is based on the general framework of thousands of interviews I have conducted on radio for more than a quarter of a century. I regard the individuals whose work is presented here and all the others I have had the pleasure of interviewing (but did not have space to include in this book) as companions in the journey on Earth. Some of these experts have passed on since I interviewed them. Among the living, most of us have never met in person.* However, we share a passion for new discoveries and a greater joy in serving the Earth, the animal kingdoms, and our fellow human beings by cultivating knowledge—a prerequisite for wisdom and loving action.

The Future of Human Experience explores the importance of being aware of the intention behind any act, as it is the energy that drives the quality of our actions. *The Future of Human Experience* examines our ability to look ahead and to see where we are going, showing that *how* we do what we do is a vital aspect of our lives. In fact, by our sheer presence each one of us is changing the world every moment. Our nature, our character, and our actions shape the future now. Our thoughts impact

---

*Please note that if there are any errors of fact contained herein, regarding the work of featured individuals, they are solely the fault of the author in the transcribing or interpretive process.

and create possibilities. Our words shape matter. We humans are godlike and possess the keys to the powers of emanation, creation, formation, and action, as taught by the Kabbalistic alchemists for centuries.

Throughout human history, oral and written records show us that prophets, shamans, and gifted local visionaries are as indigenous to the world as are its rocks, rivers, and trees. And yet for as long as we have walked the Earth, we have also been sky walking—looking for the way in which the cosmos is reflected in our lives and how our own *beingness,* meaning our very essence, our biological and spiritual makeup, is reflected in the universe. Humanity now seems to be emerging from a long period of forgetfulness about our own interdimensional natures: our godlike or divine beings in mortal bodies. The task before us is, in my opinion, to live and act with the awareness of our genuine oneness on Earth. We have all the tools we need for this.

The art of integralism as I call it—the integration of all realms of existence and fields of study—is a basic worldview. Integralism recognizes that all life is interconnected and choices are best made when the results of those choices are honestly evaluated in terms of how they affect the collective world because everything that exists is embedded in the same life field of existence.

The Future of Human Experience is a positive and scientific declaration that shows how we are divine beings capable of manifesting a balanced world on Earth and elsewhere. We are all part of the energetic expression of a perfect divinity and, ultimately, an active appreciation of the inherent oneness of all life is the path that we share. This book examines not just what futurists envision for humanity based on current trends in the world, but also what kinds of wild cards or unknown events could dramatically alter humankind's course on Earth. What kind of natural, extraterrestrial, or man-made events have either altered a civilization's course in the past or might do so in the future?

Having been a student of philosophy, spiritual disciplines, and sacred esoteric teachings since a young age, I, like many others, have found affiliation in the worldview that places human beings in direct relationship to the creative power that makes the manifest world stable and reveals the immaterial realm as one full of light and potential. Given that we humans are divine light beings and are, just as we have been told, made in the image of deity or perfection, we have within our makeup a minireflection of how the cosmos operates as well. The laws that govern the stars also govern the atoms of which we are all made.

So, what if in this scheme of things, the force that we call *love*, or the law of affinity and coherence, is the divine energy that endows each created form with spiritual vitality—the sustaining essence of the universal matrix? What if we are designed from love, to love? This is not a romantic love dependant on special situations or people, nor is it a passive love as in appreciating someone or something from a distance. Rather this love is one that invigorates each person to willed action—to serving each other and to showing reverence in all realms in which we have presence on Earth and in the cosmos.

Specifically, what if love is what does the synapsing between will and body in order for the highest good to be manifest? The love I refer to is not especially personal, though each person can experience this type of love. Rather, it is universal and unconditional; it is a state of being, not just a way of feeling. Such love pulls things together and creates unity—making beauty and peace. This is a primary perennial teaching and the end goal of the practices of all sacred lineages. It is consistently taught as a truism by indigenous people everywhere on Earth. Scientists today are confirming that this unified reality impacts how the manifest and immaterial realms interact.

As a state of beingness, this divine love is experienced consciously by an awakened human. We know that consciousness is both local—existing in a fixed moment of time—and nonlocal, occurring beyond the constraints of either time or space. This means that we can each be doing something physical in the world while also thinking about something else not yet manifest. *The Future of Human Experience* explores how this skill—the ability to imagine and then individually and collectively create a renewed world—is what makes us unique as humans.

The idea that we are made in the Creator's image is often used as a metaphor to express our potential. However, I believe that this is also a literal statement that clearly shows us our innate powers and responsibilities. *The Future of Human Experience* articulates how people of science throughout the ages and seekers on the numerous spiritual paths to wisdom share a common reverence for nature. People of both disciplines know that, above all, wisdom is found, beneficial understanding is discovered, and knowledge is cultivated when one takes part in harmonized, loving engagement. In other words, the consciousness of the human and the disposition of our hearts determine not what the forces of nature are, but how they will be utilized once discovered.

The Future of Human Experience shows that this power of unity consciousness, meaning our essential presence both when we are alive and when we are not incarnate, is itself a natural force that when harnessed on Earth has effects as great or greater than the rain or the sun. In fact, the full and conscious revelation of our innate powers of body, mind, and soul will be humanity's greatest accomplishment; it is this precipice of awareness on which we now stand.

Suggesting that we are divine beings requires substantiation. *The Future of Human Experience* delineates the many ways that our natural innate skills—such as nonlocal consciousness, remote viewing, and healing at a distance—are as integral to our being as walking and sleeping are to our dense physical body and the soul that temporarily inhabits it. That we are immortal beings whose consciousness continues after the death of the body has been demonstrated in thousands of case studies on reincarnation, past-life recall, near-death experiences, and afterlife communication.

We find that ancient civilizations developed rituals and practices for integrating man's multidimensional aspects. They understood that our thoughts and feelings are the mediator between the immaterial realm and the manifest world, between heaven and Earth, between what is seen and not seen. They knew that the question of what the future will be like can be answered by focusing our attention in our hearts and minds and seeing what is reflected there. I believe that in our souls we all share the same reflected image or archetype, a perfect unity of being between the divine source of life and all created life-forms. It is this perfect pattern within each of us that sustains all of humanity's longings and hopes for an existence with less suffering and for a life that is meaningful and good.

The soul, it seems, can be both inside of time in our bodies while also existing outside of time in eternity, and as research in the laboratory increasingly proves, all past and future exists in the present. As a waveform of light suspended in the etheric field of life, the soul receives information as to what has already happened and what is coming into being. When we think about the future we are changing it in the present moment, which is also expressing the past. The scientific observer effect makes clear that what we study or focus our attention on is changed by the focus of awareness itself. This fact tells us how important our thoughts and feelings really are.

The universe is reflexive, as Arthur Young posited in 1976 in his seminal work *The Reflexive Universe: Evolution of Consciousness*. The laws that govern this reality are karmic laws: what the Hebrews meant when they stated, "As ye sow, so shall ye reap" (Job 4:8). Given that our divine inheritance allows us to choose what we do and understanding that karma is the great equalizer, it is wise to recall that what we do to the Earth, we do to ourselves. What we do to any creature, we do to ourselves. What we do to any other person, we do to ourselves.

Each chapter in this book examines a different aspect of what it means to be alive on the planet today and offers up keys to our shared journey. In my own mind and heart I believe that we are being asked to assist in creating the "Good Earth Society" now, and that the Good Earth Society is our truest manifest destiny—what some traditions call paradise. This is the natural habitat of the soul and the natural state of the Earth that each soul is informed by.

If one were to summarize the majority of the interviews I have conducted over the past quarter century or so, one would find a consensus that says that *now* is the time for union and collaboration. Now is the time to integrate all of the wisdom traditions, sciences, and technologies as Ken Wilbur, author and founder of the Integral Institute, posits in his integral theory—allowing us to draw from the premodern, modern, and postmodern paradigms to integrate the best of all aspects of consciousness and human endeavor, thereby elevating our current understanding and practices. Now is the time for peace between nations and religious communities to occur. This is the moment for the truth to be told about our relationships to other cosmic-traveling societies, to understand our own ability to heal the Earth and its ailing systems, and to learn about the connection between our minds and hearts as great forces in the universe and in our lives.

Now we can articulate how we are metaphysical beings of light and how our ancient cultures foretold of these days when humanity would awaken and be asked to take another step in our evolution. Creating paradise now means taking that one giant (quantum) step for mankind. The chapters of this book break that one giant step down into smaller steps: ones that are just, sustainable, and universal.

- Chapter 1, "Uncovering Catastrophe in Paradise," raises the specter of cataclysm as a nursemaid of transformation in human history. It asks us to look at the collective memory of catastrophe and how our collective and individual memories of the past and visions of the future overlap. Here we examine our ancient stories and the modern view of catastrophism as a vital part of the human story.

- Chapter 2, "Predicting the Future," introduces us to future visions of the Earth. They are both paradisical and apocalyptic. By utilizing the gifts of visionaries and strategic planners, it is clear the future is in part known now.

- Chapter 3, "Remembering Our Nature: Operators of Spirit and Matter," opens the doorway to our soul, showing that our consciousness can be put to deliberate use in affecting matter. Experiments in prayer show that alignment with a unified field of divine right order amplifies symmetry. Memory as a function of the human soul and future imagination is the way in which the dream of the world is seen, indicating that we are a multidimensional consciousness participating in a cosmic phenomenon.

- Chapter 4, "Using Ancient Software: Interpreting Patterns Is Key to Seeing the Future," explores the way in which ancient civilizations used patterns of meaning as divinatory tools, such as the I Ching, astrology, numerology, and the archaeo-sky matrix of today. This chapter shows that we are pattern makers and recognizers. This seems to be the way in which consciousness operates in relation to cosmic reality and mediates between the now of the material realm and the potential of the immaterial realms.

- Chapter 5, "Becoming Earth Beings," examines more closely the Earth itself as a biosystem. When nurtured in devotion, it unfolds its greatest potential. From biodynamic farming to sonic bloom, to the consciousness of plant life, to the importance of the honeybee, and the welfare of all sentient animals, we are called to view the Earth body as an aspect of our own. It is not separate from us or our consciousness. Soft technologies like Wilhelm Reich's cloudbusting demonstrate that we and the Earth are one living beingness and that science, which unfolds from a point of reverence, will end up creating a refined, just, and sustainable society.

- Chapter 6, "Knowing the Divine Body and the Sacred Heart," begins to look at the artificial adaptation of the body—suggesting that artificial organs do not diminish the importance of our consciousness as the integrator of well-being. Using heart and heart transplant patients as examples of the challenges bioengineering engenders again returns us to consciousness as the primary capacitor in the human biosystem. There is a union between mind and heart, consciousness and feeling, within the individual and between the individual soul and the world. As demonstrated by several modern leaders in complementary medicine, we possess a spiritual heart.

- Chapter 7, "Examining Science and Technology: Brave New Tools," begins by examining artificial intelligence created as a result of genetic and robotic engineering. These new tools give us an opportunity to begin playing what some have called God games. Other new tools will usher in the new energy age on this planet.

- Chapter 8, "Being Consciousness: The Link between Everything," reveals that our human biosystems are divine capacitors. From dowsing to experiments in human consciousness, it is clear that we have the power to both create and divine the future. Examining why our innate inner powers are diminished by culture gives us a chance to awaken societal and personal attention to their cultivation.

- Chapter 9, "Experiencing the Immortal Soul," shows us *how* we are immortal. The near-death experience, after-death communication, and between-life descriptions suggest we never die, nor does our soul. In fact, we are always having conversations in the fields of life.

- Chapter 10, "Traveling Off Planet," asks what we will take with us as we move into our true space age, how we will interact with other civilizations, and how will we address the issue of other intelligence and life-forms engaging our own? Paradise on Earth is not just a memory; it is our future potential to make our home planet healthy and whole.

They say that radio waves last forever. If that is true, then no doubt some day in the future the broadcasts I hosted will be drawn down from the Akashic radio beam we once rode together and new generations will enjoy the healthy dose of laughter and compassionate optimism we shared in the need for reclaiming planetary unity. In the meantime I hope you enjoy *The Future of Human Experience* and find in it some inspiration for your own journey on this sacred planet we call terra firma, our home planet Earth.

1

UNCOVERING CATASTROPHE IN PARADISE

Who among us hasn't wondered what the future will be like? For almost three decades I have interviewed people on the numerous potentials being forecast and imagined for the near and far future and spoken at great length with representatives of ancient wisdom traditions, think tank prognosticators, laboratory-tested psychics, and many others. Sometimes the similarities in their forecasts are striking, while the methods they use to "see the future" are significantly diverse. In fact, the striking similarities between ancient teachings and modern quantum physics can teach us quite a lot about effectively creating a sustainable future.

During these decades I have explored many issues with brilliant guests and often notice a common theme among mythologies and prophecies from around the world, geological history, and various Earth sciences. They show a recurring cycle of catastrophic Earth changes and the rebirth of new civilizations. Cataclysmic destruction and renewal has occurred many times on this planet, perhaps for billions of years.

This gives us a clue that the secret of our future may lie in the mysteries of the past. So it is here, in the past, where our exploration of our future will begin. Most Westerners are taught that history is a linear progression of civilizations rising from primitive man ever upward to societies

Fig. I.1. On January 25, 2012, NASA released what it said is the "most amazing high-definition image of Earth" ever. It is a composite image that uses a number of swaths of the Earth's surface, taken on January 4, 2012. The original Blue Marble image, taken by Apollo 17 astronauts on their way to the moon in 1972, may very well be one of the most viewed images in the world. Image courtesy of NASA.

that are increasingly developed and evolved. We're taught that the history of humankind is separate from the history of the Earth; that somehow, one is a study of culture and the other a study of matter. We have been conditioned to believe that the logical progression has been from more primitive to more evolved systems, a type of indefensible evolutionism. In truth, however, science shows us that actually the reverse is true, as manifested in the smallest atom or the largest galaxy. The law of the universe is for evolution to proceed from greater complexity toward more harmonic, elegant, and simplified systems.

The record of Earth's soul—the beautiful and horrifying phenomena of creation—is recorded in humanity's myths. Rather than originating as imaginal entertainment, the myths and legends of our ancient ancestors have been revealed to describe actual events that took place on Earth. This has been shown by many who have studied the correlations in various myths from all over the world. When looked at this way, Earth history indicates that there is a cosmic phenomenon that repeats cyclically in rhythm with the fall and rise of human civilizations. It seems to me that the Earth's regenerative power, or what could be seen as the Earth's breathing in and out, inside a larger cosmic body of extraplanetary events has played an important role in bringing humanity to cosmic consciousness. The cosmic role of Earth's cycle of destruction and creation pushes humanity to emerge from catastrophe to enjoy long stretches of opportunities for cultural and social refinement. We see this in the various golden ages of past civilizations. By understanding ancient stories of catastrophes, we may find some keys to our own potential role as divine co-creators of a prosperous Earth and assist in supporting the world's soul in the cosmos.

Mythologies and Earth sciences agree that world history is cyclical, not linear, and there is support for the proposition that humanity's history on Earth spans billions of years, not one to six million years as often taught today. Lifelong student of world mythologies David Talbott, Ph.D., has devised a unified theory of mythologies that tells of a time when our solar system was a much more dangerous place to be, leading to a cycle of destruction and rebuilding that one can read clearly in the myths. Michael Cremo, Ph.D., and Richard Thompson, Ph.D., present proof in their book *Forbidden Archeology* (rereleased in 1993 in abridged form as *Forbidden Archeology: The Hidden History of the Human Race*) that humans like ourselves have existed on this planet for tens of millions of years. They also show how this evidence has been suppressed, ignored, and forgotten because it contradicts generally held ideas, both Darwinian and creationist, about human evolution. Darwinian thought maintains that we are evolved from single cell amoebas through a progressive cellular development until, from apes, we became humans. Creationists see our existence as a divine act of a Creator God who created the world, the light, the seas, the sky, the animals, and humans over a period of six days or six thousand years ago. Humans like to have explanations, but sometimes by clinging to them we miss the truth.

Geologist Robert M. Schoch, Ph.D., has exposed the vested interests of traditional archaeologists who cling to their shortsighted dating theories when clear and obvious new evidence is presented to them that pushes back the dates of advanced civilizations further and further into Earth's past.

Systems scientist Paul LaViolette, Ph.D., has shown in a series of books how ancient creation myths describe atomic physics and the waveform phenomenon. There is enough fossil and material evidence to necessitate the rewriting of human history and our time line on planet Earth as shown by Jonathan Wells, Ph.D., in his book, *Icons of Evolution: Science or Myth?*

DAVID TALBOTT'S UNIFIED THEORY OF MYTHOLOGIES

Comparative mythologist David Talbott's unified theory of mythologies summarizes the results of two decades of research into world history. With Australian physicist Wallace Thornhill, David Talbott has coauthored a book entitled *Thunderbolts of the Gods* in which they show that the creation myths from India, Egypt, Asia, and indeed from every corner of the Earth are not simply fantastic parables, imaginary dramas, or symbolic journeys. Many are recordings of actual events.

Talbott sees in their correlations a time when our solar system looked nothing like it does today and was a much more dangerous place to be.

Following the groundbreaking work of Immanuel Velikovsky, Talbott and Thornhill have pooled their disparate fields of study to show the role of plasmic energy in the tales of great thunderbolt Gods—devastating destruction and horrendous electrical scarring of the planets. Talbott asserts that looking for a scientific explanation of myths and examining their symbols could offer a greater scientific understanding of the past.

Following a rigorous historical investigation, he proposed the Saturn model—a radical vision of great spectacles in the heavens recalled by ancient races around the world. He says this acts as a unified reference point by which to understand world mythologies and the role of electricity in the universe. Looking at the doomsday archetypes that are prevalent in all the world traditions, Talbott shows how they reflect an ongoing course of planetary disorder and are expressions of humankind's greatest desires and fears. "The environment we live in today is not the same environment our ancestors lived in," said Talbott, "and their stories beckon us to recall horrifying experiences that have been part of human civilization as long as stories have been told and preserved." To really understand them, however, Talbott asserts, "the prime requirement for investigators in this field is an independent attitude, free from theoretical prejudice and eager to consider all patterns of ancient memory—even when the mythic themes make no sense under prevailing assumptions."

Both Talbott and coauthor Thornhill were influenced by Immanuel Velikovsky's book *Worlds in Collision,* published in 1950. In addition to the great founder of anthroposophy Rudolph Steiner (1861–1925), Velikovsky (1895–1979) was one of the few outspoken men in the twentieth-century era to suggest that our solar system has gone through radical changes during humanity's lifetime on Earth, which affected civilization's history in ways sometimes overlooked and not just on Earth, but on other planets as well. During one of our interview conversations, Talbott summarized Velikovsky's conclusions. "Planetary history was marked by vastly greater chaotic and catastrophic episodes than has ever been acknowledged. The planets in the solar system were in greater proximity to each other, posing serious threats to each planet's stability—whether it was from pieces of planetary bodies breaking off and smashing into other planetary surfaces, or the ejections of great fields of plasma and other impacting energies and gases."

Talbott points to two overarching concerns expressed in the ancient Babylonian, Hebrew, Asian, Chinese, Nordic, and other cultures: a longing for a return to a paradisical state and a tremendous fear of a great catastrophe. The saturnine orientation of the Hebrews, Egyptians, Greeks, Chinese, and other mythologies show that humanity experienced a paradisical epoch followed by world-destroying calamities. Talbott believes that if we look carefully at the ancient symbol systems, their pictographs and stories, the same themes repeat concerning threats to the planet from space and a longing to re-create or to preserve their piece of Eden.

"No comprehension of world mythology is possible apart from the memory of planets extremely close to the Earth, accompanied by earth-shaking electrical activity," Talbott writes. "It was not that long ago that heaven was alive with electricity as planets moved through a rich plasma environment. Ambient electrical activity gave rise to unearthly sights and sounds for which natural experience today can only provide the faintest reminder. In the wake of these events, cultures around the world strove to reckon with the forces unleashed, to interpret the meaning of cosmic catastrophe, and to remember."

Pretending to be a three-dimensional observer on Earth makes all these stories clear, suggests Talbott. "The chain of arrows event is a story about an ancestral warrior or hero who launches arrows toward the sky, and each arrowhead embeds itself in the one above it. The chain of arrows then becomes a ladder by which the hero ascends to heaven. Numerous examples of this theme are found in the Americas alone, but other examples occur from Africa and India to the South Pacific. In the Kathlamet legend of a hero named Many Swans, this great ancestor launches a stream of arrows heavenward forming a ladder of ascent to the sky. In the Hindu Ramayana, the arrows of Arjuna form a bridge capable of carrying the mighty Hanuman, the traveler between worlds."

At first, Talbott saw the chain of arrows as a series of toroids (see the image in figure 1.1.) stacked along a central spine. He believed "these toroidal forms had evolved violently from a luminous filament spiraling up the polar axis," until Thornhill told him about Peratt instability. "When Tony Peratt, one of the world's most accomplished plasma theorists, described the violent evolution of a plasma discharge [a configuration actually named the Peratt instability after him] there was this immediate correspondence between the global pictographic record [our reconstruction based on historical testimony] and the extraordinary forms of the evolving discharge in the laboratory." Quoting others in the plasma sciences, he said they found the same correlation he had between the mythological chain of arrows and the way plasmic fields actually emit their discharge. Simply put, he said it was "too specific and too precise to be due to accident." Ancient mythology describes what we are only now able to understand as plasmic discharge in the ethers of cosmic space.

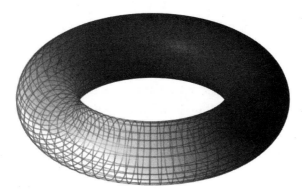

Fig. 1.1. Toroidal form

In *Worlds in Collision,* Immanuel Velikovsky expressed his own doubts in the status quo's supposition of planetary electrical neutrality, saying that he became skeptical of the accepted theories about celestial motions. He pointed out that celestial mechanics stand only if the sun is electrically neutral, which we know to be untrue. He earned the status quo's wrath when he pointed out that Newtonian celestial mechanics was based on a theory where gravitation, electricity, and magnetism had no role. It was also Velikovsky who posited that ancient mythologies describe a much more violent atmosphere on Earth as a result of proximity to Mars and Venus especially. In other words, he too found that Earth's space odyssey is not always smooth sailing given that records of meteorites and other near-Earth objects (NEOs) striking the Earth and upending civilization are apparent.

Many modern astronomers and quantum physicists, like the researchers mentioned in this chapter, would say that Velikovsky was right to challenge the dogmatic position that planets have some sort of neutral electrical state. As both physicists and mystics have maintained, space is not empty, but rather a seething energetic matrix with charged cosmic particles. Electricity is very much a part of the solar planetary story; the very field in which we have subtle existence is a field of cosmically charged particles. Like the bioelectric and biomagnetic human, the Earth is also in a constant state of etheric flux.

Talbott maintains that these ancient cosmic spectacles produced an explosion of human imagination: a myth-making epoch that has no counterpart in later times. Our ancestors attempted to portray in stories what today would be recorded in film and on video and on paper. Because of this systematic connection between civilization's imagination and the cosmic events themselves, I believe humanity was more essentially engaged with nature. They had a feeling of intimacy with the sacred and the mysterious that we no longer have in Western culture in general, and perhaps this gave our ancestors a chance for intimate conversations with nature and the cosmic world surrounding and invigorating it.

Following on the idea that the ancient community's imagination and sense of awe were part of the world drama, I'd like to further propose that perhaps in some instances natural events were an epic drama unfolded from human hearts and minds, rather than the other way around. Not only were natural events reflected in human epic dramas, but also humanity's inner imagination, visions, actions, feelings, and fears could have shaped matter and been expressed in natural events. Is it not possible that both could occur simultaneously, that nature unfolds from us and we are enfolded in her? If this reciprocity is accepted, it makes all thought potent and consciousness a cocreative matter-shaping force. Our efforts to record our history are essentially attempts to guide others, and in some fundamental way, our effort to act as witness is also an action. Might humanity have some fundamental purpose in sustaining the world both physically and spiritually, both as observers and doers?

Are we to interpret mythologies as actual historical descriptions of events? "The lightning Gods of old have a story to tell," Talbott says, "and that story, when traced to its substructure, points to extraordinary natural events." It is essentially a story of centuries of cosmic fire raining down on Earth. Here are a few of Talbott's almost two dozen examples of the symbolism of lightning utilized in ancient myth:

- Lightning is seen as a frightful weapon: a sword, arrow, mace, club, spear, ax, or hammer.
- Lightning appears as a great bird or "thunderbird" with heaven-spanning wings.
- Lightning is launched from a great wheel turning in the sky; the "chariot" of the Gods.
- Lightning streaks along the world axis, acquiring the form of a towering column, the axis mundi. It is the pillar of the sky, which at the beginning of time separated heaven and Earth.

My purpose in drawing attention to a few of the electrical thunderbolt motifs in world mythology that Talbott, Thornhill, Velikovsky, and others talk about is that they provide a vivid example of why we must expand our way of looking at our ancient cultures. Rather than being less evolved than our own modern society, the ancients were in many respects highly evolved and deeply engaged in being a conscious part of a much greater cosmic drama. We can trace history in part by what the ancients saw in their skies and on the Earth around them as described in their stories and narratives.

Consider our current civilization's intensification of research on threats from space. These threats include solar flares, meteorites, and other NEOs such as comets and asteroids, three hundred of which have been identified as having orbits crossing Earth's path, making our planet susceptible to massive catastrophe. Mirroring the stuff of science fiction, this is nevertheless a very real threat that NASA maintains oversight of.

In our modern era are we not creating little tales about this concern in our popular culture, with "end of the world" films capturing public attention? Indeed, there is growing scientific acknowledgement that it's time to seriously address preparation for and protection from off-planet threats to the Earth, for which NEO defense and deflection systems are being promoted.

THE FORBIDDEN ARCHAEOLOGY OF MICHAEL CREMO

Michael Cremo and Richard Thompson's *Forbidden Archeology* proves that humanity is much older than we are taught. Unearthing and analyzing clues in Vedic literature, they have shown that our civilizations have risen and fallen in ways most people today would be stunned by. According to the collected anomalous archaeological evidence presented in their book, the world as we know it today is at least 2 billion years old, and the history of *Homo sapiens* is far older than the 1–6 million years of ape-like hominids commonly taught. Cremo and Thompson have upset the time line for our presence on Earth in our current genetic and physiological forms by cataloging hundreds of finds, such as the 2.3 billion-year-old round, metallic, grooved spheres from South Africa, which suggest that metallurgy was practiced on Earth long before this cycle's Iron Age (1200–550 BCE).

Trying to put our extensive life cycles on Earth in perspective, Cremo states: "According to the Puranas [Vedic histories], there have been innumerable creations in the course of cyclical time. The basic unit of Vedic cyclical time is the day of Brahma, which lasts 4.32 billion years. The day of Brahma [also called a kalpa] is followed by a night of Brahma, also lasting 4.32 billion years. The cycle of days and nights of Brahma goes on for Brahma's lifetime of one hundred years [36,000 nights], equivalent to 311.04 trillion of our human years. During the day of Brahma, life [including human life] is manifest. During the night of Brahma, life is not manifest."

Cremo described, in one of our several interviews, the project of gathering this information that rewrites history. "When I started I thought it would take me about eight weeks, but when I got into it I found that the eight weeks turned into eight months and the eight months turned into eight years. There is such a huge volume of information that has been subject to this knowledge-filtering process. It involved getting all kinds of scientific publications that have been put out for one hundred and fifty years. And knowledge filtering has been going on that long, ever since Darwin wrote his *Origin of the Species*."

Cremo continued telling us about his own amazing odyssey. "When I started traveling and going to different parts of the world, I became very interested in the ancient Sanskrit writings. That's what really got me started thinking that things might be a little bit different than we are told. You can go to India, Egypt, or China or South America to the Aztecs, Mayan, and Incan places," he continued, sounding like a travel guide, "and you find the local people will tell you that some temple has been here for millions of years. And if you look into their writing you find actual histories that go back vast stretches of time. For instance, the Babylonian kings list goes back over four hundred thousand years. The pharaoh lists are older than that. What modern historians will say is that they are accurate up to a certain point, say maybe ten thousand years, but if you go back any further than that, they're not."

Cremo wondered if there was any evidence from any of these very ancient people. After all, these writings indicated human origins far predated what is commonly accepted by Western science. "If there was any truth to these ancient wisdom teachings and what they say about the age of human civilization," he decided, "then there might be some visible evidence to back it up." He and Thompson began to look for any "scientifically verifiable things that could show us that human history is far older than we are told." Their work is another approach to proving the cyclic nature of humanity's history, rather than a linear historical trail. Given this, I asked Cremo, during an interview, to contrast the normative worldview of the age of humankind with some of the ancient teachings on the subject, like those from the Hindu or Sanskrit writings.

In the accepted time line, "village life would come in around ten thousand years ago. And the first organized urban areas or cities began sometime between six thousand and eight thousand years ago. They would say that human beings like us in our current form have only been around for one hundred thousand years." The Vedic literature, by contrast, "presents what is called cyclical time. These are far greater spans of time than we normatively consider when speaking of our human history. These cosmic time cycles go back billions of years. . . . If you carefully study the cosmological literatures in ancient India, you'll find that we are about two billion years into the current day of Brahma. This means that a Vedic archaeologist would expect to find evidence of human presence going back just about that far."

I was anxious for others to hear some of the examples they cataloged in *Forbidden Archeology,* as it is modern heresy to challenge the linear model of history. "What you find is that scientists *have* found a continuous chain of evidence showing that humans like us have been present on the planet for all of recorded Earth history. The oldest discoveries that I encountered in my research actually go back to two billion years ago," Cremo indicated. Unfortunately, whenever anomalous evidence emerges of civilized humanity older than the accepted ten-thousand-year-long time line for humanity as we know it, these findings are snared by what Cremo calls the *knowledge filter*—designed to keep the current paradigm in place—and therefore anything that challenges it is not publicized. Archaeological discoveries from one million, ten million, and one hundred million years ago are regularly dismissed.

"The oldest things found in my research," Cremo told us, "were some very old metallic spheres that have been found over the past twenty or thirty years by miners in South Africa. . . . These objects are 1 or 2 inches in diameter. The one I had analyzed by some metallurgists turned out to be made of a naturally occurring form of iron called hematite. The amazing thing about these objects is that they have parallel grooves right around the center of them, sometimes one, two, or three grooves. The scientific analysis showed that these grooves were original. They were carved [at the same time that] these things were incorporated into the layers of rock where they are found now—and they are found in layers of rock over

Fig. 1.2. Klerksdorp spheres are small objects, often spherical to disc-shaped, that have been collected from two- to three-billion-year-old mineral deposits near Ottosdal, South Africa.
Image courtesy of Robert Huggett, Wikimedia Commons.

two billion years old." These balls have been cited by some alternative researchers and reporters as inexplicable out-of-place artifacts that could only have been manufactured by intelligent beings.

In fact, as Cremo showed us over and over again, this type of documentation already exists in the scientific journals from around the world and, when viewed as a whole, shows clearly that the approved theory of humanity's time line is largely erroneous. "In 1852 the *Scientific American* reported that a beautiful metallic vase was found fifteen feet deep in solid rock near Boston, Massachusetts, in Dorchester, and according to the U.S. Geological Survey the rock is from the Cambrian period. That would be about six hundred million years old."

My next question addressed the most regular criticism lodged against Cremo's argument by the mainstream archaeologists. I suggested the possibility that objects of a later date get mixed into layers of Earth of an earlier date due to the shifting nature of Earth changes. "Of course, that's possible," he responded, "but we looked for that. You'll find the scientists who have written these reports have taken that into account." This is best illustrated by the find of several skeletons in Italy, buried in Earth that is dated at three to four million years old. One explanation is that a few thousand years ago when these people died, their friends dug graves deep into the ground and buried them in ancient layers of rock. Cremo refutes this argument, pointing out that, "the original discoverers, most being geologists, paleontologists, and archaeologists, are aware of this problem called intrusive burial. But when this occurs, all the covering layers of rock would be disturbed. That was not the case [with this find]. Instead there were undisturbed strata of layers of rock. Scientists then check for faults, for evidence of earth movements, and in this case, as in many others, there is no earth movement explanation. These are ancient skeletons in ancient layers of earth."

Cremo went on to point out that the famous multigenerational, anthropological, and archaeological Leakey family has made some amazing discoveries. In 1979 dozens of footprints were found at Laetoli, in the East African country of Tanzania. Meave Leakey herself said that the footprints were indistinguishable from those of modern human beings. "These footprints were found in layers of rock over 3.7 million years old, and they were totally modern," stressed Cremo. "This is exactly the same age as the well-known Lucy and the new hominid that was found not long ago by Meave, known by the name of Platyops or Flat Face who is 3.5 million years old [from the middle Pliocene era]. It appears that when these little ape-men were walking around there were also humans like us walking around." We did not evolve *from* apes, but resided on Earth side by side.

What impact will this reversal of facts have on our view of our place in the world, relative to our way of looking at our future? "The linear progressive concept of time is what modern science is based on," pointed out Cremo, emphasizing that "there you always get the idea that things had to start out more simply, more primitively, and then move forward in an evolutionary way. . . . It's as though people want to explain things as cosmic accident that only happened once, which is the linear [and fabricated] sense of time. Whereas, if you have a cyclical sense of time, with things happening over and over and over again, that leaves us with an understanding that there has to be some intelligence behind it." It looks like after paradise is destroyed it then shows up again a million years later. There is periodicity, a pattern, and a suggestion that there is purpose to life. We didn't evolve from single cell amoebas; there is design and purpose to creation, a pattern to this epic drama that repeats itself over a period of millions of years.

As Cremo explained, "what's really at stake is our whole definition of ourselves. The way we set our goals for ourselves depends upon, in part, who we think we are and where we came from."

"It also impacts what we do with our natural resources and how we treat other sentient creatures," I said.

"Absolutely," Cremo agreed. "If we think that we are just a combination of chemicals that arose by chance and arose in this linear progressive fashion, then we don't accept that behind it all is some intelligence, some spiritual principle that transcends the whole thing. If we don't have that, then our whole purpose in life becomes dominated by exploitation of the resources around us. If we accept the other concept of ourselves and where we came from, then it becomes obvious that we will look at ourselves in a different way. We will concentrate on the development of consciousness rather than the domination and exploitation of matter."

In discussing why such falsity is maintained as scientific gospel, Cremo pointed out that there are different types of power in the world. There is job power, political and economic power, military power, and also intellectual power. It is very subtle power and those who *have* the power bring to bear great pressure on those who might be inclined to speak in opposition. It is an issue of great consequence, as we will discuss with Ingo Swann in chapter 8 on the secrets of power.

"What all of this leads to," concluded Cremo, "is that we need a new explanation of human origins. Basically, before we even ask the question of where did human beings come from, we should ask *what* is a human being. An idea that has been very prominent in science, and very closely tied to this whole Darwinian theory of evolution, is that we are simply a combination of chemicals. That's all there is. This linear, progressive sense of time is self-organizing. We are a machine and that's our business and entire purpose—to dominate and exploit the resources available to us." Some factions are even already planning to travel to Mars, other planets, and asteroids in order to mine them and turn them into commodities. "Trash the universe if we can," I said.

"That's the plan," he answered with a sarcastic chuckle we both understood. "That's the only plan put out there for us. But we are more than just ordinary matter. If you look at us . . . we are composed of three things. There is ordinary matter, but there is also mind and there is also spirit or consciousness. . . . We didn't evolve up from matter, but *devolved*, or came down, from the level of pure consciousness. That's where our identity is. We are conscious selves that have somehow or other departed from the realm of pure consciousness and have become covered over by denser energies. I think we should make it our main business to reverse the process. Let's purify our consciousness. Let's develop our consciousness. . . . That's what all the great wisdom traditions of the world have been about. They have developed technologies, not for dominating and exploiting matter, but for elevating consciousness back to its original position."

Cremo is certainly not alone in this conclusion. Increasingly, members of the scientific community find reason to assert, like those of the planet's spiritual traditions, that we are faced with a choice on which the Earth hangs in balance. Will we apply all of our talents to preserving the biosphere by refining our consciousness and how we use everything we have both spiritually and physically, or will we participate in instigating catastrophe, perhaps sooner than in its natural time?

I closed one of my discussions with Cremo with a brief examination of the extraterrestrial genetic engineering hypothesis, something we will examine in a later chapter. I asked Cremo if there was any archaeological evidence of intergalactic "seeding" of human life. Did he think humanlike life was confined to this planet? "We should expect the phenomena of life to exist off this planet," he said. "It is my conviction that there is humanlike life on other planets and in other solar systems in our universe. This is a conclusion I have drawn from a study of . . . ancient wisdom traditions like the Vedic writings, which tell of 400,000 human species scattered all over the universe." In other words, I thought during our discussion, we are not home alone. Interestingly enough, in February of 2013, NASA announced that the Kepler space telescope mission data revealed that there may be billions of Earthlike planets near us, some as close as thirteen light years away, which astronomers say is "practically next door."

ROBERT SCHOCH ON THE ROLE THAT CATASTROPHES PLAY

Following in the footsteps of R. A. Schwaller de Lubicz and John Anthony West, geologist Robert Schoch, Ph.D., was responsible for bringing the redating of the Sphinx to the level of appropriate scientific inquiry. Schoch has proved *geologically* by looking at water weathering marks on the Sphinx that this mysterious monument was constructed several thousand years before what is traditionally recognized as the beginning of the Egyptian dynasties. He says the weathering patterns on the Sphinx date its creation to around ten thousand, five hundred years ago, or 8500–5000 BCE, rather than the more normative claim of 3000–2500 BCE.

In his book *Voices of the Rocks: A Scientist Looks at Catastrophes and Ancient Civilizations* written with Robert Aquinas McNally, Schoch turned his attention to the role catastrophes play in the course of human history. *Voices of the Rocks* makes clear that Earth-shattering changes have resulted from the periodic rain of extraterrestrial objects (like meteorites), which could be the explanation for the sudden and mysterious demise of many advanced and legendary cultures.

I asked Schoch to repaint human history with the inclusion of catastrophism in the larger role it deserves. "The accepted view is that world history is progressive and piecemeal," he told us in one of several interviews, "from primitive [cultures] progressing incrementally, learning a little bit more, continuing to grow over the last thousands of years until we get to today with the Internet—all based on this long progression of incremental changes. There are no big jolts, no big surprises." This long incremental progression is just not supported by the bigger picture of planetary history, he points out.

"I think it is very clear, as I have been analyzing the geologic record and the historical record going back to ancient times and up to the present, our Earth has been impacted by extraterrestrial objects (meteorites and asteroids) numerous times, and not just millions of years ago. It was first recognized among geologists who put this way back in the past. But when you start looking at the record it is very clear that human history, human civilizations, have been affected by near-Earth objects that impacted Earth or came into the atmosphere, from which there were major environmental effects and disturbances. . . . Just because we haven't experienced this in the past five hundred to a thousand years, doesn't mean it can't happen again. In fact, everything indicates it *will* happen again," Schoch stressed, bringing to mind many of the images from the popular films like *Deep Impact* and *Armageddon*.

"In fact it could return with a vengeance," explained Schoch, considering our highly technological society whose economy and life-support systems are almost totally dependent on the electric grid. A loss of the electric grid alone would change the way in which humanity abides on Earth today. We discussed current understanding of solar flares, coronal mass ejections, and other solar-related impacts, aware that when we talk about the weather today one can actually go onto the Internet and get a basic forecast for various quadrants of the solar system. Indeed, we are a space-oriented society already.

I asked Schoch to tell us what evidence he has found to show that human beings have witnessed and recorded these types of calamitous, civilization-ending events over time. "When you start looking at the record," he said, "it seems that we have numerous examples and testimonies in recorded history (in terms of archaeological sites) where humans have experienced this. What I think is a very classic example is the collapse of the Bronze Age. From the sixteenth to the twelfth centuries BCE the worldwide devastation, as we can reconstruct it now from the archaeological record, used to be attributed to some sort of horrible wars. That just doesn't stand up to scrutiny. It looks like it was, basically, interaction of near-Earth objects, particularly meteorites and comets, with the surface of the Earth and the atmosphere of the Earth. This caused major devastation, climatic changes, and actual touchdowns on the surface of the earth."

Around 1200 BCE in the area throughout modern Turkey and Israel and the general region accepted as ancient Troy, Schoch says, "cities were absolutely leveled, destroyed, and wiped out. There is a lot of evidence of fire. It is very inexplicable why everything was wiped out in a matter of decades. What I think was happening was that we were passing through a meteor stream and Earth was being hit heavily. It was not just warfare among some rivals. I think all evidence indicates that, essentially, there were a series of comets that may have wiped the cities out. . . . Mike Baillie, Ph.D., from Queen's University in Belfast has taken the tree ring data of Ireland that show a tremendous environmental catastrophe around 1200 BCE, which he too believes to be the result of cometary events."

Another example of our misinterpreting archaeological and geological evidence that Schoch offered is the belief that the first humans to inhabit the Americas came across the Bering Strait around 9500 BCE. "But I believe," Schoch said, "that if humans came through the Bering land bridge, they had to come very, very early. To get down to southern Chile by about 10,000 BCE, they must have crossed the Bering land bridge before it iced over, about 18,000 BCE. There is other evidence in the form of charcoal and linguistic evidence, and I think we are going to find that humans were in the Americas since at least 30,000 BCE, or maybe longer. This is opposed to the classic paradigm that humans have been in the Americas only since 9500 BCE."

Hardships endured due to extraterrestrial forces are not limited to our Earth. When we travel off planet, we also find evidence of catastrophe there. For instance, looking at the surface of Mars, where once there may have been a thriving civilization, one can see another planet bearing the marks of catastrophe. I asked Schoch what he thought was preventing us from using our prevailing knowledge to address the reality of potential catastrophes with their devastating scenarios? "The problem is largely a psychological one," he said. "I think we tend to be very shortsighted. Mars is an incredible example of where there was once life. There is some evidence that whatever was happening on Mars in the past, the final straw may have been some sort of extraterrestrial impact, some kind of meteorite or asteroid. At least that's one possible explanation. But again, it seems we are very shortsighted. We have little perspective on history. When most people think back, they only have a concept of the past couple of hundred years. These past hundred years have not been difficult as far as human history or planetary civilization goes," he reminded us, despite man-made wars. He went on to point to the widely publicized cometary impact that scarred the surface of Jupiter a few years ago. If that can happen there, it can certainly happen here.

Describing the possible scenarios of cometary disaster on Earth, Schoch explained that a comet hitting land would kick up a huge ball of dust and create a type of nuclear winter effect, blocking the sun and lowering surface temperatures. Reflecting sunlight in what is called an *albedo effect,* cold areas would continue to cool and warm areas would begin to go through a cooling stage. "If an asteroid or comet hit the ocean," he continued, "and we were already in an ice age, it could turn it off. But either way, regardless of gradient Earth temperature, there would be huge earthquakes and tsunamis, probably wiping out all coastal cities, certainly any of those surrounded by ocean. If it penetrated the ocean floor and broke it open, it would release magma. Molten rock would literally flow from the ocean bottom to the surface creating tremendous steam, killing off aquatic life and much of life on the surface of the Earth and in the air."

Once again showing that history is not uniform or linear, Schoch concluded that the "uniformitarian point of view is defenseless because we already know there have been five major extinctions and in all likelihood they were all the result of this type of impact. Sixty-five million years ago in the Cretaceous-Tertiary (K-T) extinction the dinosaurs were wiped out. But that wasn't the biggest extinction. The one at the end of the Permian period two hundred and forty-five million years ago eliminated, we think, 96 percent of all life on Earth. There was also one at the end of the Ordovician period, four hundred and forty million years ago; the Devonian period, three hundred and sixty million years ago; and the Triassic period, that was about two hundred and fourteen million years ago."

With the Arctic ice sheets melting, the overall global warming, the aridification of desert lands, and the flooding of others, the Earth is already expressing upheaval. Also there is the depletion of stratospheric ozone and the dying off of certain coral reefs. Unfortunately, the Earth is not currently enjoying a very bountiful time—in large measure the result of greedy and reckless human behavior. By the time we finished speaking, I felt ever so grateful to be alive. At the same time, though, I am thankful to be more attuned to the possibility of a catastrophic scenario that could upend our world. It is wise to be open to many possibilities. John Petersen, whose work we will examine in chapter 2, calls such an event as a comet hitting the Earth a wild card that would create overall devastation.

MELTING DOWN DENIAL

Lonnie Thompson, Ph.D., is a paleoclimatologist from Ohio State University's Byrd Polar Research Center and, as such, he is responsible for some of the early discussions about global warming. When he returned to Quelccaya, Peru—the largest ice cap in the tropics—to sample a location he had last measured more than twenty years earlier in 1977, he was surprised to find a lake where once there had been an ice mass. Thompson, like the hundreds of scientists worldwide who agreed with the consensus finding reported by the Intergovernmental Panel on Climate Change (IPCC) representing the opinion of one hundred nations, asserts that, "there is new and stronger evidence that most of the warming observed over the past fifty years is attributable to human activities."

To make their case clear, the IPCC stated in their Third Assessment Report, *Climate Change 2001,* that "the planet's average surface temperature increased by about 0.6°C during the twentieth century, and is projected to increase another 1.4°C to 5.8°C by 2100." Is that just another cycle? The report makes clear that the rate of warming they can now measure has occurred "without precedent during at least the past ten thousand years." February 2012, according to NOAA's *State of the Climate Global Analysis,* marked the 324th consecutive month with a global temperature above twentieth-century averages.

By using satellite mapping techniques and taking direct samples, Thompson and his team noted that between 1998 and 2000 the glacier Qori Kalis at Peru's Quelccaya was retreating at a rate of more than a foot per day, thirty-two times faster than in 1978. "You can almost sit there and watch it move," he said in one account. Africa's Mount Kilimanjaro has lost 82 percent of what is called its *ice field* since first being mapped in 1912. As reported by Dawn Stover in her article "The Big Melt" in

Popular Science (May 2001), "At the current rate of melting, the snows of Kilimanjaro that Ernest Hemingway wrote about will be gone within 15 years."

While the world is growing aware of the diminishing ice sheet in the Antarctic and the melting of the permafrost in Europe, there seems less interest in realistically addressing the rising sea levels that will predictably accompany them. Flooding worldwide and a warming trend on Earth could also mean greater famine and widespread contagious diseases in some parts of the world. Institutions such as The Johns Hopkins Bloomberg School of Public Health and the U.S. Centers for Disease Control and Prevention have identified some basic problems humanity faces from current weather extremes or predicted future global climate change: heat-related changes; the impact of extreme weather on health in general; and illness from air, water, food, or vector-borne diseases, such as those that come from rodents and other animal or insect host populations. After Hurricane Sandy in 2012, the Caribbean islands and the United States' shore communities of New Jersey and New York, including New York City, got a taste of what the power of surging water does to our life on Earth. In a couple of hours entire neighborhoods are flooded and decimated, and cities are put off grid. Put this on a global landscape and we can better appreciate our human ancestors' stories as an effort to inform us of possible events on Earth, which may happen again. In a time of scarcity, drought, super-cold or super-hot temperatures, all life-forms compete for resources.

Bestselling author Graham Hancock has joined me several times to discuss his influential books. In *Fingerprints of the Gods* and *Underworld: The Mysterious Origins of Civilization,* he focuses on the shoreline civilizations that were inundated the last time the glaciers began to melt. He explained that "the new software-like inundation mapping makes it possible to line up the flooding of shorelines worldwide and trace where we should expect to find the remains, underwater, of prior civilizations." Unfortunately, the current equipment can go "no deeper than about 150 feet while many of the submerged sites around the world that are being located are as deep as 450 feet. According to almost a thousand ancient myths around the world, these civilizations were obliterated in a universal flood. When the glaciers melted between seventeen thousand and seven thousand years ago, sea levels rose and more than 15 million miles of habitable land were submerged underwater. This entirely changed Earth's geography and the conditions in which humans could live."

Hancock and numerous other guests on the various radio programs I have hosted have highlighted the abilities we're gaining due to technology. These gains help us to access parts of our past that up until now have been unavailable to us for research—a significant factor as we go about learning from our past in order to better create a stable future. However, it is worth reminding ourselves that even without material technologies we have inner technologies that can divine the whereabouts of everything, in any time: a subject examined in the coming chapters.

THE LOST ATLANTIS

When one thinks of lost or ancient civilizations, the legendary Atlantis is one of the first that comes to mind. There are many contemporary investigators who believe they have discovered the "real" Atlantis and candidates include the North Pole, North America, South America, and various

Fig. 1.3. The location of Atlantis in Bolivia, according to Jim Allen's research. Image courtesy of Jim Allen.

islands in the Mediterranean. Some of these discoveries begin, as it did for Jim Allen, with a new decoding of Plato's fourth-century account of the Atlantean civilization, which he wrote about in his *Timaeus* and *Critias*, as allegedly told to him by an Egyptian priest.

Of particular interest to our discussion of catastrophism was Plato's statement that "In a single day Atlantis disappeared entirely." Allen believes he's found Atlantis in Bolivia, as detailed in his books *Atlantis: The Andes Solution; The Discovery of South America as the Legendary Continent of Atlantis* and *Decoding Ezekiel's Temple*. Allen shows how a site in the Altiplano reveals all the geographical conditions described by Plato's account. As he related in our discussion on the subject, "The capital city [of] Atlantis was on a large rectangular plain connected to a canal that the king of the city had built. There was a central mountain and concentric rings of land and water." Allen relied on ancient measuring systems and texts, using them much as one would a treasure map if looking for buried treasure, and he makes a convincing argument that has also been documented in film.

Fig 1.4. Jim Allen with one of the black stones at Pampa Aullagas, Bolivia. Image courtesy of Jim Allen.

PAUL LAVIOLETTE'S *EARTH UNDER FIRE*

Physicist and systems scientist Paul LaViolette, Ph.D., also believes that the Earth has been subject to cyclic periods of catastrophes over a long period of time, but rather than their being simply meteorites or comets, LaViolette sees cyclic cataclysms resulting also from massive ejections from the galactic core center of our galaxy. He has combined modern astronomical knowledge with a search for clues found in ancient mythologies and symbols in a most interesting way. He even shows how the signature dates in the Great Pyramid demarcate this long engagement of ongoing disasters. His conclusions as expressed in our lively on-air discussions show that not only did our ancient ancestors know of this particular danger, but that they left warnings about it for future generations, meaning us.

Though it's true that core explosions at the center of our galaxy are not a top priority for most scientists and astronomers, LaViolette contends that it should be. Galactic core explosions "have and could affect us," he insisted. "We see them going on in other galaxies similar to our own. There is evidence that the core of our own galaxy has exploded in the past. The last major explosion was at the end of our ice age." LaViolette's three books *Beyond the Big Bang, Earth under Fire,* and *The Talk of the Galaxy* rely on mythological as well as geological and astronomical evidence to make his point. "At the center of our galaxy there is believed to be a massive object. Whether a black hole or a super star, they've determined it's a few million solar masses, a few million times the mass of our sun. It radiates cosmic ray electrons, X-rays, gamma rays, and radio waves, but we can't see it visually because it's covered with dust. However, at times this core becomes very luminous. It can increase its energy output by a hundred thousand times or more, and this is what poses the threat. When this emission of radiation reaches us, it comes as a wave, so to speak, which I call a *super wave,* and could last anywhere from several hundred years to a few thousand years. So we're talking about a cataclysm that spans many generations. It's not like an asteroid hitting the Earth and its impact is seen in a few days. In legend we see generations of humankind going through this catastrophic engagement."

LaViolette asserts that these cyclic, generation-spanning catastrophes are in large measure the result of a regular, major galactic core explosion. It is a cycle occurring roughly every twenty-six thousand years, putting us on a course for this type of cosmic radiation and potential devastation in the near future. "We had one of these events thirteen thousand years ago," LaViolette attested, "and some have said we are quite due for another one." He wants more scientists to get involved in the study of these phenomena, because he also is suggesting that the devastation of a cosmic super wave striking Earth could be prevented by building a special kind of shield. Indeed, the age of NEO deflection technology is upon us.

"The big wave would carry these cosmic ray electron- and proton-charged particles," LaViolette explained further, "along with gamma rays, X-rays, and radio waves. You would actually see a bright star, which would appear between the constellations Scorpio and Sagittarius. In fact, a Hopi myth talks about the appearance of a blue-white star, which would herald the next catastrophe." Here once again ancient Earth traditions are telling us about the past and the future. "Now, it's not so much the radiation that would affect us directly," LaViolette continued, "but what it does is create a chain of events. It pushes cosmic dust into our solar system. Our solar system is kept clean by solar wind, which is always pushing dust out. Beyond the orbit of Pluto there is a lot of cometary debris and other stuff in a frozen state. So when this super wave arrives with all these cosmic rays, they would form a sort of radiation belt in the solar system. They are able to reach such a high density of energy that they can actually vaporize the frozen material out there and push it in. So the energy in the solar system becomes clouded with dust, unlike anything we've seen before in our lifetimes. Imagine the tail of a comet. Imagine seeing that haze throughout the sky—so much that it would block out the stars and even obscure the moon and the sun. You could actually have a shroud around the sun and it would become reddish."

"And what could we then expect to see happen on Earth?" I wondered aloud. "It would change the Earth's climate," LaViolette explained. "It would activate the sun and the sun would begin to erupt enormous flares unlike anything we've seen. Even at the peak of our solar cycles, we haven't seen anything like it. . . . We see evidence in the geological record of a huge increase of carbon-14, which could only be explained by cosmic rays or solar cosmic rays. In an extreme case, the sun's increased output would have melted the ice sheet at the time of the Ice Age. We do find evidence of very rapid melting of the ice sheets, flooding of the continents, and the rise of sea levels. You look at the mammoths in the Arctic, and they are buried by catastrophic flood. They are still in a frozen state in the Arctic. . . . Essentially," he said, "I do not believe that comets were the main cause of the end of the Ice Age. They could not have changed the climate like that. The evidence in the ice core records of actual cosmic ray increases shows that, indeed, there were these cosmic ray peaks, just as I predicted in my thesis in 1983."

As LaViolette made clear, it's not that comets, asteroids, and meteorites were not hitting the Earth, but that the ongoing destruction over a period of several thousand years, impacting multiple civilizations worldwide, would make these solitary events merely the punctuation points while the solar radiation was the daily affair.

LaViolette told us, as he does readers of his book *Earth Under Fire: Humanity's Survival of the Apocalypse,* that at the closing of the last Ice Age "our ancient ancestors endured one of the most lethal global catastrophes to have occurred in the course of human history." He emphasized that the intelligent minds of those times thought it imperative "to construct a message that would endure through time and be understood by the descendants of those who survived. Using sophisticated cryptographic puzzle techniques similar to those modern astronomers use in designing extraterrestrial communications, they created a time capsule message that described the elusive celestial cause of this tragic disaster, alerting us that it could recur at long intervals" and arrive at Earth's doorstep virtually without warning.

"This ancient cipher is today displayed in the heavens in the form of the twelve zodiac constellations (Greek, Egyptian, Babylonian versions), its informational content having been passed down orally in the lore of astrology. Also certain esoteric keys were handed down to help unlock its message: the Sphinx being one and the tarot being the other."

These keys are added to other systems as described by the late John Michell (1933–2009) in his book *The Sacred Center: The Ancient Art of Locating Sanctuaries*. Michell shows that "there is a cosmological code, model, or prototype for all the examples of astrologically ordered societies and landscapes" of sacred sites in which the Milky Way held a prominent position. In the same manner of clearly articulated measuring devices, even the galaxy has such markers left for space-voyaging societies alerting others to catastrophe.

That this devastating cyclic phenomenon in history is known, LaViolette explained further, is revealed by ancient mythologies pointing to three identifiable pulsars within a radian arc second of the galactic center, behaving potentially as intergalactic travel beacons and warnings. LaViolette believes the ancient Egyptian creation myths were direct expressions of the cosmic wave phenomena that our universe is propagated from. It is the same waveform propagation that the Mayans reveal in their calendar as an explanation of creation and the manifold created life-forms, as Carl J. Calleman, Ph.D., shows in his book *The Purposeful Universe*. Ancient civilizations were not primitive. They understood cosmic and physical laws that we modern-day humans are only now coming to terms with. LaViolette showed us that pulsars mark the region in the galactic core that would be dangerous for space travelers today. He believes that extraterrestrial civilizations have engineered the field around stars—creating these supraluminous pulsars to act as directional beacons. In a similar way today, we have directional signals in airports to enable planes to "fly in on a beam."

Referring to the apparent sophistication of an ancient civilization, LaViolette carried on. "For example," he added, "in the creation myth [of the Egyptians] where Aton creates the universe and there is a separation of two children, Geb and Nut, (the earth and the sky) . . . the myth is describing very advanced science that was discovered in only the last fifty years."

I had to ask him to elaborate on that. "The creation myth shows us," he continued, "how a subatomic particle forms. In other words, the wave theory of matter as we just discovered in the twentieth century [was known by] the Egyptians around 3000 or 4000 BCE. You see that the physics they are describing is how a waveform emerges through the existing ether. It's very taboo in physics today to admit the existence of the ether, but there have been so many experiments showing, in fact, that there is what is called an absolute reference frame. This is a proof of the existence of an ether." LaViolette is corroborated by the work of Paulo Correa, Ph.D., and Alexandra Correa with an aether motor, enabling scientists to examine the etheric realm and how it functions.

As we will see later in chapter 7, the questions we ask determine what we look for. Accepting the ether as the ancient cultures have is vital to understanding how thought and feeling impregnate matter with potential outcome, direction, and amplitude.

LaViolette expounded on the importance of the ether to his theory. "The Hermetic tradition views the universe as an open system. That [view] requires a sustenance—for the Earth to be continually sustained by some force or energy. It wouldn't be something we could label as energy because it would not be physical. It would be whatever activates the ether, affecting the ways the ether, as something dynamic and alive, would be continuously creating matter." Many Earth traditions call the sustaining force of the ether God, Great Spirit, or the Holy Creator.

THE QUESTION TO BE ANSWERED

From Talbott's ideas of plasmic discharge to these broader descriptions resulting from galactic core explosions, the picture is clear: the Earth has gone through tremendous cosmic assaults resulting in catastrophes throughout our billions of years of life on this planet. Whether looking at ancient mythologies or ancient precepts of science with modern laboratory confirmation, we find more and more that we are at a fascinating crossroad where ancient writings and modern sciences reflect one another. As we turn our attention to the sacred and secular record of human history, we find a great diversity of wisdom and methods for recording them. What can we gain from these ancient teachings and planetary history?

Some see the ancient past in our near future and suggest the future will be apocalyptic while also transformative, indicative of a new humanity on Earth. I have come to accept catastrophism as an expression of radical change, be it man-made or a result of natural disasters. These traumatic memories are still held in our DNA. The study of NEOs tells us to be mindful that we are living on a planetary body that is hurtling through space.

The researchers in this chapter have exposed the flaws in approaching humanity's history as though it were linear by collecting the evidence showing that it is cyclic. Human civilization on Earth is a serial unfolding of civilizations rising and disappearing. If we view the Earth as a living being, I'd say her soul contains the memory of many periods of creation and dissolution. It appears to me that paradise and catastrophe are partnered, much as there is partnership between an inhale and exhale in our bodies. And there is a planetary cycle that dictates what the planet itself will bear of humankind and extraplanetary forces.

While it is clear that civilizations rise and fall, how they do so is the question I am concerned with in *The Future of Human Experience.*

2

PREDICTING THE FUTURE

Many world teachings predict that the events of this century will make the Earth a radically changed biosphere. By collecting and studying the various predictions for our immediate future, perhaps we can pool our efforts to significantly improve the long-term welfare of the Earth and all life on Earth—from the forests to the skies and all that live and depend on the waters as well. Although we focused in chapter 1 on the record that history gives us of extraplanetary influences on us, there are of course other factors that will impact the human experience.

There are predictions of decades of war and global shortages of essential staples in our near future, of famine and plagues: partners to colossal Earth changes over a period of decades. There are also compelling prophecies worldwide of a great change in humanity that will usher in an enlightened age, when despite great Earth changes a more conscious and inspired Earth people will arise.

From my many years covering global politics and the rise of the "corporatocracy" (as a layer of this epoch in time), as well as a rise in human trafficking and various types of enslavement, every person can ask himself, "Do we really need to go through a phase of global collapse, alarming terrorism, and brutal exploitation of humanity before insisting on our divine birthright of shared freedom?" Is this kind of future really *our* future? Perhaps when we imagine such a dark drama and we watch it in modern films and television shows that present a brutal future, we are being programmed to be part of creating this global mayhem. In this scenario those who have the best weapons and most intolerant fundamentalist regimes will thrive. This is not a good option and, in fact, is part of a cultural indulgence in visceral images that neurophysiologically elicit fear and trauma in each viewer. These images are not *nothing*. They are images impacting our inner life and daily experience; they affect the nervous system of each person and the imagination of people of all ages. Children's games and propaganda promoting violence and death and the manner by which our culture celebrates war is not good for us. I have higher hopes for the world and greater faith in humanity and pray that those in the media and the entertainment businesses will take more seriously the roles they play in manufacturing images people become informed by, stimulated by, and oftentimes corrupted by.

Is it not possible to see the great challenges we face on Earth today as an opportunity to re-create our entire world in a better fashion? In this chapter we will meet many individuals exploring *how* we shape the future, even unconsciously, and why each one of us is actually affecting the future right now.

THE ARLINGTON INSTITUTE: MENTAL MAPS TO GUIDE DECISIONS

John Petersen is a professional futurist who says you can't predict the future. Instead "what can be accomplished is to create possible or probable scenarios and to account for as many contingencies as possible." Petersen's Arlington Institute helps military and other government institutions and corporations do just that. His book *Out of the Blue: Wild Cards and Other Big Future Surprises; How to Anticipate and Respond to Profound Change* presents a dizzying array of eighty-four possibilities of things that could happen in our near and distant future. In creating a database to examine what our future could be like, Petersen ranked the impact any one change in society or our environment might have. He rates the length of time its impact will last and to what degree it is capable of altering the life of the individual, a certain societal sector, or society overall.

"You can't predict the future," he insisted in an interview. "There is no way you can do *that,* and anyone who says they can do that hasn't thought about the underlying science. There are too many variables that can make the future different than you thought. The best process is to build alternative pictures in your mind: logical, credible routes or thematically designed pictures, which we call scenarios. These are not things you draw out of the air; you build a spectrum of possible futures. Once you do this, the images that lay in your mind are put against current events in far more effective terms. You can see them in terms of already possible futures."

Describing how the material world is impacted by thought, Petersen continued, "You have already thought about what you are seeing suggestions of. That puts you in a position to anticipate and see the implications of things." As theoretical physicist Fred Alan Wolf, Ph.D., explains it, these are the things that will pop out at us. Sports psychologists have demonstrated convincingly that when an athlete visually rehearses a sports task in their mind it makes for a more effective execution of it. In the same way imagining the future by running through various situations in our minds prepares us for various possibilities. Wouldn't it seem logical, therefore, that we could *better shape* the future by already having thought about the outcome of certain actions?

In this, the Petersen model presents a clear structure for the input of data. As Petersen himself explained, "You have to come up with a system that, given the least number of factors, can account for and adapt to an unknown number of situations." Most interesting to me was the category Petersen calls *wild cards* for their low probability but very high impact.

Petersen writes that wild cards have "a scope and magnitude for which we have neither the experience nor the tools to respond effectively. The Arlington Institute tracks the early indicators that might lead us to anticipate the arrival of selected wild cards. We are also developing computer-based tools that would provide new insights into the behavior of these events." Petersen explained during one of our many interviews that wild cards "have a direct effect on the human condition. They are large, tend to be broad, and cause important, if not fundamental, changes. . . . They happen so suddenly that there just isn't enough time to deal with the impact—no matter how much preparation you do." The Petersen system approach to the future is formulated by evaluating even what the impact would be in the case of a wild card like a global food shortage or a civil war in the United States. A comet striking the Earth would be a megawild card. "Something as big as a comet would have the greatest rate of change and the highest impact of reach. Our vulnerability would be high because of it and it could basically upend our civilization, depending on where it hit."

Many military analysts are concerned with our infrastructure's increasing reliance on our power supply and computerized networks. From municipal watersheds to national security, local factories to emergency rooms, the electric grid is a lifeline. Weapons that can deliver an electromagnetic pulse from a distance, shutting these systems down, are more of a threat today than in decades past and present the looming specter of another wild card event.

I spoke with Nick Begich, Ph.D., founder of Earthpulse Press, when he was also the director of the Lay Institute. He told me, "Just a few decades ago, there were manual systems with technicians trained to wind a crank or push a lever." Today, most systems are operated by people sitting at keyboards telling computers what to do. "A shutdown of the grid," says Petersen, "would really mess things up. Almost all business would come to a halt. Imagine what you could do to an economy. There would be no fresh food and no running water in urban areas. The municipal services, like fire houses and police departments, would be handicapped by lack of power." If terrorists or weather events were to eliminate a major piece of the power grid, the "impact would be global. . . . Given our great vulnerability and the scale of its impact, it should be one of those systems things that our society takes a better look at." Surprisingly playful, he also added, "But there would be more babies conceived so there just might be a population boom later on!"

Petersen looks at power factors and rates of change when evaluating the impact of a future possibility; therefore he is able to show how a global community or single person can plan for a wild card event. "What you need to do is decide which wild cards are the most significant ones. You pick a dozen characteristics, how fast is it coming, how much effort is there to offset it," and what its reach or impact might be on the world. I pointed out as an example, "from there you can run mental or physical exercises like we did worldwide to prepare for Y2K in the year 2000. The advance planning enabled us to address most situations before they arose as well as preventing most from occurring."

I asked Petersen what he saw concerning the use of paranormal skills by people in the future. "There's no question," he said, "that we will have more people exercising their powers in a new way. Remote viewing, which we already know is used around the world, would have a near-global reach, but its popularity will be curtailed, in part, by opposition to its development." In other words, it will probably be quite some time before you'll see any government-sponsored billboards advertising the power of nonlocal mind, or what author Gregg Braden (*The Isaiah Effect, The God Code,* and *Secrets of the Lost Mode of Prayer*) refers to as *inner technologies* and renowned psychic Ingo Swann calls *biomind superpowers.* As Swann points out (see chapter 8), there aren't many "power schools" where you can go to learn how to perfect the use of your nonlocal mind, which is unfortunate because tests on Swann and other natural psychics prove we are wired to function at levels far beyond our current understanding and normal practice. Our nonlocal mind, or our access to the universal mind field, makes it possible for us to see across great distances, effect healing from afar, and even view distant planets.

These traits are the traits of the soul making itself visible in our very real human form. As I see it, manifesting these great human powers is the path of the future. There may even come a time when telepathic talents will be one of the few ways we can stay in touch with each other, as we may not actually have cell phones or landlines that work. By practicing now to perfect these latent talents in all of us, we can begin to ensoul the world and therefore improve our potential futures.

Some of the potential futures the Arlington Institute looks at are beneficial, like the end of a carbon fuel economy, showing just how important changes made today can be. I couldn't resist asking a man who says nobody can predict the future, while simultaneously showing us how accurately you can estimate it, to tell us the major trends he saw for the future. "If you want the most fundamental condition I see for the future," Petersen noted, "it's the haves and have-nots and that's not just economic. It's nations not having access to technology and medicine. So the issue that I think is most problematic for the future is how do we deal with that? There is a growing, accelerating hazard in this separation."

Petersen agreed that we have no choice but to bring disciplines together, such as a developing synergy of talents for finding solutions to some of our greatest environmental challenges. "All problems are interdependent, interlaced systems and there is encouragement that comes from new sciences like chaos theory or science of complexity or new technology, making complex issues and databases presented in three-dimensional forms. It makes issues easier to see." It seemed Petersen had landed upon what his work was fundamentally about.

"What any of us see as the future has a lot to do with what it will be like. Looking across the horizon and creating normative scenarios of a desired future—if you do that as an individual or a kid deciding what he wants to become or a nation planning their own future you need to envision; you need this idea of where you want to be downstream."

From a systems point of view, the question is how to create an action plan to reach a goal or prepare for a possibility. The actual physics of imaging in our minds tells us that what we envision has a greater possibility of manifesting than something we have never even considered. In short, Petersen was explaining—from a function of systems—why others have counseled humanity to imagine ourselves richly and to consider others' needs. I suspect the answer will lie in what the Buddhists identify as compassion or dependent co-arising and what ecologists call sustainability. Humans are designed to exercise free will and that is one of the reasons we can't entirely predict the future, but a semblance of the future is already present today, within each one of us.

THE RISE OF THE CORPORATION

W. Warren Wagar, Ph.D. (1932–2004), wrote *A Short History of the Future,* which gives us an opportunity to examine potential scenarios in the near and distant future. As professor of history at State University of New York at Binghamton, Wagar conducted "History of the Future" classes for several decades. I asked him in one of our broadcast discussions what changes he saw in his students' view of the future (his findings were compiled from the 1980s to the year 2000). His response was not surprising, but disconcerting nonetheless. "Students are more pessimistic about the future. They seem to think of the world with a great deal of skepticism. Yet I have to say that there are still those who are deeply engaged in making a difference in the world, who want to repair the world, want to be part of something positive."

Wagar predicts three different periods just ahead for humanity based on current trends. "The first phase," he explained, "is what I call *Earth Incorporated.* Looking at the next forty some years [we] anticipate a rising tide of globalization, but also of accumulation and concentration of capital in larger and larger multinational corporations. There will also be more and more effort by industrialized nations to bring law and order to the less developed parts of the world, even at the expense of exploiting those countries. The whole thing culminates in a clash between the rich and the poor nations in 2044, a terrible catastrophe that starts with a nuclear war and finally leads to the unraveling, temporarily, of civilization."

Wagar's descriptions of the future are almost clinically precise, though you can hear his discomfort with the possible scenarios he details. My instinctual concern is that we not become attached to either his scenario or its time frame, as this may make it a more solidified possibility by our sheer imaging of it in our minds. "Listener beware!" I felt like saying. "Wipe this out of your mind!"

"Second phase," he continued, "which I call the *Red Earth,* is the rise of the world republic, which nationalizes wealth, puts all corporations under the control of a world republic, and attempts to rebuild the shattered Earth, to restore the environment: the great housekeeping effort. In part three of this progression, the world republic becomes unnecessary. It had been vital to rebuild the Earth, to make technological advances, but finally in part three, in the twenty-second century, we have the House of Earth—where many different communities form that are independent of one another with closer relations, but everyone goes their own way. The Earth is free for social, political, and spiritual experimentation."

What current events, I asked, already identify our near future as one of schism between wealth and poverty? "The enormous resentment that is felt towards the U.S. and Britain and other developed nations," continued Wagar, "is the sense that these developed countries are exploiting the poor countries, permanently keeping them underdeveloped for the sake of their own enrichment." Like Petersen, Wagar appreciates that this perception is a justified one and that "until that sense of difference recedes and until there is a better distribution of the world's wealth and resources, I think that resentment is only going to grow." From space colonization to changes in religion, education, and health care, Wagar essentially paints a portrait of great disassembling, then a government consolidation, then eventually a hundred years from now—after going through decades of war—there will be world peace and mutual collaboration. During this last phase, we will respect our differences as a richness rather than something that should be altered.

My own personal concern about the loss of representative government in America inspired me to spend ten years as a daily radio broadcaster, three to five hours a day, five days a week, speaking out about globalization and world affairs. I thought that if light were shed on the decimation of the rule of Constitutional law—that which makes us a republic in America—then we would collectively rise up to change things. Wagar and I agreed, however, that although it is important to challenge the things that we know to be unjust, unethical, and wrong, and that a shift in consciousness would be the biggest wild card of all, if humans remain locked into the consciousness of dominating and exploiting matter, it is clear that we will continue marching into a period of geofascism with a system of homogenized economies. This will necessitate a type of global-political homogeny in government as well. I still hope my several decades of air work concentrating on these and other civil liberty and environmental issues with many activists in every state ignited a passion in some people, for the republic and representative law making and keeping, as it was ignited in me and which motivated me to join the Libertarian Party in July of 1996.

Though he made no note of it, Wagar was also relating what many prophetic traditions have proclaimed. Only after great suffering will the people of this world come to know that we are one humanity. The Hopi say we are living in times of great change and that we all must learn to swim in the middle of this raging river, letting go of the shoreline, of what we know and are comfortable with. Many traditions state clearly that we have a great choice, between a path of harmonization or a path of destabilization for us as individuals and as a planetary society. The path all sacred traditions point to is one wherein we consciously pursue a reverent life that inherently requires ethical stewardship and action compelled by the awareness that duality is an illusion. There is no *us versus them,* there is only *all of us:* you and me, river and otter, forest and town, nation and planet. To know where we want to be in the future, as Petersen points out, we have to be honest about where we are now, individually and collectively.

Continuing with Wagar's view of the global corporation having greater power than nations is what John Perkins details in the books he has written about his life, *Confessions of an Economic Hit Man* and *Hoodwinked,* which we discussed during two different broadcasts, the most recent in 2012. Perkins was a chief economist at a major international consulting firm. He advised the World Bank, IMF, and the countries of Africa, Asia, and others in the fine art of what Perkins calls *predatory capitalism,* which he noted, "has created truly the first global empire. And it's really not an American empire, it's a corporate empire . . . whose only goal is to maximize profits regardless of the social and environmental costs . . . and that has really created a failed global economic system. It fails for everyone except the very wealthy [corporation]. They are really predators on the rest of us."

We currently function under an *institutionalized death economy,* a term

I created and have used for over a decade. It's an economy of destruction based on warfare and disregard for the environment, healthy food systems, adequate health care, women, children, and animals. We have a poisoned agriculture industry, species declination from human impact, and billions of people living in subsistence poverty, slave workshops, sex indenture, and civil wars. And where these things go on there is also big business.

Perkins filled in the blanks of this reality. "Just as it was my job as an economic hit man," he explained, "to identify countries with resources that our corporations coveted, like oil, we arranged huge loans to those countries through big international banks. The money doesn't actually go to the countries [though they will be responsible for paying off these banking debts], it went to our own corporations to build projects in those countries, infrastructure projects like highways, ports, electric power grids," clarifying that this was not for the benefit of the people in these communities who cannot afford a car or pay for electricity in their homes.

In my years as a whistle-blower I referred to this calculated process as *extreme politics,* as it leads to "nation taking." When a nation cannot afford to pay its debts to these banks, it forfeits its autonomy. Sometimes its resources are privatized through the banks to foreign companies and the bank then indentures the citizenry to repay the nation's loan, with severe consequences to their own low-wage economies. "So this corporato-cracy," Perkins continued, "saw how successful this was in Asia and Latin America. And that's what we've been experiencing" here in America, referring to the recession that began in 2008, which led to so many Americans' forfeiture of their homes and loss of jobs.

"It's the same as our banks telling a person who can only afford a $300,000 house that they can buy $500,000 house, and the house is the collateral—telling people it would be worth a million dollars in a few years, to tighten their belts and buy the house. And then of course the bottom fell out of the market and the house is now worth $200,000 and they still have debt close to $500,000. When people are in deep debt they become slaves to the system." We both noted that many younger people worldwide are aware of this corporate plantation that has made every-thing a utility to exploit, all the way down to our very DNA.

So, people are right to protest the lack of representative lawmaking, the decimation of natural resources, forests, waterways, farming land, our air, and now even space. But we as consumers, the *all of us* wherever we live, have choices and our choices help shape the corporations' capacity to influence legislation and to mislead workers and consumers without regard for the long-term or even the short-term welfare of anything but their profit margins. Thus the future of this corporatocracy is, in part, in our own hands. Identifying its methods is a start to changing it.

Slave labor, for example, is alive and well in the world, both in the so-called free market and in the industrial prison systems where indentured servitude goes without challenge by the general public in the United States, which imprisons more people than any other nation on Earth.

In America one in every one hundred people is behind bars. According to the Pew Center on the States *Issue Brief, Prison Count 2010,* while state prison populations are declining slightly, federal prison populations have doubled since 1995 and by 2008 immigration cases accounted for 28.2 percent of all federal sentences. Twenty-one thousand foreign nationals were imprisoned in America at that time. Enslaving immigrant populations behind bars is big business in America.

From smuggling and indenturing people of all ages to field labor, sweat shops, and sex and drug marketing, the globalization taking place results in part from the enormous movement of people worldwide looking for work or safety from oppression and war. In 2011 there were 71.3 million migrants residing in Europe, 57.2 million in North America, 61.3 million migrants in Asia, and 19.1 million in Africa. These are people traveling from their homes to either foreign lands or foreign countries to obtain work. However, the United Nations High Commissioner for Refugees has estimated that there are currently about 43 million people forcibly displaced worldwide by war. Why is it that the more global our communication and impact can be, the more egregious the appetite for domination and exploitation in some humans becomes?

In an ecological model of dramatic change, more people will be relocating across the planet. Given the reality of global warming, and with it rising oceans, these immigrant numbers could include those people currently occupying waterfront areas who will be forced to move inland. This future migratory population could impact much of the east and west coasts of America. My own state of Maryland and our nation's capital of Washington, D.C., along with the Naval Academy, could be partially underwater in the decades to come.

Kathleen Newland, writing for the Migration Policy Institute in 2011 in *Climate Change and Migration Dynamics,* shows how a change in sea level, increased temperatures, a disruption of water cycles, and severe storms will change all nations. And some nations—such as Egypt, Bangladesh, Vietnam, India, and China—have lowland farmland that will be at risk as well. The report makes clear that in terms of sheer numbers of people who may be on the move in the decades to come, sixteen of the twenty-two largest cities in the world are seaports. It's not just small island populations that will need to relocate; it's also the populations of Calcutta, India; Bangkok, Thailand; Shanghai, China; New York and Miami; and other major urban and rural areas. Studies show that by 2070 hundreds of millions, maybe billions, of people could be displaced, looking for higher and drier land, while trillions of dollars in lost assets could collapse economies worldwide.

Yet, as shown by many other guests on my radio programs, including well-known futurist Gerald Celente, we are poised on the brink of a revolution in technology that can help humanity avert global chaos, but we are heading into troubled waters first. Globalization and economics divorced from the valuing of all life is a serious threat to everyone. And as Celente reminded us, "In the end, there is no doubt that there is a driving desire in most human beings to do good and to make a difference in the world." As an example, Perkins is quick to show that new economies based on bartering, on worker-owned factories, and on sustainable energy systems are sprouting up in some of the most decimated places. "We are our future," he said with great hope, reflecting—from my point of view—the bottom line about the future of humanity: we are its primary architects.

MASS DREAMS OF THE FUTURE

Echoing the values of the dreamers in the Greek temples of Asclepius, Chet Snow, the late Helen Wambach (1925–1986), and R. Leo Sprinkle began a series of meditation workshops in the 1980s in an attempt to see if there was a consensus vision of the future. Some of the 2,500 participants possessed varying degrees of intuitive talents. Snow and Wambach's book *Mass Dreams of the Future* presented the results of their study and some of the vivid, personal mass dreams they recorded, which, when gathered together, make the landscape of tomorrow seem ever present. Focusing on the two time periods of 2100–2200 and 2300 and beyond, they utilized the data of 133 participants for purposes of valid statistical analysis. The results fell into four distinctive general categories or types of habitation in the future: (1) in-space habitats off the Earth's surface, either in space stations, spaceships, or in experimental colonies on other planets; (2) seemingly new age communities on Earth, usually in the mountains or near the ocean shore; (3) high tech urbanites, mostly living in artificially enclosed or underground cities; and (4) rural survivors in nineteenth-century-style villages. According to these visions, the future is as varied as are feelings about them.

When I first interviewed Snow he told us that "one gets the overall impression from many of these reports from the 2100 era that there are large unpopulated areas of the Earth's surface in that time period." Explaining that only 5 percent of participants claimed reincarnating during the twenty-second century, 11.5 percent saw a future life in the following century, the twenty-third suggesting the possibility of a greater population base in the 2200s. Most participants talking about the former time period reported that there was a smaller population on Earth. What remained consistent during both time periods reported on (2100–2200, and then beyond the 2300s) was that the high tech city inhabitants' limitation to domed and enclosed interior spaces and underground housing was accompanied by a sense of unhappiness over that fact, even though great central gardens throughout the biodomes were described.

I asked Snow to elaborate on the various types of space communities that participants had described. "They are not all the same. Some found themselves living in interplanetary shuttles while others found themselves living in experimental stations on Venus and Mars. Several claimed to be residing on an asteroid or simply not on Earth." Of the space-dwelling respondents, many reported an alliance with other space-voyaging species or aliens who helped supply humans with resources for living in space. As we will examine later, using Mars as a way station is just around the corner. Indeed, as briefly described in chapter 8, Ingo Swann and others have also presented compelling evidence suggesting that there may already be a colony of humanoids on the moon involved in some type of mining operation, much like the one that our current American space program is promoting for the near future.

In past-life regression therapy, to be discussed later in this book, subjects are put into a slightly altered state and then often directed to look at their feet or hands and clothing in order to help identify where in time they are standing. I imagined it would be the same in future-life progressions, so I asked Snow how people saw themselves dressed in the future. Some of those living on Earth and in space saw themselves dressed in loose fitting tunics or robes. However, 77 percent of those who saw themselves residing in a space-type environment were wearing one piece, tight fitting uniforms or jumpsuits, often described as metallic-looking and usually gray or silver. Interestingly, this description matches that given by thousands of people reporting contact with UFOs and ET (extraterrestrial) beings. This same type of outerwear is described as the garb of the alien species that are reported as most actively engaging humans all over the globe.

And what did these space-bound, jumpsuited humans of the future eat? Artificial and prepackaged pills that looked like "high tech, high-protein minerals and vitamins served in cubicles on a plastic tray, like butter quarters in plastic blocks."

The data regarding emotional states of people living at least one hundred to several hundred years from now revealed a mix, just as one would find on Earth today. Some reported feeling good about space habitation, while others felt a great sense of loss and of missing Earth. Even those who found themselves in high tech, golden cities were distraught over a sense of emotional deprivation and of seldom being able to go outside. Those who saw themselves living in natural environs on Earth, the new age–like communities, reported the greatest overall satisfaction with their lives and the future. This study group suggested that what would be perceived as great Earth changes could also be the catalyst for a new spiritual age to unfold.

There were a great many correlations in the locations identified in the study where communal villages would exist after 2100. These included the Rocky Mountains, the Himalayas, Greece, the Peruvian Andes, Finland, a Pacific island, Ireland, New Hampshire, Western Africa, and in North Carolina and Florida. While some seem illogical, even land masses underwater currently might rise again. The monumental work of Edgar Cayce, psychic and founder of the Association for Research and Enlightenment, which was carried out almost entirely through the use of trance mediumship, produced a volume of data, which suggests that some of these same locations could become safe havens after enormous Earth changes take place. Actually, some of us believe these enormous Earth changes have already begun, evidenced in the melting of Arctic glaciers and the erratic weather that is increasingly taking place all over the world today.

I AM AMERICA

Lori Toye grew up in a small rural farming community in conservative Missouri, so what happened to her when she was in her twenties was not something she was prepared for. She had a series of visions that introduced her to some profound spiritual teachings.

Although she did not participate in the Mass Dreams of the Future workshops, she has meticulously detailed her many future visions, which include some imagery of very detailed maps. In fact, one of the maps Toye says she was shown in her mind is called the *Golden City Map,* which also identifies what areas in the United States may become centers of spiritual rebirth after certain land areas are submerged beneath the ocean and others rise. Some of these golden cities correspond to the areas identified as spiritual sanctuaries by the participants of the Mass Dreams of the Future workshops.

When her first dream about future Earth changes occurred, Toye was frightened and unsure what to make of it. "My work with Earth changes began with a reoccurring dream that started in the early '80s. It was a very interesting dream," she said. "Four beings in white robes came to me and gave me a map of the United States. But it was not a typical map. The map showed very drastic Earth changes." At first these dreams unnerved her, Toye explained, and she remembered commenting to a friend, "'This is a very scary thing.' I was the mother of three small children at the time. It was very frightening for me, until my friend reminded me that prophecy says that after such changes we will have a golden age."

The first map that Toye was shown was called the *I Am America Map,* which she shared publicly with the world in 1983. It shows a map of what the United States may look like "after this time of great change. Much of California is gone, the Northwest—Oregon and Washington are gone. . . . They talked about the opening up of the Mississippi from the Great Lakes to the Gulf of Mexico and opening up Texas into this new huge bay." If you recall the midwestern floods of the late 1990s, 2007, 2008, and 2011, such a division down the center of the United States seems within the realm of probability.

It was this very same image that my husband, Bob Hieronimus, drew in the early 1970s as a result of a waking vision he had.

The devastating hurricanes, tornadoes, and floods in America and around the world, the increasing instances of typhoons, forest fires, volcanic activity, earthquakes, droughts, landslides, and even tsunamis—such as the Indian Ocean tsunami that followed the Indian Ocean megathrust earthquake of December 26, 2004, and took the lives of over 230,000 people in fourteen countries—support the reality of Earth changes from natural disasters affecting where we live and how we live. The up to twenty million tons of debris crossing the Pacific Ocean in the aftermath of Japan's March 11, 2011, 9.0 earthquake and tsunami shows another way in which the planet is all connected (as does the floating garbage in the North Atlantic and Indian Oceans).

Toye continued, saying that the great teachers in robes who appeared to her, known as the *ascended masters,* "said that global warming is now

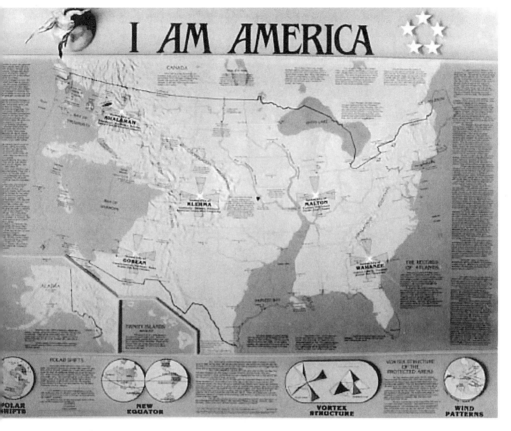

Fig. 2.1. The map of America that Lori Toye saw in her visions of the future. Image courtesy of Lori Toye, I Am America Publishing.

happening all over the world and is a prelude to these coming Earth changes: global superstorms, high winds, greater extremes in all weather." Unfortunately, three decades after this information was imparted to Toye, ecological science studies are confirming these predictions about the effects of global warming, a topic I first covered in the early 1980s.

When I interviewed Toye for an update on her work in 2011, she stressed what she believed were the reasons behind her visions of the future. When they first started happening, she felt like she was "working almost like a telephone, taking information. There were eighty sessions total. But I came to realize that the maps were also about changing our way of viewing the world. We have amazing power to change the world simply by what we do today." Toye was confirming what Petersen and others tell us is so: humans have an amazing capacity to shape the future by what we do today. This is a logical statement, but it is also a spiritual one. It affirms that how we look at the future is also shaped by our values and feelings, not just by information.

PROPHECY AND PERCEPTION

Toye emphasizes that the Earth changes shown to her may not occur as presented, depending on "what humanity does to address our genuine and critical environmental challenges. . . . What *is* clear is that these changes will occur to some degree so that a new consciousness can occur on Earth. It is very, very important for our evolution," she believes. Indeed, historical records agree with the predictions of prophets, psychics, visionaries, and dreamers: catastrophic Earth changes and the birth of a new civilization go hand in hand.

As we know from scientific tests—as described by William Marks (who is now known as William Waterway), author of *The Holy Order of Water*—mankind has the ability to purify water with loving intentions and prayers. Consequently, forestalling or altering catastrophic Earth changes should be within our spectrum of potential. It is also this awakening that Barbara Hand Clow has addressed over the decades and writes about in *Awakening the Planetary Mind: Beyond the Trauma of the Past to a New Era of Creativity,* which emphasizes that we are awakening to our multidimensionality and global mind and global heart. Catastrophism, Hand Clow points out, is a memory-based tendency originating in historic catastrophic events eleven thousand five hundred years ago. These events separated humanity from its prior prediluvial world of a highly developed and benign seafaring culture. This trace memory remains in our DNA and inspires fear and duality, although we can alter its influence by our thoughts and actions today through many steps we can take.

One step in particular that we can take toward positive cocreation might be to recognize what the aborigines, ancient Greeks, and modern-era dream counselors teach: to value our dream time just as we value our waking time, for they both are real even though they operate in different domains. What we think, say, and do shapes the material world because the material and immaterial world interpenetrate at all moments. As Petersen and Toye and numerous guests of mine suggest, what we imagine or daydream about or experience in sleeping dreams makes certain things possible. Perkins calls it, as do many tribal peoples, shape-shifting. We can become what we imagine. Having held an image of something in our minds makes it potent. It has an effect like turning up the volume to a song one is listening to.

The material and immaterial realms of life are reflexive, that is, they reflect one another. This aspect of how consciousness interfaces with the immaterial potential in all life is one aspect of quantum physics that is being studied today. These scientists' efforts hark back to similar pursuits by the alchemists of another era whose common goal was the purification of oneself and the transformation of matter. The mandate of ancient wisdom teachings is to refine the material world and one's personal nature in order to reach divine revelation and create a paradise on Earth. Clearly, this is not a new pursuit. Seeking refinement and harmony between disparate life systems seems to be a natural tendency, if not the purpose of humanity.

I have found over the decades that many of us are engaged in this alchemy of consciousness as a deliberate pursuit, one which juxtaposes the eternity of the soul with the expression of life we encounter in our daily lives as thoughts, feelings, and actions and attempts to synthesize or bring together numerous sciences and talents in order to address our shared challenges. Such a focus by any person ultimately leads to a finding, by way of example, that if we want to see peace in the world, we also have to manifest peace within ourselves, in our individual lives.

In the esoteric tradition of Judaism, from the Chassidic lineage of which I am a student, it is said that in the afterlife we wear the garment made of our accumulated thoughts, speech, and actions. Our lives and how we live them create the design, style, and color of the wardrobe of light we will be known by when the denser body is cast off. As described in Judaic teachings, our lives are a corridor to the world to come. Life on Earth is the living classroom that nurtures each person's development from lifetime to lifetime.

Within this living classroom that we call Earth, and specifically within the physics community on the planet today, there is a wonderful group of functional mystics. The laws they have discovered or modeled are in complete agreement with the teachings of many ancient spiritual and indigenous traditions. Fundamentally, everything is expressed as a refraction or part of an inseparable whole. As well, through the law of similars, all manifest and yet to be manifest states are related through the octaves of similars. Much like a piano keyboard, where there are eight different variations or octaves of a note, our thoughts are like these musical notes when put into a musical frame of reference. They have beat, they have frequency, they have a shape and sound to them. Some call them *thoughtforms*. According to clairvoyants who can see them, these thoughtforms emanating from an individual can literally reach out and affect the shape of the material world.

Certainly we know from personal experience that we can get what in the sixties were called good and bad vibrations from people and places. This is a real sensation based on real energetics. When you remember the basics of physics, that all material things are vibrations and that our own bodies are primarily biocapacitors that respond to acoustical, electrical, chemical, and magnetic forces to name a few, all of which produce various states of vibration, it's easier to picture how we all interact. It's as if we are in an ever-seething matrix of energies interconnected all of the time. This "all connectedness" is facilitated through what can be thought of as a life field, or the L-field, although scientists call it by many names. Many of those whose work is presented here are studying this particular aspect of science.

In summary, dreams, meditations, and visions have potency just as waking "reality" does. What is physical and not physical are related and our thoughts and emotions can bring harmony into a community or life, or inversely, disharmony. We are powerful creator beings and our destiny is to become aware of this capacity. This renewed awareness of the role we each play, as both observers and doers in our world, shows us why we should each strive to manifest our highest ideals, dreams, and loving hearts. We are all actively participating in the future of our world, all of the time.

THE PHYSICS OF CONSCIOUSNESS: WHERE MIND ORGANIZES MATTER

Fred Alan Wolf, Ph.D., author of *The Dreaming Universe: A Mind-Expanding Journey into the Realm Where Psyche and Physics Meet* and *Mind into Matter: A New Alchemy of Science and Spirit* and several other books, has a wonderful sense of humor about quantum mechanics. As he often points out with a chuckle, "everything we perceive is real; it's just in varying rates of vibration."

A physicist would talk about the same thing from the quantum perspective, explained Wolf. I had asked him to explain the hermetic axiom "as within, so without, as above, so below" in the terms of physics. "Quantum physics is the study of atomic and subatomic matter and energy. It's also the study of light and its relationship to matter and energy. It's also the study of what happens on the very small time scale, space scales. It appears to be the overarching theory, which governs the whole material world."

Wolf is decidedly what I would call a thought adventurer. In his book *Mind into Matter* he asks, "So where does the new information providing (for instance) the choices for natural selection come from? How does this information come into the world? I'll tell you: New information is not generated from the past; in terms of space and time it must come from the future." He is certain that we live in parallel universes and that we are multidimensional beings that can be expressed in mathematical equations, or even the ancient Hebrew alphabet. Our lives have a mirror reflection from the vacuum of space, or as he so eloquently puts it, "the world depends on what you believe is real. If the many worlds' interpenetration is real, then you exist in more than one world and every event in every universe affects you. More than that, you affect everything else in all of these universes in countless ways."

Our language of today has its roots in the Hebrew alphabet, where each letter is an energy state, a state of being. As Wolf said, our alphabet, or Alef Bet, can be traced back to the Hebrew where "each of these letters actually is a word itself, meaning something. *Aleph* (A), for example, meant great power or ox. *Bet* (B) was house or that which separates something from the outside and the inside. And *gimel* (G) meant movement or, in Hebrew, a camel.

"Here we have these remarkable letters that are also words and they give us a hint as to their spiritual nature. I found that when I went back deeply enough into the roots of alchemy Hebrew was really a basis for a lot of their discovery." And he relates that when he went looking for the roots of science, "I found it in ancient Kabbalah, which is really a spiritual understanding of the nature of reality."

Repeating that reality is not limited to the physical world, he reminded us of the ancient Egyptian and Hebrews' understanding of the power of sound or word. When we examine certain rituals, "we are given

ט	ח	ז	ו	ה	ד	ג	ב	א
Tet	Chet	Zayin	Vav	Hay	Dalet	Gimel	Bet	Alef
(T)	(Ch)	(Z)	(V/O/U)	(H)	(D)	(G)	(B/V)	(Silent)
9	8	7	6	5	4	3	2	1

ס	ן	נ	ם	מ	ל	ך	כ	י
Samech	Nun	Nun	Mem	Mem	Lamed	Chaf	Caf	Yod
(S)	(N)	(N)	(M)	(M)	(L)	(Kh)	(K/Kh)	(Y)
600/60	500	50	40	40	30	20	20	10

ת	ש	ר	ק	ץ	צ	ף	פ	ע
Tav	Shin	Reish	Kof	Tzadee	Tzadee	Fey	Pey	Ayin
(T)	(Sh/S)	(R)	(Q)	(Tz)	(Tz)	(F)	(P/F)	(Silent)
400	300	200	100	900	90	800/80	800/80	700/70

Fig. 2.2. Alef Bet. The twenty-two letters of the Hebrew alphabet are powers and qualities hidden in words.

a place to start looking at language, to perhaps identify how they went about selecting tones." For example, the story of Joshua bringing down the walls of Jericho with his trumpet blasts demonstrates that all matter is either held together or dissembled through frequency. Each note, sound, or word has a reflective shape. Current developments in energy weapons and energy healing operate under these same principles.

Mastering how our minds shape matter is the key to our future habitation of our bodies and the Earth. When we understand this process, it will be easier to appreciate our individual and collective power and divinity and appreciate just what it is that animates our soul and what spirit does in the body. Wolf tried to explain how our thoughts could manifest on the physical plane by using the analogy of how a computer thinks. "In the language of the computer there is something we call a *bit*. A bit is just a smidgen of information. You might call it the primary distinction: it is either a zero or a one. From piles of these bits you can make a number of different arrangements, which turn into words, pictures, sounds, lights, and feelings. . . . The bit represents the change from outside to inside, or from what is unmanifested [not manifested] to what is manifested. It represents void into something, suggesting that the first bit came about like the [theory of a] big bang. It turned zero into one. Thus the bit became an *it*." Though this is good descriptive language for manifestation, just for the record I don't personally consider the big bang as a comprehensive enough description of creation.

As it relates to the new alchemy, however, Wolf explained that when you realize that even before there were bits (zeros or ones), there was something that was neither a zero nor a one, but merely the *potential* to be a zero or a one. Today this is filtered into a science he called quantum computers. "Quantum computers operate not with bits, not what we call zeros or ones, but with what we call Q-bits, quantum bits. There are values in between zeros and ones, and they are capable of manifesting later as zeros or ones. They are encoding a tremendous amount of information." It may be that if we ever discover a technology that reflects God's creation of the universe, "it may be to some extent Q-bits that manifest in the physical world, or in the unmanifest world, or what we call the mind world, the mental world."

I pointed out that one way to see this universality, via looking at the computer language of bits, is that whether one speaks Russian, Chinese, or English the computer translates each language into ones and zeros.

Here quantum science begins to sound like numerous occult teachings. "There are also other subtle vibrational patterns," Wolf continued. "We call them quantum waves, or the quantum physical aspects of the physical world. These things are vibrating and are really rather remarkable. They are like pure magic. They are waves of probability, waves of possibility. These possibility waves go through peaks, they vibrate, they undulate, they dance . . . and when things become vibratorily maximum or peaking, so to speak, in these vibratory fields, then things that are likely to occur have a greater chance to occur, providing," and this was the hitch, "there is someone there to observe it. . . . When an observer comes onto the scene, the things which more or less tend to pop out are the things more or less likely to occur. So there is a kind of consciousness guiding the whole process."

Perhaps because they still appreciated their own divine and immortal natures, people in ancient cultures placed more value on the power of thought than we do today. There seemed to be a greater understanding of the role that thought and feelings played in making things happen in both the immaterial and material worlds. Physicists like Wolf are rediscovering the science of how this power manifests. "The whole body is a recording device," he points out. "When information comes into your body, your body reflects it as a vibrational pattern. Our bodies have been designed to reflect and cognate upon incoming information. As new things come into our lives, there is the opportunity to change some of those patterns. When we do change them consciously, we begin to evolve along a story line. We start to tell a different tale by what we observe and how we observe things. There are definite predilections. There is a side of us that is part of the history of the whole human race. This is the constant dance that consciousness plays. The body is there recording things and gives information, when requested by consciousness, to be played back into the world. The whole point of new alchemy is to learn to use different ways of appreciating information, so you don't necessarily see the world the same way all of the time. Most of us are stuck in ruts. We have limited belief systems operating that tell us we are limited to some large extent."

The reason Toye says the maps she has foreseen of the future Earth changes and their aftermath are not fixed in stone is because the extent to which changes occur and how they occur depends on us. When individuals look to the future intuitively or psychically, the scenarios they observe through the veil of time are not fixed realities. At any moment of looking we perceive only what exists at that moment, based on the current congruency of thought-wave patterns circling the world and of deeds taking place. A group of people focused with good intention and doing good works in the world can make a profound difference in terms of what happens now and in the future. "The whole universe is vibrational," as Wolf says. "Every human being, by observing and by learning how to observe, can actually alter these waves, these possibilities, so that new possibilities can emerge." In essence, we are all minicreators making the world every moment what it is; it's just that most of us aren't aware of it. Most of us think that the world is simply happening to us, but it is also true that *we* are happening to the world.

3

REMEMBERING OUR NATURE

OPERATORS OF SPIRIT AND MATTER

I was a very philosophical child, always asking "why" and "how" about things I didn't understand. This got so annoying to my mother that she came up with a saying that she would often use in exasperation whenever my questions or those of my three siblings got too tedious. "The message is, there *is* no message," she would say emphatically. Or, "the answer is, there *is* no answer."

Despite my innumerable attempts to understand the underpinnings of my universe and why everything in it behaved the way it did, I can't say today that I completely know how the universe really works or what the role of consciousness is, ultimately, in the greater scheme of things, but I have found confirmation that it is multidimensional. I know that it can exist outside the constraints of time and space and it changes when any of us looks at it or attempts to describe it. It also seems to me that consciousness is a vehicle by which our soul acts upon the world, by becoming imbued in matter, feeling, willing, sensing, observing, synapsing, and so forth.

The visible and the invisible collaborate. There is balance between the immortal, spiritual soul and the mortal body and physical world. It seems that souls cycle and twist, repeat and reprise and, in so doing, echo ancient themes common to all human beings. The Gnostics called this constant "circling home" the homesickness of the soul. It yearns for its own milieu, which is not of this material world. In the Western world we are brought up to believe that the "not visible" realm is illusion and the material realm is real. However, as taught by most esoteric religious and spiritual systems, life is a combination of these two realities. That's why we're called multidimensional beings. Many of my guests over the decades are scientists whose findings corroborate what the spiritual traditions of the world have said all along: spirit and matter are partnered in this dance and drama of life and what is thought of as "not life"; they interact through varying states of resonance, frequency, and vibration.

Furthermore, the individual and the society are bound up in one another. We human beings are animated by a type of spirit force that is nonlocal and immortal yet always present in our embodiment. We are immortal beings in mortal shells simultaneously. We are each a spark of the divine—a spark of God. This is called in Judaic Kabbalah, the *yechidah,* a Hebrew word meaning the singular spark of the originating soul of each person.

What would occur if humanity suddenly remembered its divinity by remembering its world stories in a way that was instructive in the present? What if we recalled that creating and destroying paradise is a collaborative process? Whether to create or destroy paradise is a choice we are making now. We are being shaped by the future spirit of the planet as much as we are being unfolded from the past of the world's soul.

Given this, I have often wondered what might happen if modern science suddenly confirmed and accepted that the imaginal realm is potently informed? What would happen if our culture truly appreciated that it is from the imaginal realm that the world is made, the soul is nourished and made whole. Would the culture of Hollywood change? Instead of perpetuating a constant stream of deadly and violent images as seen so frequently on the nightly news or in the movie theatres, would we see positive and creative images that build up society, the individual, and the world? The soul, as a part of the world soul, is always in the process of becoming; that's why it is always known and unknown. Mind creates the world and so do our hearts. A perfected will, trained to align with love, is godlike.

I have made a general study of consciousness by reading and interviewing others who have studied the phenomena of how consciousness operates. I did this because I wanted to know if there was a consensus, in a modern sense, of what consciousness is, what it does, what underlies it, animates it, invigorates it, qualifies, or defines it. How does it do what it does? Can we identify formative forces?

QUANTUM CONSCIOUSNESS

Candace Pert, Ph.D., of the National Institute of Health (NIH) describes in a miraculous way that we humans are "wired for bliss." Her work, articulated in *Molecules of Emotion: Why You Feel the Way You Feel,* and which she discussed on one of my broadcasts, tells us that from synapse to synapse as a chemical and bioelectric event, we are designed to imagine deeply, to experience profoundly, and to enjoy our bit of paradise on Earth; we are an integral combination of body, mind, and soul. In fact, our minds not only affect our cells, as in the way visualizing can impact bodily integrity or lack thereof, but also our emotions direct our body in the same way a captain does its crew. In addition, our minds can alter our emotions the way the ship builder alters the shape of a ship. Our breath and will, like the wind, can make the ship sail or lie still with no wind at all. We can build the ship, be the wind, and navigate our own unique and particular journey.

In the 1960s one of the first persons to tell us that the answer to consciousness would be found in quantum physics was physicist Evan Harris Walker, Ph.D. (1935–2006). His book *The Physics of Consciousness: The Quantum Mind and the Meaning of Life* describes the synapsing brain in a slightly different way: he suggests that it is the will, as the essential driving force behind the soul's action in the body, that decides whether to synapse or not. This means that brain activity is not as independent from the soul and its desire (will) as it might seem. This is also the same description one finds in Kabbalistic teachings on the soul. In other words, conscious thought, expressed in pointing one's finger at something or shaping ideas, is directed by will. It is neither simply mechanical, by accident, or without purpose. It is not just chemical happenstance, but also a spiritual process. There is an immortal "I" directing these actions.

Walker suggests that, in fact, reality is the result of the observer observing the world. Reality does not exist outside the observer; mind instigates matter to take shape—it *forms* matter. Of course, this is completely in harmony with the ancient hermetic teachings and first people's teachings worldwide and raises the age-old question, if a tree falls in the woods and there is no one there to hear it, does it actually make a sound? Or one could add, does it actually fall?

The material world reflects an immaterial potential, just as a seed contains the potential of the flower or the tree yet to blossom. Consciousness seems to reflect both potential *and* will, while it may be the mind that generates the sustaining wave that each thought is carried on. Mind participates in what Rupert Sheldrake calls a *morphogenetic field,* an environment in which all life talks. Like a telecom provider that gives households their phone lines, mind gives us the current to talk on and consciousness dictates the way we use our minds—what we think, say, and do.

Clinical psychologist and bestselling author Karen Nesbitt Shanor, Ph.D., is a leading expert on the mind. In Shanor's book *The Emerging Mind: New Research into the Meaning of Consciousness,* which was based on the Smithsonian Institution Lecture Series she designed, she shows how our understanding of spirit and matter is finding definition in our scientific laboratories and in our awareness as well.

She says she helped organize the Smithsonian Institution Lecture Series to demonstrate "how very important spirituality is. The Western world [has been] trying to set that aside for quite a while. We thought that we had to separate science from spirituality, but, in fact, we are mind, body, and spirit. Quantum physics gives us a way of studying and under-standing a lot of what most of us knew went on anyway—that is the spiritual part, the nonphysical communication that goes on and even how our thoughts become reality."

Lynne McTaggart is another researcher who is unraveling the mysteries of consciousness. Have you ever had the experience of thinking about a person you haven't been in touch with for a long time and then they call you out of the blue? How thoughts travel, how they make connections, how we really do communicate with anybody anywhere in the world is clarified by her book, *The Field: The Quest for the Secret Force of the Universe.*

Shanor corroborates McTaggart's findings. "We go beyond time and space," Shanor said. "I purposely created the scientific groundwork for it so people will see that science and spirituality are not different." Shanor went on to acknowledge her mentor, Dr. Karl Pribram. As she told me, Dr. Karl Pribram "is my mentor and was my professor at Stanford years ago. [He] has been way ahead of all of this, talking about the quantum parts of the brain, the waveforms of the brain, what parts of the brain hook into the consciousness of the universe, et cetera. Now we are sophisticated enough to show a lot of this."

Shanor went on to describe laboratory experiments that are going on these days in teleportation. "The whole idea of what we call tele-portation, for example, that we can change matter back into wave-forms, change matter and energy back and forth all the time. Einstein knew about that, but now we can . . . demonstrate how this happens. Teleportation is where something disappears and then reappears again simultaneously. Evidently, to 'beam me up, Scotty' you'd need to be standing near a beam and your body would disintegrate and then reappear again somewhere else. In Austria a few years ago, scientists were able to actually demonstrate a form of teleportation within the lab. They didn't do it with a body. They took a little packet of energy and they had it disappear and then reappear simultaneously again in a different place."

This capacity for switching on and off is also present in the human mind. Psychiatrist and leading authority on dissociative disorders, Dr. Frank Putnam has looked at how we change states of consciousness by studying the mind, multiple personality disorder, disassociation, and how a person who is healthy can switch states of consciousness on and off. For example, Shanor related one could be "driving on the road, semiconscious, thinking about something that happened at work or humming a little tune and suddenly somebody quickly darts in front of us and we change our consciousness state very quickly. We don't do it gradually. In fact, it is a quantum leap. Our hearts start beating very quickly. We go through many of these each day. However, most of that happens at the waveform level first and then it becomes a physical reality. We have this quick change of states of consciousness and we manufacture billions of new molecules."

How we shift so suddenly may be explained by what Pribram believes is a place in the brain that responds to the vibrations of the cosmos. "We go from one state of consciousness to another," explained Shanor, "but there is a part in our neural synapses, just before you get to the gap between the neurons—a place in the dendritic web that Dr. Karl Pribram believes is the place that is so subtle. It is like a little spider web that picks up vibrations and he believes that this is the place where the physical part of the brain gathers information from the consciousness of the universe." A more recent book that Shanor coauthored with Jagmeet Kanwal, Ph.D., *Bats Sing, Mice Giggle: The Surprising Science of Animals' Inner Lives* details how vibrational communication from echolocation to singing can be found in nature as a regular method of knowing what one needs to know and sharing it with others. They show how nature is an integral system that uses many different forms of resonant communication.

ERVIN LASZLO'S KIND OF INTEGRALISM

Ervin Laszlo, Ph.D., is the founder of the Club of Budapest and the author of seventy books, including *Science and the Akashic Field: An Integral Theory of Everything* and *The Chaos Point: The World at the Crossroads*.

In an interview he described that he, like others, was asking, "What is the meaning of the world, where are we going? And so I decided to try and find answers to these questions."

"One of the ways to describe it fundamentally," Laszlo said, "is through a kind of *integralism*," a term that I had been using unaware that others were using it to mean other things. Essentially however, Laszlo's integralism and Ken Wilbur's and my own share a basic premise in common: to integrate the sciences and the arts, politics and mechanics, the centuries and the dimensions. I asked Laszlo to describe his use of the word and what it meant to him. He replied, "What is obvious is that what happens in one place affects what happens in another. We have known this happens in the physical body, but we didn't think of this in terms of the world at large. Now it turns out there are these nonlocal effects. This nonlocality simply means that what happens in one place is in fact affecting someplace else almost instantaneously, which means that a signal is traveling much, much faster than the speed of light. . . . We have much better instruments now and what we are finding is that the world is much more subtle than we had thought."

Of course, the ageless wisdom teachings of the world have always given terms to these invisible planes of existence. These terms include the physical and etheric, the astral or emotional body, the causal or the mental body. They also include, as per Hindu theosophy, buddhic or atmic bodies, which in Judaism would be classified as the five components of the soul that are made of different layers of vibrating energy: vital force (*nefesh*), spirit (*ruach*), soul (*neshamah*), living presence (*chaya*), and singular spark (*yechidah*). In turn, these interpenetrating five layers exist in the five worlds of action (*asiyah*), formation (*yetizirah*), creation (*beriah*), emanation (*atzilut*), and the universal archetype of humans (*adam kadmon*) in ascending order. Today, scientists in the laboratory show that these various fields and their pattern-making influences exist and that we are interacting with them.

"The key word is information," Laszlo continued. "We are getting information from the Internet, but also there is information coming from the cosmos." What Laszlo says reaffirms the viewpoints of so many other guests of mine on Hieronimus & Co. radio shows—they have also found that our multidimensionality is both local and outside of locality too. The universe is always interacting with us. Consciousness is the apparatus of the soul as well as all beingness. Consciousness is not confined to the brain or to the body. It seems to be the milieu in which everything that is coming into existence, or otherwise exists, finds itself.

This changes the questions we ask, and therefore the answers we are getting. "When we look at the world as a living system," Laszlo added, "we see that it is our job to help it and maintain it, to help it to grow." We are biocapacitors and we are cosmic capacitors. We digest the light, called vitamin D, as much as we digest an apple and from it get vitamin C. We are invigorated when we do this, when we use our personal will in positive action. Just as healthy soil invigorates the food chain and formic acid is used for development, the cosmic ethers, the local weather, the air in one's household are all collaborating in any given moment. So is each person's body, mind, and heart (spirit)—people who are alive on the planet today and people who are not presently incarnate.

What holds all of this together? It seems to be a sense of interconnectedness between everything. This "everything" responds in harmonized beauty when human feelings and actions, intentions, and thus forethoughts are rooted in compassion and generosity—what in English we might codify in the word *love*, the vitalizing energy of life. A reverent nature and attitude puts us in the proper relationship to life. The job of the human is to be humble, to be reverent, and in so being, to elevate the world.

QUANTUM ACTIVISM

In 2012 I hosted a two-hour conversation on air with quantum physicist Amit Goswami, Ph.D., in which we examined how nonlocal consciousness—which is both personal and universal—informs our actions and the choices we make. We also discussed how, because of this reality, personal selection impacts evolution, be it of the honeybee or a space colony. We talked about how what we do today determines tomorrow.

Goswami has coined the term *quantum activism* to show just how each of us does in fact change the world and why we can change the current trends that ignore the Earth's emergency and our own. As I like to say, what emerges depends on us.

"It only takes a few people to change the world," said Goswami. "Truly, once we understand the mechanism and how the material and immaterial are interacting through us and with us, we open up to a higher level of creativity and insight." The history of science is clear that in the last quarter of the twentieth century there was a "coming to realize that consciousness is the field through which what is immaterial becomes material." We now can see that discovering the quantum reality has shifted the questions we are able to examine, has shifted our own perception of what reality is.

"When I had my own revelation in 1990, I realized that consciousness is the mediator and that there is no dualism between the material and the immaterial realms." While schooled in the Hindu tradition of his family, which honors and recognizes the immaterial realms of life, "I was actually a real materialist but over time this changed."

Goswami told us that there are four worlds, or realms, in which the quantum possibilities of consciousness fall: "Physical for sensing, vital for feeling, mental for thinking, and supramental for intuiting." These four categories show up in many esoteric disciplines, such as Hinduism, Buddhism, Judaism, and other spiritual paths, and are the various octaves of life by which existence becomes self-evident. In Kabbalah one's entire life goal is to come into mastery over one's emotions through the refinements of the mental body guided by the ability to use yet a higher mental faculty than rational thinking—intuition. This intuition seems to be an organ of perception that taps into the cosmic life field where what is not yet seen can be felt and what is possible can be impressed in matter by human will. It is this same field that the I Ching, the ancient Chinese divinatory system, relies on.

To show us that we are not as solid state as we sometimes think, Goswami pointed out that "we don't really live in our body all of the time. Most of the time we are living in our thinking and our feeling realms. Most people have only fleeting experience of their intuition. Major progress has been made though, in our understanding that all of our life experiences are important. All types of experience, physical, emotional, intellectual, and intuitive, are true experiences. Since 1990, we have found that the material sciences that said that everything is happening because of the brain, we now know that this is not the whole story. . . . Most cultures talk about the heart a lot, about our feelings of romantic love. While the heart is just a muscle it is also capable of feeling. Even people with artificial hearts [as we'll examine in chapter 6] have feelings."

Goswami continued with enthusiasm, saying that "fortunately now we have a better understanding. Rupert Sheldrake started a new trend in biology. . . . Sheldrake's idea was a very good one. All of us start with a single-cell embryo, but how then do things become differentiated? What tells the cells to multiply into two, four, and so forth? There is also differentiation between the liver cells, the kidney cells, the brain cells. How do the cells know where they belong in the body? Sheldrake found the answer in what physicists call nonlocality, which means information exchanged without a signal, in other words signalless communication. But there must be something making this interaction happen. Material things aren't supposed to have this happening but Sheldrake suggested there is something called morphogenetic fields, which are necessary to make form. So we get this idea that all biological organs are made in conjunction with morphogenetic fields, and in quantum physics you can put consciousness into the game. This morphogenetic field is what traditionally we call the vital body."

Essentially what Goswami was telling us was that an expression of modern physics is also an ancient teaching about the vital force that supports life on Earth, the same vital force Steiner talked about in the plant world and Christopher Bird (author of *The Secret Life of Plants*) and others showed is so. They are referring to this same vital force accessed in acupuncture and numerous laying on of hands techniques. It is the same vitality captured from plants and minerals, whose essential signatures are stored in water, which in turn is made into homeopathic medicines. "How do we know that this [vital force] explanation is correct?" Goswami asked. "Well, can it explain the chakras [the Hindu system of vital forces in the body]? What we are finding is that we can say, for instance, about the heart chakra that it has something like a soul," something other than the material elements participating in its well-being. The morphogenetic field sustains each form and when it changes, via evolution or personal selection, it then changes all the other forms it will support thereafter. This is one explanation for how changes can happen very quickly in individual lives, worldviews, personal likes and dislikes, and even in biology. It is perhaps why spontaneous remissions can happen or Earth changes can be averted.

As I see it the immaterial realm is informed by quantum bits of consciousness observing itself. Here all life flows endlessly in and out of void and form—consciousness is what grabs the particles and makes form. Action, as will that is applied to form, is a creative endeavor mirrored by the cosmos and by each person. It is a godly undertaking to shape matter into form, to educate a child to become self-aware and a self-managed person. Such a person is more open to love, to helping others, to being honest and kind, to solving personal and communal challenges.

This is a very important finding, Goswami emphasized. When people first meet on the street and hypothetically have an attraction, what is it that makes them feel this affinity? "From a quantum point of view they are collapsing the possibilities and it is the morphogenetic field that is causing this natural congruency, and so then we feel this romantic love." This means that "affinity is taking place outside the locality of the moment, otherwise why would there be this sense of me in you and you in me, and this desire for union when we have no conscious history of knowing each other?" Of course, past lives and karma play a role in this kind of phenomenological model, "but the ground of being is not simply cells doing what they are programmed to do, but cells responding and changing based on things that are not measurable" and may not even be material substances but are invisible influences nonetheless.

This understanding both enables and calls on each person to be stewards of their thoughts, their feelings, and their actions. Why? Because we are all influencing the life field; it is being shaped and determined by us. This is why when one person comes into self-mastery they change the morphogenetic and other fields that people will engage in. When one person finds peace within, they contribute to peace in the world as well. We then can be said to entrain others to a new pathway through this new personal or communal advancement.

All sacred societies tell us that sacred ritual and holy storytelling serve this purpose in society; these are methods that help each person to refine themselves. If one individual improves the way they respond to the world, it is easier for the next person to do the same thing. We see this type of progressive improvement in sports and how world records are broken by succeeding generations—each becoming more proficient and more adept at something that several centuries earlier no one could do. Why? Like the person creating a new path in the woods who has a harder job than the people who will come later, once the trail is made and the path cleared anyone can walk through the woods. Evolution is influenced in a similar way by leaders in every human endeavor.

The world evolves because each person is slowly awakening to the divine life within and the divine life without. Humanity is becoming aware of the ancient culture's due diligence in aligning sacred sites with astrological phenomena, not because they were primitive, rather because they understood how the physical world is influenced by the spiritual forces of the stars, planets, and galactic phenomena—how nature has an immaculate design of relations. Modern civilization is slowly integrating the material with the immaterial sciences that the sacred societies of Earth have preserved and kept alive from century to century, for the benefit of all life on Earth. While climatologists are alerting us to a tipping point regarding global warming and potential global collapse, humanity is not without solutions to these problems. The real challenge remains our desire and our will to change our economy, our education systems, our energy technologies, political and agricultural practices, and what I identified earlier as part of a larger, much more conscientious and vibrant life economy.

Goswami too is calling for quantum activism that shows us that once we change our mind about something, like an attitude that is not helpful, and instead open our consciousness to divine right order, we become vehicles for positive transformation.

Now that we understand the importance of thoughts and feelings as components of evolution, moving toward unity consciousness is necessarily the current impulse needed for our development. If we are wired for bliss as Candace Pert attests, we are also wired for unity and peace. May we each be an addition to the world and the world's future by coming into loving rapport with life.

THE SOUL FIELD OF ROBERT SARDELLO

How then does a person develop a loving rapport with life and become an important addition to another tipping point, the tipping toward good? How do our souls take part in this process? Spiritual psychologist Robert Sardello, Ph.D., author of *Love and the World: A Guide to Conscious Soul Practice,* put it this way during our conversations. "The fact is," he said, "our souls are not separate from our bodies. They are our ongoing substantial connection with the world around us. There is a soul field you can enter. You can feel this. Physicists speak a lot about fields these days. They're real. You can walk in a room and know if there is love in that room or not. You can feel the grieving of the world that is under so much difficulty these days."

But what is our essence as a physical, emotional, and spiritual being? "The essential nature of the human being," proclaimed Sardello, "is that none of us are finished. We are always in the process of becoming who we can fully be. Psychology has always had a very strong bias towards the past and has this view that we are who we are because of what has happened to us in our past. That is only half of the story. There is actually a time current that is coming towards us from the future that we all experience but we don't know how to pay attention to. For it has more to do with who we can become, than who we are due to our past."

Perhaps the key to our reality is that it has as much to do with remembering our past as feeling our future. As Sardello explained, we can step into this place of what is coming to meet us from the future, which has more to do with our destiny. "If we live from only our past, we are fated to do what we do. We become subjects, like a chair," he added. "We become objects to ourselves. . . . The way you can experience the time current from the future is not through our head and thinking. It is experienced through the heart, and if we can be in the place of the heart it's kind of a place of not knowing. It's an ability to allow events and experiences to unfold according to their own design. We learn to pay attention to them rather than direct where we think they should go."

Describing what physicists call interpenetrating but distinct fields, Sardello reminded us that we are not souls inside bodies, but soul-animated bodies. There is no duality because everyone's souls are connected. Together we express the world soul, that part of the world soul we participate in shaping, or that part of the cosmic mind that we collaborate in. Given that we are godlike collaborators, utopia is our perfect state. It is by envisioning the world through our hearts that we are utilizing our godly inheritance.

"We belong to a wider world," continued Sardello. "We are part of the world process. Everything that goes on there, also goes on with us. It's a matter of becoming more sensitive to that." His practice of spiritual psychology "is also a world psychology; it means we can develop the ability to see the oneness of all the world around us. We have to remember ourselves as part of the world; feel the world in us."

For instance, I believe that to have sympathy for something or someone is to be in sympathetic rapport. It is a state of resonance. In sympathy we feel someone's pain. We have let that pain into our heart, but we also know it by comparing it to our own memories, both our body memories and our emotional memories. Thus, sympathy seems to me as much about ourselves as about the subject of our sympathetic exchange. Because this act draws down memories from the biochemical nature of the sympathizer, our act of sympathy can be said to have neurological and biochemical impacts. We are experiencing *other* in a deeply personal way.

On the other hand, when we have empathy toward the world, we are completely surrendered. The *I* has no specific boundary as defined by our usual "me-ness," so to speak. The *I* will is replaced instead by surrender to *thy* will. We are not responding from memory, but from an openness to the unknown, to the mystery of other. It is not related to us from memory; empathy is broader and unlimited in scale. It is related to us from a sense of wonder, awe, and compassion.

If sympathy operates as a partial construct coming from our memory, coming from our past, then might empathy be unfolding from the future? We go out into the universe and we take the image of the encounter (which is a frequency) back into our hearts. When we hold that frequency image there, as Sardello describes in his book, we encounter it in its etheric countenance, in its potential state—much closer to its ideal state than the physical. I like to think of this heart envisioning as a way that we can engage the future before it is totally manifest as a physical reality. To be in empathic entrainment, we go out toward other and other pulls us into their presence, much like a vessel and what fills it.

This imaging process through the heart and the mind allows the future to be altered now. It's as though we allow our hearts, our conscious soul, to repair the world with our attendance. Not a witnessing without action, however, but a witnessing in surrender—a use of will in a selfless movement and intention—a loving of the all and the all within us. We are, in effect, teleporting into the future and reassembling it now. All of these activities meet, however, in the present, in the now.

"The soul's most fundamental activity," said Sardello, "is to make connections between ourselves and others and in the world. This is the inherent power of making things unified. It's love. The opposite of love is fear. It tears things apart. It makes things very isolated. Fear is the exact opposite of love."

The *I* that Sardello speaks of as integral to the soul and our activity in the world is "distinct from our ordinary ego consciousness," he said. "The *I* is the capacity to be present to the world as it unfolds before our eyes, rather than seeing it by what we already know about it. . . . If you look at our lives and try to find a destiny moment, which is something that has happened to us that suddenly changes the direction of our lives, like when people fall in love, that is a destiny region. When you are thrown into your heart everything is new and alive. The center of the *I* is the heart. The challenge is how to live more consistently in that region: in the heart where the world is alive and active. We don't exactly know where we are going," he said, "but indeed it is more of an odyssey than a path. Paradise is in our hands and in our hearts and in our mind's eye."

SWEET'S LANGUAGE OF THE HEART

Communicating from our hearts is one way of conducting prayer. William Sweet talks about prayer the same way a farmer talks about good soil. It is with a familiarity, intimacy, and an acknowledgement that the laws of nature impact us all. Sweet is the former director of the Spindrift Institute founded by the late Bruce and John Klingbeil. Father and son Christian Scientists, the Klingbeils were interested in the actual science of prayer that seemed so effective in their lives and the lives of millions across time. So the Spindrift Institute set out to make a study of prayer.

When Sweet and I spoke, he commented that funding for human experiments would have been cost prohibitive, so they designed studies on plants. Their studies are designed to be replicable using standard scientific protocol for testing theories, designing the tests, and then evaluating the results. As Sweet said, "Anyone can do this and see the truth for themselves." Between 1975 and 1993 the Spindrift Institute conducted thousands of tests on various types of seeds. They prayed over rye, mung beans, and soybean seeds. They prayed for yeasts and molds. And they recorded just how prayer affected each living system. After thousands of tests and test cycles on various plants, they discovered what kind of prayer produces the most beneficial outcome.

Sweet told us about one of the particular tests they ran on mung beans. "We called it the XYZ test," he said. "We would put mung beans in cups and a control group [of these cups was put] out of sight. Daily, one of our Spindrift researchers would pray for the X and the Y cup of mung beans and then later in the day pray for the Y and the Z cup of beans. What happened over a period of time is that this middle cup, the Y cup, was getting double treatment every day. The more we applied prayer, the more effect it had."

> Control sprout growth: 11.5 percent average
> X beans additional growth: 2.0 percent
> Z beans additional growth: 3.1 percent
> Y beans (double treatment) additional growth: 5.4 percent

Spindrift did not test group prayer in this instance, but its XYZ experiment suggests that with one person praying the double treatment or additional quantity of prayer produced increased results.

In one of their soybean tests they added various stresses to the seed, such as extra water or too little water. The task of the people praying over them was simply to pray for the seed's welfare. Some doing the praying were told which seeds were under what kind of stresses while others were not told. Sweet was excited when he shared the results: "Spindrift is probably most well known for our testing of two types of intentional thought," he said, "goal-directed thought and non-goal-directed thought. What we found is, consciously or unconsciously, most people pray with a goal in their mind. . . . The non-goal-directed thought, the one we found to be the holier type of thought, involves more quality and is of a higher intention of what's being prayed for." It is the "thy will be done" kind of prayer that they found over and over again was most effective in creating beneficial results.

"The difference between the two," continued Sweet, "is that when we think in our minds what we want, usually our own ego and our own goals get in the way. We either directly or unconsciously have these goals. We tried to set our experiments up in a tricky way so it would catch our goals. When most of us pray for something or someone, we are praying for a change towards improvement, so we thought it best to deviate the seeds from their healthy norm." The catch is that oftentimes the specific improvement someone is praying for may not be in the best interest of the subject. As Sweet put it, "what we want versus what the plant or persons we are praying for really needs. What we want to happen may not be in the best interest of that which we are praying for."

So even though our intentions are good, perhaps our own will acts as a formative force. I wondered if, by entering our willing volition, we were creating what is called in physics an *interference wave*. Indeed, the Spindrift experiments noted this same quality. "The Klingbeils considered goal-directed prayer to be like particle prayer, and nondirected prayer to be wave prayer," Sweet said. "They found that in non-goal-directed prayer, the prayer's actual impact was shown on a graph as an amplified waveform. Directed prayer, the kind where we determine what we think would be the best outcome, did not, in fact, do so."

"When they prayed a wave prayer," he explained, "to support and love that soybean, they found that type of prayer released the stress in the soybeans. The soybeans that were over-soaked gave off moisture and moved back towards normal and those that were undersoaked started to take on moisture." I commented that the key word seemed to be *love,* and Sweet was surprised. "It's amazing that you even said that. I was going over some of Bruce's original writings today, which I have read many times, and just never saw this before. He says prayer is the love of God. . . . John Klingbeil said we often grab the particles in our prayers but we should learn to catch the waves."

In a similar way this is our goal-directed thought showing itself in the placebo effect. Our faith in something builds a big expectancy, whereas prayer pulls us toward our best outcome or "pulls for a fit," as Sweet called it. This is similar to what happens in empathic experiences. He explained the Spindrift experiments with stressed yeast, wherein the yeast is giving off carbon dioxide gas. "This test was run over 500 times and what was shown was that within a two-hour period a person's effectiveness of prayer could be measured. . . . We have to give up what we are praying for, give it to the universal stream of love, and let love do the work that is required by the organism to achieve its greatest balance." In this case the prayer enhanced the gas being given off when being prayed for, meaning the yeast is being assisted by prayer to become normal again.

One of the most important studies to have taken place, in my opinion, addressed the energetic reality of humanity's undertaking of genetic bioengineering in crops. There is currently a massive effort by Monsanto and other corporations to force the world to accept GMOs (genetically modified organisms) like Roundup Ready soybeans, bred to withstand the chemical named Roundup that is used in agriculture. They also want to prevent any labeling of products in which these GMOs exist, knowing that labeling impacts consumer choices. In addition they are constantly lobbying Congress to be exempt from any further but necessary testing of GMOs, which are already failing safety and efficacy tests worldwide, so much so that some nations, Ireland, Russia, Peru, Japan and Egypt to name a few, have banned their import or use. Spindrift attempted to discern the resonance that the universe, a much larger body than the U.S. Congress, might find for genetically engineered seeds by testing a seed called triticale. Triticale is a self-pollinating hybrid of wheat and rye currently grown primarily for animal feed as either a grain or forage crop. Molecular biologists and others say that they are attempting to improve grain quality to expand the market for human consumption. Designed theoretically to withstand extreme heat and drought, its creators are marketing it as a way to alleviate world hunger. In fact, however, studies show its damaging impact on wildlife reproduction, livestock health, and farmers' actual crop productivity.

The triticale seeds were stressed like the others and then prayed for, but eerily enough there was no change at all. The Klingbeils felt that this suggested an inability of the natural force of love to transform these manufactured organisms. Or, as Sweet said, "The universe did not approve of it. There was no resonance." I believe this finding to be highly significant and something we should be following up on. It gives us a fairly low-tech testing method for all kinds of other things like the Dow Corporation's Enlist corn, designed to withstand 2,4-D herbicide, a main ingredient in Agent Orange, which is the same defoliant that caused cancer, birth defects, and neurological damage in the Vietnamese people and U.S. soldiers who were exposed to it in the 1960s.

Returning to the subject of the Klingbeils' research center, they chose to name their institute *Spindrift* after the froth at the edges of violent sea storms, because thirty years ago it was, indeed, mightily heroic to have ventured into the science of spirit. Our dear friend Christopher Bird wrote about their courageous venture and subsequent confirmation so long ago in his book *The Secret Life of Plants* as he chronicled others experimenting with plants and showing that they absolutely do communicate with humans. Made of similar organic compounds, we resonate our essence of light. Love brightens it and puts it into an entrainment. Bird was right about so many things. We must protect the natural seed bank of our planet. We should sing to our plants and our forests and pray for the seeds of the Earth that they take hold where they should.

Non-goal-directed love will nourish both the seed and the planet. Love is a natural force that all natural life systems benefit from. The Spindrift experiments showed us that loving prayer is a restorative power. The significance of what they found can be utilized by us in our own lives as well.

THOMAS MOORE:
REMEMBERING TO LISTEN

Former Catholic monk, theologian, and well-known philosopher and author Thomas Moore writes about our human nature so exquisitely that at least once a year for close to a decade, I invited him on the air. He is a gifted communicator, authentic in the moment, and we never feel rushed to make a point or ask about one. He has commented that as a therapist the greatest thing he can do for his clients is to listen to their stories and give them the opportunity to share them. "Remembering is important," he declares, "not so that we can recall everything that happened with precision, but it seems that reflection, recalling, or calling forward to the present is nourishing for the soul." As he puts it in his book *Original Self: Living with Paradox and Originality,* "memory holds us together as individuals and as communities. When we forget who we have been, we lose the full sense of who we are. People who have drifted apart from the soul or who want to defend themselves against the pain of experience, often make an effort to erase memories."

The kind of remembering Moore is talking about fits right in with the context of the primary goal of *The Future of Human Experience:* to show that we are divine beings, but that we have forgotten who we are. We have forgotten our godlike powers and we no longer believe that we are truly made in the great Creator's image. "Memory," said Moore, "is potent. It does something to us. It makes us who we are and gives us depth." Indeed, it connects one generation to the next, one month to the next, one life to another, and one moment to all others.

To really appreciate what memory is, Moore says we have to "get rid of a common misconception that we are always trying to learn something, take new information, and make advances. That's one way we think of the progress of the soul, but that's not the only way to look at it. So, when I talk about the value of remembering the past, I'm not talking about learning something from all of that, getting some new insight or anything, but that memory itself is of value. Remembering, itself, is a form of contemplation. Not an open-ended kind of contemplation, as in a condition of nothingness, but looking at your own life and being present to all the parts of our life experiences. Being present to them and allowing them to sweep over us once again, not to learn anything, but simply to be connected to all of those memories. All that stuff is the stuff of the soul."

Distinguishing between soul work and spiritual practice, Moore pointed out "that the spiritual practice people often imagine is a way to get somewhere, because people want to make a very careful advance. In this other case, we go backward and I think we are deepened by it. When we get beyond personal memory, then we get into the collective memory, which is deeper than that."

DOES ARCHAEOLOGY HELP US REMEMBER WHO WE ARE?

From Carl Jung to Joseph Campbell, many observers have pointed to our loss of mythmaking as a reason for forgetting our own divine origins. Certainly my husband, Robert R. Hieronimus, has made a strong case for this matter over the years, particularly in his book *America's*

Secret Destiny: Spiritual Vision and the Founding of a Nation. I wonder if archaeological findings can't help us figure out who we really are
and what humanity's purpose is. Just like finding an old family picture
of relatives who have passed on can bring back memories of celebrations
and other events shared, can we remember our collective past through
these artifacts? Perhaps so, if the physical world acts as a repository for
recalling nonphysical feelings. Perhaps the immaterial soul's experience of
any moment across time and space can be remembered like home videos,
allowing us to reassemble ourselves, recall our other phases of life or even
past-life events, and rearrange the members of our psyche. Perhaps ancient
ruins and artifacts act as amplifiers for forgotten memories. Maybe using
ancient software connects us to the particular past that that system grew
out of. Perhaps memories, more so than the facts of an event, are the filter
through which we see the world and the residue that lingers in places,
engendering what is called place-memory, or resonant signature.

Place then has a "historic feeling" and feeling in us has history too.
The world is as we remember it and, in fact, it seems that how we recall
something is more potent than what may have occurred. In the imaginal
realm it lives on and is replayed and retooled until it fits into a story we
may or may not be conscious of. It takes on an energetic life of its own.
It is drama infused into cellular memory. It contributes to the collective
unconscious and is a field of activity, not a static picture.

Our memory is a filter we apply to our observations. Memories elicit
feelings and biochemical reactions, and we are allowed to relive, in a reflective sort of way, the experiences of the past, both pleasant and unpleasant.
By retracing the steps we deepen their tracks in our own minds and, thus,
the immaterial world becomes imprinted with our reflection. Recalling or
retelling stories is a way to invigorate the influence of their content in our
lives. That is why, in most sacred societies, the oral tradition is protected
by assuring that enough people in each generation are properly schooled
in the way of ancient storytelling. It is why, for instance, in Judaism the
Torah is called the *living* Torah. Every week, for thousands of years, Jewish
people have read a specific section of the Five Books of Moses and from
it examined how each historic event is reflected in personal and collective

lives now. It is not just a record of the past. It is a reflection of various states of the human condition and its potential. As we will see in the next chapter, this is also the premise of the I Ching and the Aztec calendar and the art of astrology. "In our ordinary lives," elaborated Moore, "the problem is we tend to think of the future and to think that the future is more important. But to remember, to act on memory, gives us a grounding and support all the time. To remember an anniversary, to call friends, or to send cards is a form of adding cohesion." It is likely that part of the function of stories in our past was to keep us from forgetting. The world's stories exist to remind us of what occurred. The world's sacred oral traditions are humanity's insurance policy against completely forgetting our past. They are our sacred stories and are preserved in the world's religions, ethnic tribal practices, and even seasonal community and family rituals. Moore continued, "When that memory breaks down, there is the loss of a very individual support that goes with that loss of recall. Orientation is not just physical. There is orientation in meaning and orientation in the world in a general sense; so with any problems of memory, what we could do is look past the physical aspect and try to imagine how to surround others with our own memories if they have lost the key to their own."

Rituals, especially those performed in the same way for centuries, show us that memory is also a community process. Moore agreed, saying, "Memory is not just an individual thing." Like snapshots in memory, ancient software (rituals, calendar synchronizations with the cosmos, and stories) can remind us of our inner technology and our design as simulators of the cosmic world. Our inner structure that serves as a filter is, in part, modeled after the divine processes of creativity, loving compassion, and merciful justice. Storytelling in our society has traditionally been nurturing to the soul of the individual and the community. It is a shared memory, a shared story that we each embellish within our individual imaginations.

Lamenting that modern stories told on TV and in movies, books, and plays very often are not really stories, Moore said, "We've lost that in our society. They are ideas put into story forms or they are stories to please, but they are not stories. They are an illusion of stories." And he's right. Most of the stories in popular entertainment these days do not well up from communal experience of some major celestial event or personal triumph or collective resolve. "They are inventions for commercial intention," he said. "It gives the illusion of storytelling . . . so even where we have our stories there's a breakdown there." This acts as a sort of inducer of societal amnesia or a collective forgetting of our soul's true nature.

Does this mean that to remember our real nature, our humanity's role in the cosmos, we have to rediscover our ancient and celestial stories or terrestrial ones that reflect those divine powers? Might we not look within ourselves this very day and see there the entire celestial drama of Earth and other planets in collision, of halcyon days and years of loss, a waning and waxing of our own, each of us and together? Perhaps the ancient divinatory systems or ancient software programs we will explore serve the purpose to remind us of how we fit into a larger world process. They remind us that our tools are for deepening and perfecting ourselves and the world.

Our modern-day treatment of the soul is to lock it up or to discard it completely. As Moore agreed, "If we allowed [the soul] to inhabit our culture, we would have a whole different world. . . . If we allowed more soul into our culture, I think it would be transformed overnight."

With civilizations and individuals, soul development is not linear. There is a continual rise and fall and rise again in ever-changing octaves of manifestation. If we are composed of the spiritual light essence that animates the entire world, then forgetting about our origins in that divine source results in a collective sort of amnesia with dire consequences, even to life losing its meaning. Remembering catastrophe and paradise might be one way of better understanding the history of the cosmos and our part in it. We each take part in sustaining life on Earth by sustaining the life spirit inside of each other and also by loving Earth, divinity, and all relations.

The interest in formative forces highlights the integration of mind and heart as a source where will may draw purpose from or a place where the world moves through us and from us. Life meets in the mind and heart. It is our bonding mechanism with all life-forms, our individual and shared beacons. How we feel about something or someone has a great deal more to do with how we act or react than simply what we think; that is until we overcome our selfish desires. Thus no thought or image, no feeling or desire, is without potency. A single good deed fulfilling the spiritual impulses of love, empathy, and compassion expresses the integral synapsing of mind, heart, and soul.

One question this inquiry has facilitated is, could matter be the stuff of soul out-picturing itself as it gains potency from the immaterial into the material realm via consciousness? In making the conscious mind the designer and our heart the transmuting alchemical fire, do we not breathe life into the invisible and make it real? Is this not an example of our godly bliss, the ability to imagine and then to manifest, to realize and then to shape, to breathe life into matter, to make that which is hidden revealed?

Everything matters, even the mystery my mother gave me by instigating a lifelong effort to demonstrate that "the message is, there *is* a message." In fact, there are infinite messages. My mom might have been more accurate if she had said "the answer is in the question" or "the message is that there is no single message, but rather messages happening everywhere and all of the time." Conscious minding is a godly process.

4

USING ANCIENT SOFTWARE

INTERPRETING PATTERNS IS KEY
TO SEEING THE FUTURE

The range of choices we have in this world is altered by the conscious-ness we can apply to any given task—whether it's caring for our home or our sacred places, speaking to family members or leaders of nations. With greater focused attention, one is given more information. There are countless tools available to us to use as vehicles for consciousness to move through and there are countless ways of taking information in and interpreting it so that it endows action with mindfulness. In this chapter we will examine a few of them and how they are related to one another: the I Ching, the Aztec calendar, astrology, and sacred ritual sites interpreted with the archaeo-sky matrix.

These are some of the myriad spiritual and astronomical sciences that are just as valid as the technologies that help us manufacture or travel or process materials. There are soft technologies that help us use awareness to materialize celestial or spiritual forces. I like to call them parascientific software, as all of these systems are means by which the immaterial world can find expression and by which we can know the larger picture of what exists and of what is coming into manifestation.

These pattern-revealing processes show up in divinatory or matrix systems all around the world and are similar in that they all organize information into meaningful patterns that can be understood. Some of what shapes us is taking place in our solar system and beyond. We and the universe are one. Universal languages use shapes and patterns to express universal truths, much as today's crop circles reveal truths about proportioned manifestation in their beauty and mathematical harmony. What this all leads to is the fact that there is a sacred geometry by which life is organized and reflected. It has been said that God geometrizes. What is clear is that we, as well as nature, are designed to operate as reflections of these patterns, which the Greeks and other cultures explored in sacred geometry or Plato's music of the spheres. That is why one finds these related patterns throughout humanity's history in so many ways.

Humans are driven to create, and to create in harmony with divine measurement makes the form and its maintenance in line with cosmic forces. Like the great spirit of the Divine that we are an expression of, and the active forces we engender through our thoughts, feelings, and actions, we cogovern our own lives and the life of the Earth and the cosmos. There are maps for these systems, but to activate them we must accept that we are, in fact, divine beings and worthy of our inheritance of cosmic and Earthly well-being.

THE CHINESE CODE OF TEN THOUSAND OR SIXTY-FOUR

The Chinese Book of Changes, or I Ching, escaped the savage book-burning crusade of tyrant Ch'in Shih Huang Ti in 213 BCE. That was fortunate for the world, for in it we find the common roots of the dominant Chinese philosophies of Confucianism and Taoism. From the late third century BCE until almost the end of 220 CE, formal esoteric schools were devoted to the study of the I Ching. But it was not until the young scholar Wang Pi (226–249 CE) wrote his commentaries that it finally blossomed, no longer encumbered with the societal suspicion that it was an unreliable oracle. By then, also at odds with the more politically connected thought of yin/yang (the school of absolute dualism) and the magic schools it generated, the I Ching was elevated from a contested book of divination to become appreciated as a Chinese classic of great wisdom.

According to what is still considered the best translation of the I Ching from the original Chinese—Richard Wilhelm's German translation—the Chinese were looking for a way to express the world in a number symbol system. They came up with what are called hexagrams, which are made of solid and broken lines. All sixty-four of them express different states of energy. As the hexagrams change, they reflect the movements and changes of the macrocosm as well.

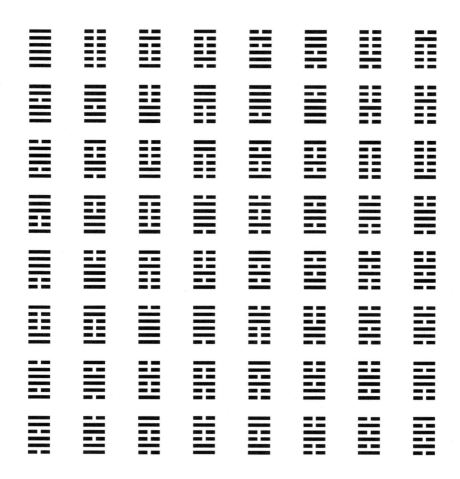

Fig. 4.1. The I Ching hexagrams

Much like today's computer software, the I Ching operates on a system of dots and dashes, or solid and broken lines, which represent zeros and ones. The sixty-four various ways in which a solid line and a broken line can be arranged comprise the whole universe and its workings. Throwing yarrow stalks to derive a hexagram in order to answer a question was itself an application of the principles of the vibrational world and word, which is known to be active though unseen. According to Wilhelm, "The nature of the yarrow stalks is round and spiritual. The nature of the hexagrams is square and wise. The meaning of the six lines change in order to furnish information." These divining sticks were considered receivers of some sort of subtle energy representing heaven and the spirit, making the invisible world cognizable. The yarrow stalks themselves were also prized for their sacred nature in healing.

The sixty-four hexagrams (which can also be divined by the repeated tossing of coins as well as yarrow stalks) represent the Chinese version of the universe's ten thousand variants. Lines are considered either at rest or in motion. They represent natural forces that are building up, breaking down, or standing still. The ones building up depend on the principles of light and the ones breaking down depend on the power of darkness: not in the sense of good and evil, but rather reflecting that natural forces of the material and immaterial world. As Wilhelm writes, this is "the expanding and contracting phase of the underlying life energy. These are the ebb and flow in the great ocean of life."

The pattern in which the tossed stalks or coins fall reflects the answer to the supplicant's inquiry. The I Ching hexagram "enabled the person to survey the condition of things, making even the unconscious man conscious." Seeing man as a microcosm of the macrocosm, the I Ching made the laws of heaven and Earth knowable, observable, and tangible. The I Ching, acting as a computer to access information, made it possible to see what had otherwise been unseen. The key is learning to properly center one's mind and intention in order to ask the most advantageous question. If done properly, this produces an "emotional life of harmony."

Finding an ultimate formula for the I Ching's endurance in the words "wisdom, love, and justice," Wilhelm shows how the Chinese realized that one can, indeed, shape the world with loving intelligence. By correctly interpreting the patterns we can know what is best for Earth and heaven, the living and the dead, and the born and yet to be born. The I Ching enables one to peer into the future and into the spirit world as well, that which underlies and interpenetrates the physical. It takes events or current tendencies that are not yet manifest and shows their potential outcomes as well as the type of action or nonaction a person or community should take.

It appears to be the microphysical events, or what physicist Fred Alan Wolf calls Q-bits, that make the natural falling of yarrow sticks or tossed coins part of the immaterial and physical realm, which is the essence of thought and consciousness. Dr. Carl Gustav Jung (1875–1961), the Swiss psychiatrist and psychotherapist who founded analytical psychology, expressed this relatedness as synchronicity: when two seemingly unrelated events occur simultaneously but are not coincidences, though at first glance they might seem to be. Petersen's modeling for the future expresses the same process. What Petersen calls the wild cards simply tell us what can happen based on what we can identify at the time of the inquiry, just as the sixty-four hexagrams are, according to Wilhelm, "the instrument by which the meaning of the sixty-four different, yet typical, situations can be determined."

Similar to the way that astrology arranges the world into patterns that a person is familiar with, the I Ching reflects stages of movement and, by pointing to their correspondence in nature, reveals deeper meanings. They both ascribe relationships to mundane events and spiritual essence, again showing the "as above, so below" formula as well as "the here now" and the "not yet here." To stand still is not to do nothing. To stand still is to observe, to watch; it counsels patience. The I Ching, like other esoteric systems, integrates a human being's emotions, senses, intellect, will, and soul, addressing all aspects of the spirit body simultaneously. And it is this multidimensionality that gives the I Ching its universal applicability as a divinatory tool.

The I Ching is one of many types of ancient software that assimilates and reflects energies derived from the vacuum, translating the Q-bits and bits into images and meanings. When we interpret the hexagram's meaning, what we are capable of perceiving is what will pop out at us or, in other words, what we are inclined to see due to similar things we have already become aware of. Thus, our effort to perceive activates that which is being perceived—it is a sort of two-way recognition. Like two actors in a mime mirroring show, our conscious acknowledgement gives whatever we are looking at a certain potency.

The Heisenberg uncertainty principle states that one cannot precisely measure the location and speed of anything simultaneously and offers an explanation, at the quantum level, for the principle known as the observer effect, which notes that the act of observing alters what is being observed. It is a modern-day acknowledgment that all life is interconnected at varying rates of vibration and that, at least where humans are involved, there can be no such thing as a totally objective science.

AZTEC CALENDAR AS ANCIENT CALCULATOR

On the other side of the world and over a thousand years after the I Ching was formalized, the ancient Aztecs left behind their example of ancient software that would enable generations of human beings to calculate significant events in the planet's history. The Aztec sun calendar, a carving from the middle of the fifteenth century, is now in the National Museum of Anthropology in Mexico City. It is a mathematical calculator made from simple elements that reveals that the Aztecs had an advanced knowledge of both astronomy and mathematics.

"But more than anything," says John Mini, author of *Day of Destiny,* "the calendar is about motion, or movement." In fact, the very center glyph (Ollin) of the most decorative and highly organized calendar circle portrays the universe in motion. It is made from the face of the Sun, whose name is Tunisia, "which is further described by his hands and the symbols of the four Noah or ages of the Suns." It is also demarcated by the four directional symbols of east, north, west, and south. The entire center of the Aztec sun calendar is surrounded by twenty images comprising the ring of solar archetypes, which includes images for the crocodile, the wind, a house, a lizard, a snake, death, and herbs, among others.

"Each of these," continued Mini, "represents a state of being and energy pattern. Outside the ring of archetypes is the ring of fives and then the ring of eagle feathers. The former is masculine, divided into four parts and again showing the cardinal directions, and the latter is feminine and describes the points in between the masculine cardinal points. Layers of

Fig. 4.2. The Aztec calendar. Image courtesy of Wikimedia Commons, El Comandante.

circles continue to be added until the entire Aztec cosmology is in place. As an ancient calculator it indicates cycles of life and death, creation and destruction, seasonal cycles within larger cycles and an overall balance between them all."

Number cipher keys are often used to unlock ancient software, and like many other ancient cultures, the Aztec use of the repeating pattern of thirteen is another example of their advanced scientific knowledge. Cultures like the Aztecs that made a close observation of nature realized there are thirteen joints in the body (including the most significant, the one at the occiput in the brain, which they called the thirteen cane), there are thirteen lunar cycles in a year, the moon travels across the sky each day thirteen degrees, there are thirteen semitones on the musical scale, and in the sky there is the sun plus twelve astrological constellations. On August 13, 1521, when the city of Tenochtitlan, the metropolitan center of the culture of Mexico, fell to the Christian Inquisition, ninety thousand medicines were found in their native medical pharmacopoeia. This was hardly a primitive civilization needing to be saved.

Given all of this, the sophistication of the calendar is evident, but how did this complex cosmic calendar foretell the future? Did it really predict that the Aztec culture would begin to rise again on August 13, 1999? Did anything noticeable happen that day, other than the election of a former corporate executive as president and the rumbling of the sacred mother mountain? In an interview, Mini explained, "the day of August 13, 1999, was considered by the Aztecs to be an extremely important focal point where numbers of confluences of natural forces would come together. In the Aztec world, as in most indigenous cultures, there is a real emphasis on humanity's connection as a vital role in the whole panorama of nature. That vital role is considered a force of nature, just as the wind, rain, or any of the natural forces might be. And that force, which we are sort of collectively driving, is driven by our own free will and [the direction] we put our energies." It starts to sound familiar after a while, doesn't it? Our minds, our intentions, our will, and our hearts are part of the universe, unlimited by time and space. "What they said," Mini added, "is that August 13, 1999, is the beginning of the opening of a window in time as we transition into the next solar age, which they call the sun of flower or the sixth sun."

Mini shared how the sixth sun refers to a time when there will be a cross-pollination of all cultures, peoples, and ways. "That is why it is the flower's tip that is expressed in the tongue of the Aztec God image. We live in the time period that all of their practices were to seed, having prepared the foundation for this new age today. . . . What my Aztec teachers talked about is that at the time of August 13, 1999, what we would see would be some very interesting phenomena in the heavens, in the sky. They said that if we did what nature would most want us to do, then we would enter through this window in time as we head toward 2012. This is the gap we are looking at, where our free will and the choices that we make are really going to determine the outcome and the momentum of where our planet is going to go." Mini then pointed to reports from around the world on August 13, 1999, indicating airline pilots noticing bizarre aurora borealis formations all over the planet in unusual places.

I asked Mini to elaborate on the gap in time between 1999 and 2012, and he explained it in a wonderful way. "It's very much like acupuncture," he said. "A needle by itself isn't a very powerful object. However, if you know what you are doing and you place it at the right time in the right place on someone's body, it can have very, very profound effects." I don't have any trouble with that comparison, as I have used five-element acupuncture every month since 1980 as the cornerstone of my wellness and I can see the correlation clearly. Mini elaborated: "The Aztecs believed that this was one of these acupuncture points in time that exists in a window of time between August 13, 1999, until December 21 of 2012. This is when, they say, the choices are being made that will determine where the planet is going to go. It is kind of like a chemical process. You put all the ingredients together and then a process begins, and there are only certain times for that process to work, and every small factor can end up steering systems one way or another. . . . The shamans in Mexico have taught me over time what that prophecy tells. It is science, like DNA. There are certain numbers of elements that combine and recombine in order to give us new versions of an ongoing story that is spiraling and swirling, telling itself in different ways."

Mini also explains how modern events like the eruptions of the Mexican volcano Popocatepetl are considered by many as fulfillment of ancient prophecies. "Mount Popo" has been a central figure for the Aztecs and the people who live in central Mexico from time immemorial. They look to the volcano as a beacon or a signal of what is occurring politically, geophysically, and spiritually. "For the Aztecs these phenomena are all part of one large picture. The eruption occurring at the time of Vincente Fox's ascendancy to the presidency, for instance, was seen as something really big happening."

The year 2000 was called one tecpatl, or one obsidian, which comes from the bowels of volcanoes. Obsidian was used to make surgical tools in the Aztec culture and "the word tecpatl itself means truth, or going into and dissecting things," continued Mini, concluding that now is the time for "going in and dissecting what's real and what's not real. Way back in 1988 one of my teachers told me that this would be the year [2000] when we would see all sorts of global truths come to the surface."

Physical biologist Carl J. Calleman, Ph.D., reveals in one of his books, *The Purposeful Universe: How Quantum Theory and Mayan Cosmology Explain the Origin and Evolution of Life,* that various energetic waveforms emanate from the cosmic tree of life affecting us for varying lengths of time. There are billion-year cycles, which the Vedic literature refers to and we discussed earlier, million-year cycles, and even an eighteen-day time period in evolution, which Calleman says occurred between March 8 and 26, 2012, representing the highest vibration humanity can experience, leading to unity consciousness. But "the essential thing the calendar describes," said Calleman, "is how the tree of life is the archetypal pattern from which waveforms are issued, which in turn engender various lifeforms from the cellular to the self-aware human." These ancient systems express the manifestation of waveform phenomena. The various worlds, which to the Maya are numerous, with thirteen heavens—each with their own nine underworlds—all affect humanity simultaneously. Ancient traditions could see what was not visible, name it, and derive meaningful orientation from it.

There is no doubt that we are at a critical phase in Earth's own evolution, the end of Kali Yuga according to the Hindu tradition, the dark age coming to a close. We gain strength and vision from the clarity of the work, books, and life experiences of people like José Argüelles Ph.D., John Michell, John Major Jenkins, John Mini, Carl Calleman, and others who address the cosmic patterns we are wired to. As one way of synchronizing the life processes between ourselves, the Earth, and our cosmic partners, Argüelles (1939–2011) urged the world to immediately adopt a lunar thirteen-month, twenty-eight day calendar. He did this because it reflects more accurately the cosmic alignment between the Earth and cosmos, as the Judaic, Vedic, Islamic, and numerous indigenous cultures maintain to this day.

John Major Jenkins, author of *Galactic Alignment: The Transformation of Consciousness according to the Mayan, Egyptian, and Vedic Traditions,* shows us that the solstice sun has come into alignment with the galactic center, or the center of the Milky Way galaxy. This began occurring between 1998 and 2000 and is an event that last happened 12,960 years ago. It is an event of cosmic proportion—the beginning of a window of change that will be highlighted by the very year that the Mayan calendar ends one cycle of human experience, in December of 2012, and then begins another.

Our current cycle is also portrayed in other prophetic calendars as a time of great importance in human evolution. The Jewish mystics, or Kabbalists, say that in the Jewish year 6000, or 2240 CE, we will enter the jubilee millennium on Earth, the seventh millennium or *shemittah* (Hebrew for "release," referring to every seventh year in Israel, a cycle kept since biblical times, when agricultural activity rests giving the land and trees a sabbatical year). This period will mark the last phase of material life on Earth for human beings. The Kabbalists teach that we will begin our ascension back into the spiritual realms from whence all of us came, (described earlier by Michael Cremo when referencing the Vedic teachings about our origins and eventual return). Some have suggested that the end of that period is when every human who is buried in the Earth will be resurrected and facilitated into the being of an immortal presence. For now we are tasked to become self-conscious co-creators working toward fulfilling the divine design of restoring Earth in the dense physical realm—this being both our calling and our inheritance.

MICHAEL MOLNAR'S DEDUCTIONS ABOUT THE STAR OF BETHLEHEM

Looking back at another moment in time that had been prophesied, one can turn to the events in Bethlehem two thousand years ago to appreciate, in yet another way, the connection between events in the solar system and events in our lives. The three Magi, or wise men, anticipated the future and planned for it using astrology just like the practitioners used the I Ching and the Aztecs used the sun stone. Everyone develops their own software by which to operate their culture, and the legend of the star of Bethlehem reveals an advanced understanding of astronomy in the Middle East at that time.

Astronomer, historian, and violin maker Michael Molnar, Ph.D., has written a book about this most talked about holy star, and over the course of several interviews he retold how he became interested in tracking down the astronomical significance of the star of Bethlehem. In addition to studying the stars, Molnar is a coin collector, and during the 1990s he bought a coin depicting Aries the Ram. He relates how a series of synchronicities happened to him along his path of discovery. In examining why there might be such a zodiac sign on a coin of that general time period, he said, "A few months later I discovered that the coin was from Antioch, Syria, issued about 6 CE or 10 CE. Aries the Ram two thousand years ago symbolized not Antioch, Syria, but the land called Judea, or King Herod's kingdom." Explaining how the Romans had annexed Judea and made Antioch the new capitol of Judea, he continued, "Suddenly I recalled all those other stories from astronomers and from ancient stories that the star of Bethlehem, whatever that was, had appeared not in Aries the Ram, but in Pisces the Fish or Virgo the Virgin." And yet, his coin was telling him to look elsewhere. "And here I had sources," he said excitedly, "that were telling me that stargazers back then were looking to Aries

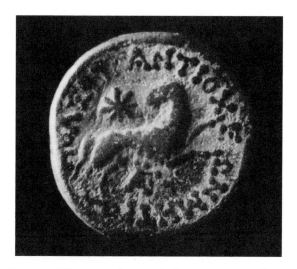

*Fig. 4.3. The coin of Antioch depicting Aries the Ram.
Image courtesy of Michael Molnar.*

the Ram to indicate the future of ancient Judea," not to either Virgo or Pisces as we've been told.

In order to discover what the star of Bethlehem really was, says Molnar, "We are going to have to think like they did two thousand years ago. If we are going to see what happened in Roman times, we cannot apply our modern ideas or religious hopes and wishes on the events of two thousand years ago. We have to consult those ancient texts." Since the ancient texts reveal that astronomy and astrology were essentially the same thing, Molnar was attempting to erect a regal horoscope for the time period in order to assess when and where a new leader might be born, just as the ancient sages of the time would have done. "The coin showed me that I had to look for something important in Aries the Ram. A sign in Aries indicated the birth of a new king."

I felt like we were traveling back in time as he spoke.

The unfolding story of Molnar's discovery itself reflects the way in which the universe speaks to us through similars, providing us with what we need. They might better be described as answers to thoughts or prayers or wishes. Answers arrive, in part, out of one's own attention and our attention then pulls for a fit. "So later that month," he continued, "I was in a bookstore and came across the Greek text of the Gospel of Matthew. I opened it up to that part and immediately recognized what the star [as Jupiter] was. . . . When I made this announcement in *Sky and Telescope Magazine* back in January 1991, I happened to cite that during King Herod's reign there were two eclipses, or occultations, of the regal planet, Jupiter, by the moon. That is, the moon passed in front of Jupiter in the spring of 6 BCE. . . . One of those dates [during Herod's reign] was April 17, to be exact."

The ancient astrologer/astronomers of the day would have seen Jupiter as a symbol for a king. "Jupiter was the most important planet," explained Molnar, "because when well positioned in space it could mean the birth of a king. . . . So I asked my computer to show me where Jupiter was relative to Aries in 6 BCE. [I found] at this time Jupiter had become a morning star in Aries the Ram. So I fired up the computer to when typical scholars think Jesus was born, from 8 BCE to 4 CE, and I found that, indeed, Jupiter was in the east only once in Aries the Ram: April 17, 6 BCE. I also had the eclipse or occultation of Jupiter, so I sat down at my computer and created an astrological chart for that day."

I was hoping our listeners were as excited as I was after reading Molnar's book *The Star of Bethlehem: The Legacy of the Magi*. What does it all mean? posed Molnar. What is the significance of the date April 17, 6 BCE? "The date was truly magnificent to the astronomer of ancient times," he told me. "In Aries the Ram, we had Jupiter in the east, the planet Saturn and the sun and the moon all close to Jupiter. To us modern people this may be uninteresting, but when this phenomenon in Aries the Ram occurred, it indicated not just the birth of a king, but a great king. I think [some] people interpreted it as the messiah."

To the ancient and modern practitioners of astrology, the world has its own rhythm and seasons of incubation and manifestation. The importance of the star of Bethlehem is that it wasn't a star at all, but the planet Jupiter. It was followed astrologically by the wise men or astrologers of the day who recognized it as heralding the birth of a great king. Once

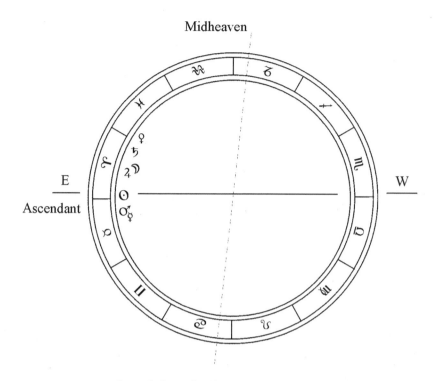

Midheaven

E

Ascendant

W

*Fig. 4.4. Astrological chart for the time period of Jesus's birth, April 17,
circa 6 BCE. Image courtesy of Michael Molnar.*

again, an ancient symbol and number system relating the movements of
the heavens enabled humans to look for a reflection on Earth. In this
case they found it in the birth and personage of the young Jewish baby,
Yeshuah of Bethlehem.

THE ARCHAEOCRYPTOGRAPHY OF
CARL P. MUNCK Sr.

A growing number of people are rediscovering a number system they say
connects the heavens to both ancient and modern sacred sites. By playing with the math, one can have all kinds of adventures discovering connections and harmonics between different locations on Earth, and even

locations on other planets. This number calculation system demonstrates a modern technique for proving the axiom "as above so below."

One new type of researcher is called an archaeocryptographer, and one outspoken practitioner of this interpretive art who joined me several times is Michael L. Morton. Morton has worked extensively with the material of Carl P. Munck Sr., the pioneer in this new field of study, expanding it into the realms of prominent (current) star positions, as seen by the naked eye, and is now applying this work to the area of crop formation research. Morton claims to have found that the "matrix numbers" of crop formations (also called crop circles, though they are far more elaborate than simple circles) and of the current sky positions of certain prominent stars. They are correlating very specifically with the exact positions of important ancient structures indicating an apparent "ancient unified field matrix."

Researcher Carl Munck, the originator of archaeocryptography, found that the "Giza meridian" or longitude (the location of the Giza Pyramids in Egypt plotted on the globe) was the true meridian marker of ancient cultures the world over. He demonstrated that nearly every significant megalithic or ancient sacred site was set up on a grid designed in relationship to the location of the Giza meridian in Egypt—not the Greenwich meridian of England. The Royal Observatory was built in 1675, at which point Greenwich Mean Time was established to aid mariners. The Greenwich, or Prime meridian that passes through the Royal observatory, was established in 1851 and adopted as the standard by most of the world in 1884 and much later by France, which officially adopted it in 1978. Prior to its adoption as a standard, each city in England (and the world) kept a different local time. Since 1884, the Greenwich meridian has been used worldwide for calculating longitudinal measurements on Earth.

To the Egyptians, the Giza meridian was the most important marker on Earth in that it reflected a marker in the sky and was symbolic of the splitting of the heavens between life (east) and death (west). Munck declared that this ancient prime meridian has been our true prime meridian since Earth's last polar shift, which, according to some researchers, took place as recently as 13,000 years ago, while others maintain this last occurred 790,000 years ago. The longitude variance between the

Greenwich meridian and the Giza meridian is exactly 31 degrees 08 minutes 0.8 seconds. Morton says that the archaeo-sky matrix "is a way of showing how any point on Earth is related to any other point, relative to the ancient prime meridian for Earth." While this change to the Greenwich meridian might not impact modern astrological calculations as some theorize, it did impact our consciousness. Industrial society was unhinged from the cosmos, no longer seeing itself as part of a greater universe.

"There are amazing things that happen with this system," claimed Morton fervently. "There are clusters of things that are alike, [such as] crop circles or animal effigies around the world, whose numbers, based on this system, are directly related to each other in harmonic ratios." As a calculator of civilizations and the precession of the equinoxes, this coordinate-based system makes many meaningful correlations between places built by the ancient Egyptian civilization, the D&M pyramid on Mars (named for its discoverers Vince DiPietro and Greg Molenaar, regular guests of mine), Stonehenge, and even the White House of the United States, to name but a few. "The Giza meridian arc even reflects the sacred measuring unit of the Greek Pi or Phi," Morton said.

Just as some native traditions worldwide show a relationship between their culture and extraplanetary life—such as the Native American tribe of Cherokees who claim affiliation with beings from the star system Sirius, as do the Dogon tribe of Mali in Africa—the work of Munck, Morton, and others is giving us a mathematical tool for uncovering this larger relationship once again. Their matrix system shows a fundamental parallel between what occurs in the cosmos and what occurs on Earth and what also occurs in each one of us. For example, Mary Ann Weaver, an online contributor to the field of archaeo-sky matrix, pointed out that the Alnitak star in Orion's belt is in all likelihood the celestial prime meridian marker for the galaxy. Robert Bauval first articulated the apparent significance of the Great Pyramids at Giza and the way they were built with correspondence to the three belt stars of Orion in his Orion correlation theory, which he made public in 1989. Robert Temple, Bauval's coauthor of several books, understood and explained their significance relative to the star system Sirius in his early masterful book *The Sirius Mystery.*

The system also points to a potential intergalactic code by which communication between civilizations may take place. What is apparent so far, at least to me, is that there is a definite matrix system by which the sacred sites on Earth are organized and that they correlate to various star systems in our galaxy. There is a universal number language and we seem to be discovering it anew.

Because I have trouble with math, I had difficulty keeping up with Morton as he dashed off numbers and computations, but we kept at it until it made sense. The differential of 31 degrees 08 minutes 0.8 seconds between the two prime meridians of Greenwich and Giza, he explained, "means that to formulate any longitude on Earth [in order to find hidden connections and patterns] we'd have to reformulate for the system that uses the Giza meridian system."

The system shows how the alignment of our galactic center (the point the sun makes its revolution around) with the three pyramids at Giza points our attention to the star system Orion. This is based, in part, on ancient Greek measurements and calculated using the 360-degree circle first described by the Egyptians. This system of relating all things to their number reveals that from the ancient Egyptians and Hebrews to the Greeks, Gnostics, Freemasons, and others, there is an ongoing expression of man and cosmos as being bound up in each other, much as an electron or a neutron is in an atom. Even the modern placement of the Washington Monument shows a harmonic relationship to the prior mentioned sites. And when Morton says *related,* he means *precisely* related through a calculation of their longitudes and latitudes and the numerical relationships between them. Using the longitude and latitude coordinates of any location on Earth, but based on this historic Giza meridian, we can calculate its harmonic.

Topographical maps and astronomical calculations both designate places by a set of three numbers: hours, minutes, and seconds. These numbers actually describe precise locations on Earth, based on the elliptic path the Earth travels during a day of rotation around the sun, and are the same coordinates the global positioning satellite (GPS) uses to calculate location. By way of numerous experiments, Munck showed that if one *multiplied together* the hours times the minutes times the seconds this provided the primary number for each location. The primary number is then used to specify its orientation to the pyramid at Giza, which is the meridian marker for calculating longitudes. These new numbers, produced as a result of multiplication, will show you the harmonic relationship between various places—terrestrial or extraterrestrial. Morton gave us several examples of the kinds of patterns that show up and I encourage interested readers to follow up with his online samples.

I knew that Morton, as a numbers man, was going to lay the golden egg with one of those *aha* moments, when, almost giggling with delight, he asked me, "So Zoh, do you know what the unzip angle of DNA is?" Was I supposed to know this, I wondered? Did everyone else? I hardly know the unzip angle of a plastic bag, let alone our DNA. "It's at 7⅓ degrees," crowed Morton. Lacking the insight to get excited about this, I asked with great curiosity and a typical degree of impatience, "And so?" Morton replied, as though everyone should have seen it, "That's exactly double the 3⅔ ratio between the size of the Earth and the size of the moon." I wondered if that means our DNA zips and unzips as the moon waxes and wanes? Do our cosmic bodies on Earth experience high and low tides as well?

I imagine the universe as a complex of vibrating strings, like keys on a piano, arranged in octaves. One could say the archaeo-sky matrix system plucks the universal strings and shows us how places in different times and spaces are connected. The heavens, as we have seen, show us what to look for on Earth. The key is to find the right system of alignment. The archaeo-sky matrix and archaeocryptography systems allow us to uncover what is not seen otherwise and seems to offer us clues for finding hidden civilizations on Earth and in our galaxy.

Thus, given that there are already clear relationships between places on Earth and other planets or star systems, by logical extension we might also be able to make better sense of the current visitations from other civilizations off Earth. These visitations are being reported worldwide, just as they have been throughout humankind's history. Studying the archaeo-sky matrix and other ancient cryptography methods might help us generate a map of orientation that will show us in what way our present civilization, and other off-planet locations, may be in harmonic relationship to one another, hence offering us guidance as we voyage into space in the future. Perhaps this is a great sacred key left behind by our ancestors as a gift to the present: a sort of multigenerational and multidimensional heirloom, a sacred timepiece or treasured journey map.

I suspect that if we were to examine the places on Earth that we know are historically important, we may be able to trace our sacred connections. We could, perhaps, use the process to collect and show these related places and times on Earth, as search engines do on the Internet. We should also be able to overlay this grid matrix on the map of the world and thereby discover buried civilizations, hidden texts, and other ancient software, or even calculate harmonics off planet and discover other planets or space-journeying civilizations related to us who may now or in the future be in contact with us.

We can see that our lives are a reflection and collaboration in the evolution of the universe, just as the Vedic, Hebrew, Mayan, and other cultures believe. Finding reflection of this cosmic pattern, one could say that spirit is in all matter. If spirit, then, is the light force that invigorates all life, knowable and unknowable, visible and invisible, we can begin to recognize that what we feel, think, and do affects the world, literally. If the unzip angle of our DNA is related to the distance between the Earth and the moon, doesn't that lend credence to the ancients who taught that the stars and planets and their relationships were also reflected in our anatomy? If this is so, then properly aligning ourselves and our civilization with the galaxy we exist in would put us in proper order to function optimally. This is the purpose of medical astrology, an ancient healing art. Unfortunately, it is seldom practiced in the world today.

As we will examine later in chapter 8 with Professor William Tiller, perhaps our bodies and souls are actually divine simulators. I like to think of them as being godlike, and these maps of consciousness indicate that we are simulating something cosmic in our daily lives. Our feelings, our thoughts, and our aspirations are nudging the future along and not just our own future, but the world's. Essentially, consciousness is a way of shaping light that is drawn from the vacuum of space, which is a repository of potential energy. It is an unlimited resource to draw from. Some call it God, some call it the Great Spirit, while others call it an energy vacuum. However, it is by no means empty, but rather brimming with all that is potential.

Some people develop the spiritual faculties to see the subtler fields of energy, sometimes experienced through second sight (clairvoyance) or through the sense of touch (clairsentience) or hearing (clairaudience). Throughout humankind's history, those with such advantages have operated their inner software by which to interact with the invisible worlds. Ultimately, these systems have a central, principal purpose: to ensoul matter with conscious light. By *ensouling* I mean to endow the world with conscious awareness and intentions, to express the soul's nature, which is to unite things and make them whole. This is what raises the vibration and, hence, the quality of life on Earth for all life systems. In my opinion our evolution is the result of consciously attending to the world within and without.

5

BECOMING EARTH BEINGS

She hangs in space like a prayer sustained by cosmic forces. It is a miracle that a planet like Earth hurtles through space spinning on her own axis at approximately 1,000 miles per hour, while also rotating around a greater solar planet at about 67,000 miles per hour. Just like our lives, her orbit has cycles and when we attune to them we integrate our lives with the life of nature. All shamanic and esoteric traditions honor this process. Through observance of this natural rhythm—the cycles of seasons and cosmological precessions—one is shown the unfolding of Earth history and perhaps our divine purpose.

At some elevated level of psyche or of heart intelligence, most humans have a very spiritual sense of the Earth, recognizing that she gives her life for us, but we also have to give a portion of ours in return. In the ancient past, perhaps humanity was closer to the Earth because the labor of farming and harvest integrally connected humans to communal and natural forces. As the Western industrial machinery relieved human hands of daily farming tasks, so too it released our hearts from loving the Earth. There has been a fundamental divorce from proper Earth stewardship—becoming instead an attitude of exploiting the Earth as an economic resource. This has been the most profound change, in a spiritual and physical world sense, to have occurred in the last two thousand years. In this sense, industrial farming paved the way for the atom bomb and all its deathly enterprises including nuclear energy and technology.

At one time, the Earth was revered. Her needs were attended to because it was understood that her bounty was what sustained life and that her tribulations were deeply connected to our own. For most of humanity's recorded history, dominating the Earth was an unthinkable transgression. Today we are stripping open nature's barrier that once had preserved the genetic bank of our destiny, the genetic map of all of nature's being. Our technological wizardry is admirable, but unfortunately it is not tempered with ethical enlightenment. The tendency to use nature bit by bit for some short-term profit exacts a serious price that far out measures any gain.

We have the knowledge to sustain the Earth. If we choose to accept the responsibility of becoming divine co-creators, we are given greater and greater challenges: many of them born of human greed, arrogance, and, on occasion, even malice toward the Earth. From underground nuclear and underoceanic weapons testing, to food irradiation and genetically engineered crops, events of the twentieth century have been incredibly damaging to the Earth and to all life systems. In many respects we have become technobarbarians, with lethal powers to interrupt the cycles of nature. Weather engineering, space weaponry, chemical and biological warfare, industrial farming, and factory farming of animals are all expressions of our indecency toward life on Earth. Each of these technologies places an increasingly greater duress on all life systems. In short, humanity is the creator of horrific suffering.

In natural systems there are always cycles of birth and death, replenishing and diminishing. Humanity is simply a part of that natural system and rhythm. While we know there are times of life and death for a planet, we have an obligation to support life where life calls for support.

I became an environmental activist at the age of fourteen and thus have been tasked almost all of my life with revealing and denouncing all that is wrong on Earth today and promoting alternative solutions in their stead. In this chapter we will look at methods of healing the Earth. Serving Earth is sacred service. It is an expression of love for life itself and a way of being part of the planet's destiny. From Earth systems to animal welfare, the Earth is an integrated system deserving our highest good.

THE JOYOUS WAY OF THOMAS LOVEJOY

When I last interviewed the controversial ecologist Thomas Lovejoy, Ph.D., in 2001, it had been ten years since our prior conversation. Lovejoy is a Yale University–trained biologist and has formerly served as science advisor to Secretary of Interior Bruce Babbitt. He was also assistant secretary for environmental and external affairs at the Smithsonian Institution and vice president for science of the World Wildlife Fund. Some destructive environmental policies had changed since the early 1990s, but not as much as many of us had hoped for. I asked Lovejoy about the media's role in perpetuating the corporate paradigm, which posits that the Earth is a natural resource to be exploited for profit, without concern for the long-lasting impact to the planet and all life on it.

In characteristic fashion he admitted that he worried less "about bad information, than people not knowing any information: at least in the sense of going through their daily existence without understanding the connection that everybody has to these problems. In terms of energy use [we need to consider] where the sources are coming from. The things we buy—are they sustainable products?" He emphasized that none of us "fully appreciates the full impact of the decision we make about what we use, what we buy, and what we do." The issues for all systems we design should be whether they are just and sustainable, but even in the environmental community *sustainability* means different things to different people. "How do you know sustainability when you see it?" questioned Lovejoy. "In a sense it's a sort of squishy concept. If you take it back to an actual piece of geography, such as south Florida, the way to measure whether the aggregate of human activity is sustainable or not, is [to determine] whether the fundamental, characteristic biology is holding its own. Well then, if it is not, it's not sustainable. The advantage of that is that we only call something an environmental problem if it affects living systems. The best way to measure the impact is in the biology of the natural world. Looking at a particular place allows you to integrate all the different stresses that are, in the end, being put on the environment. Then you can assess whether or not what is going on is sustainable."

For instance, the issue of drilling for oil in the Arctic National Wildlife Refuge is a good example of the environmental issues facing mankind. "It really comes down to whether we are going to recognize that there are certain places on this planet that we [should] only intrude on in the most gentle way, like walking in. Frankly, I think the amount of oil you would get out of that place is relatively insignificant." Indeed, it is probably less than a six- to eight-month supply of oil for the United States. But Lovejoy is emphasizing that what we really need is "an environmental strategy that moves us away from fossil fuels and towards alternative energies, energy efficiency, and energy conservation without feeding further climate change problems."

Lovejoy has earned his reputation as a promoter of sustainable and wise land and energy use. "As I look at this whole array of environmental problems, a really significant part of it is the energy scenario for the human society. The buildup of greenhouse gases in the atmosphere and the onset of human-induced climate change have reached the point where the Arctic ice cap is actually melting [at a rate more accelerated than first projected] and getting thinner. This all tells us that we need to be moving away from fossil fuels. The interesting thing is that there are some real possibilities, which are quite imminent." The big three automobile manufacturers anticipated fusion fuel cell cars coming off the assembly line in 2003, which has not happened as of this writing in 2013, although Japanese and South Korean automakers say they will do this by 2015. Explained Lovejoy, "Making a transition from gasoline and the internal combustion engine to hydrogen-driven transportation is really just a matter of scale. The effort is in bringing down the unit cost and also setting up a system of hydrogen energy supply." In moments like this I wish Eugene Mallove was alive to enjoy the outgrowth of his pioneering support for hydrogen fusion, which he advocated since the late 1980s (as discussed in chapter 7).

Another guest of mine was Donald Aitken, Ph.D., cofounder in 1969 of Friends of the Earth. He currently owns a consulting firm focused on sustainable development and building design worldwide. When we talked he made it clear that we can look at our past experiences going from wood to coal and from coal to oil to see that it generally takes sixty years for the economy to support a switch from one type of fuel to another.

Lovejoy's point is that the transition can and should begin now. "We have all these gasoline stations across the United States. To convert them to being also hydrogen efficient would cost a significant amount of money, but not huge. If we could begin to make that change very quickly, then the rest of the world would take the United States much more seriously in terms of climate change."

Germany is one country with a long-term view of sustainability. As described by Aitken, "Germany is [several years] into their sixty-year energy plan to create at least 35 percent of their energy needs from alternative fuels." Denmark, Japan, and the European Union are all making large strides to emulate this design as well. Regarding the overall increase in heat-trapping carbon pollutants since the 1990 baseline, the world's output has increased 54 percent. In 2011 only Germany and the United States had reduced their carbon emissions (by 4 percent and 2 percent respectively) while China had increased theirs by 10 percent.

Lovejoy currently is the biodiversity chair at the Heinz Center for Science, Economics and the Environment in Washington, D.C., but at the time of our conversations he was the World Bank's chief biodiversity advisor and held other positions as well. Given that he had a prominent position with the World Bank and that I had been a broadcaster focused on geopolitical activism and blowing the whistle on corporate and government crimes for about a decade from 1992 to 2002, he and I were bound to disagree on some things. This was particularly true given that some of my analysis focused on the problems the World Bank creates for nations dependent on their loans. The World Bank is made of five development institutions and claims to be the world's largest funder of education and the fight against HIV/AIDS. It also proffers strong support for debt relief, biodiversity, and water and sanitation projects. Being made up of political appointees and employees, it does not represent the people of any nation per se. Although ultimately environmental problems are global concerns, my concern about the activities of the World Bank and the International Monetary Fund is their autonomy in making decisions that impact millions of people's lives.

While the World Bank has nine thousand employees in more than one hundred offices worldwide, they have a great deal to do with environmental policies and international agreements. As a banking apparatus they wield more power than is appropriate, holding a nation's labor as collateral with no representation for the people they impact. As discussed earlier in this book during my interview with John Perkins, defaulting on any of their requirements—environmental, or otherwise—could mean the cancellation of loans, calling in of debts, or direct fines.

Again, and I am being a bit redundant because these are very important points to take in: what that can mean in the short run is that the nation-state becomes an actual property or indentured population paying off the nation's debts to the Bank just as a householder does in paying a bank for private loans. Sometimes these loans—rather than being used to actually improve infrastructure, health care, and education—go into the pockets of corrupt politicians and the population itself does not prosper. When the World Bank comes calling, the state has only one recourse: to tax its own citizens more, often diminishing individual welfare, and selling off national resources and properties to multinational corporations.

Lovejoy obviously supports the work of the World Bank noting, "The interesting thing is to see the change within the World Bank over the twenty-year period I have been part of this process. There are still plenty of things that need to happen. I was cleaning up my office a couple of years ago and I found this letter, from 1984, from the vice president of the World Bank thanking me for having come by and explaining to him about biological diversity. Well, today the Bank literally spends billions of dollars in straight biological conservation projects." These take the form of grants, loans, and other partnerships. "There is not only growing sensitivity in the Bank, there is direct action," he continued. "The president of the Bank is committed seriously to conservation."

Lovejoy has dedicated his life to unfolding with nature's need, and his activism has had results. "Biodiversity is the underpinning of human society," he says. "It's the biodiversity that generates soil fertility naturally. Biological diversity is a source of medicine and food. Biological diversity is cycling carbon around the world, preventing [situations that] would have been even more ecologically destructive—even the ecosystem service of watershed protection and disaster prevention. When you get huge storms, like Hurricane Mitch in Central America in 1998, the people who live in the places that were deforested suffer much more than those in areas where they have the natural vegetation left intact." Unfortunately, biological diversity may be the key, but we haven't been very good at recognizing it as we maintain our accounting, warns Lovejoy.

Always one known for his creative solutions to our life-system challenges and other related environmental problems, Lovejoy has integrated the appreciation for biological diversity with the need for sustainability. He created a system of land swap for nations that may be land-rich but cash-poor. In exchange for not developing certain areas, they get credits that go toward paying off their nation's debt. Taking us back to that moment of dawning discovery in his own mind, he remembered, "As I sat in on a hearing in the House of Representatives looking at the negative effects of projects of institutions like the World Bank," (laughing as he recognized how he was at the time of our interview working professionally within their structure) "it began to develop in my mind. As I listened to one of the people testifying about social impacts, it seemed to me more and more that some things were being generated by a country's desire to save hard currency to get out of its indebtedness. So I thought: why not create a way to give credits against the debt that a nation holds, for things like conservation—something they may very well want to do, but find it very hard to afford in their poor condition. So that was the origin of the debt for nature swaps. I have recently learned that it has now passed the billion-dollar mark," and this was in 2002. Hopefully the land acreage has increased since then.

It's this kind of creativity in problem solving that brings hope to all of us. Lovejoy insists optimism is necessary. "You have to be optimistic because first, if you aren't you won't try and second, human creativity can be quite extraordinary when it is challenged." The more broadly and deeply we can consider the needs of the related systems of Earth, the more likely we can create appropriate solutions. "I am counting on some really creative responses that are hard for us to even imagine at this point." Multidiscipline approaches assure the most comprehensive and swiftest arrival at positive solutions. And the creative problem-solving process itself is something we can do more deliberately by using meditation, our dreams, and open-ended discussions. We will look at this in a later chapter on the Divine Body.

Lovejoy appraised where we are at the outset of the twenty-first century. These globally connected environmental problems have developed slowly, by increments, but "when you add it all up," warned Lovejoy, "then it's a problem. The rain forest, as most are aware, best represents the challenge that we, as an association of humans, have in making right use of limited, but replenishable, resources. . . . When you talk about the Amazon, you are really talking about the world's largest remaining forest, the world's largest remaining wilderness, and the world's greatest single repository of plants, animals, and micro-organisms. So, in one sense, it is the icon of how we are dealing with the planet as a whole. It is a really significant piece of the global puzzle, of what's happening to, or to be specific, what is shaping the climate."

Inclusion must be part of the process of finding a solution in order that the solutions are founded on right relations. The needs of the indigenous peoples and the demands of geopolitical commodity or corporate pressures must be balanced between what is just and sustainable. How can we derive fresh approaches to very serious questions of survivability, let alone sustainability? "I think it has become abundantly clear," Lovejoy responded, "to people who are trying to advance the conservation and sustainable agenda, that it never works unless there is true involvement of the people in the particular place concerned. And that becomes even more important in this age of global transition and rapid economic change. It's long and it's messy, but that's where you can have real conversations and, in the end, come up with parts of solutions that are likely to last. In fact, you have hit upon the really fundamental and essential piece of what sustainability is all about. Namely, that it has to be for everybody and that it is very hard to really advance the proper agenda when there is a tremendous amount of inequity, where there are few very, very rich and many very, very poor. You really have to pay attention to improving conditions and aspirations of the poorer people on Earth, making sure that they are not getting the worst of the environmental impact."

WHAT WE DO TO THE EARTH, WE DO TO OURSELVES

On Earth Day 1990, I coined the slogan "What we do to the Earth, we do to ourselves." This was an outgrowth of the work I was doing as chair of the Maryland Earth Day Committee's fundraising and my later work organizing in Maryland for the same event in which I collaborated with institutions such as the National Aquarium of Baltimore, the Baltimore Zoo, Irvine Nature Center, and numerous smaller ecowise organizations and individuals.

I still believe this slogan couldn't be more direct and to the point. The environmental impacts on health are only beginning to draw the attention they deserve, for we are living in a self-created soup of chemicals and increasing electromagnetic and nuclear radiation for which no living system has any evolutionary experience. And the connection, said Lovejoy, "is very real. It can range from natural disaster all the way to endocrine-disrupting compounds, which are certainly affecting the reproduction of wild species as well as the reproductive health of human beings."

Genetically engineered foods pose a similar threat to the ecosystem and the health of the entire food chain. We are manufacturing things that would not evolve from their own genetic need. A stalk of corn is not likely to grow with synthetic pesticide inside its seed, nor would a rabbit find it helpful to glow in the dark (it's unlikely that a rabbit and a jellyfish would ever mate over time, though their DNA has been combined to create just such a glow-in-the-dark bunny). "What I worry most about," Lovejoy said, "is the ability to design organisms, crop species, tree crop species, that can be grown anywhere." As Lovejoy expressed it, "this means the last places on Earth, the wastelands, will also be subject to the manipulation of human beings."

What ethical intention do we bring to the act of environmental and economic stability? Is it to improve the Earth's future, or is it to improve the future as a commodity for the investors and corporations? "As measured in dollars," concluded Lovejoy, "most bottom lines do not measure the quality or future quality of life. We have to get better at that type of thinking if we are going to adequately address the challenges we now face."

FINDING SOLUTIONS NOW: BIODYNAMIC FARMING

Like our ancestors before us and our native tribal communities today, many people still regard the Earth as a living biodynamic being, with memory and wisdom. Some have called this wisdom Sophia and her body Gaia. This vision was first promoted by James E. Lovelock, Ph.D., in 1965 as the Gaia theory. It represents the integration of all fields of wisdom into an overarching principle that posits that biological responses regulate the Earth's environment. Biotic and abiotic mechanisms are interrelated and can be imbalanced by human activity, which we have now witnessed with the accelerated global warming that is presently taking place on our planet.

Agriculture has played a central role through humanity's long odyssey on Earth. How we use or abuse the Earth's natural systems determines, in part, whether we will flourish or not. Supporting life requires the growing of food crops worldwide, meaning that agricultural restoration can become the foundation for improving our global community's ecosystems and human health.

One available tool is biodynamic farming, which offers us a way to both cherish the Earth and attend to the process of growing foods and raising animals properly. According to activist and CSA (Community Supported Agriculture) owner and educator Allan Balliett, biodynamic farming is "a spiritual approach to growing" that sees the plant essentially as the center of the Earth, which is also in touch with the far reaches of the cosmos. It puts the farmer within the context of right relations to sentient life and Earth biosystems. Biodynamic farmers "try to take into account all of the forces that affect plant growth and their nutritional value."

In 1924 Rudolf Steiner (1861–1925), Austrian educator, esoteric scientist and originator of anthroposphy and the Waldorf School System, gave a series of lectures near the end of his life, resulting from his concern that foods didn't taste as good as they did when he was a boy. Steiner was concerned about the depletion of soil quality because of the use of chemicals, which can be traced to about the year 1900 in that area. As Balliett pointed out, "It's amazing to realize that as far back as then, a hundred years ago, people were already seeing the dramatic change in . . . the taste and quality of foods as a result of their introduction of chemical farming, which was beginning to replace the ancient and well-proven system of peasant farming."

Steiner believed that a plant is not isolated, but rather is in a relationship with the entire universe. The source of activity within the plant is not limited to sunlight and water and minerals, as might be taught at a less spiritually inclined agricultural college. "If it is in truly living soil," Balliett explained, "the plant will respond to a whole range of formative forces, which come through the universe and which are, essentially, the basis of life. This is a really important thing to consider, particularly for people with health issues. Regardless of how we see things in our culture, the source of life, whether [it's coming to us] through animals or processed goods, still comes down to the way the plant can process both terrestrial and extraterrestrial forces. Like most lifelong farmers, biodynamic farmers know that planting with the phases of the moon makes a difference. "I'm continually surprised," Balliett noted, "when I speak to Extension Service people who want to deny that beans will sprout faster if they are planted a few days before the full moon, or that fungus is more active a little while before a full moon. The healthy plant in healthy soil is very much an interaction between the forces in the universe. In biodynamics we use a book called the *Stellar Natura,* which tracks on an hourly basis the forces that are positive for plant growth. Many of us plan our planting, harvesting, fertilizing, and watering with these rhythms within the cosmos. One of the conversion experiences I had, [convincing me to switch] from organic farming to biodynamic organic farming, was with some pea seeds.

"When I had planted pea seeds whenever I felt like it, they'd stay in the ground for eight days. Then I used the *Stellar Natura,* saw a good day and planted those seeds next to the other seeds already in the ground. The seeds that I planted according to the *Stellar Natura* ripped out of the ground in about four days. The other peas that I had planted, I had to wait at least a week before they came up. We also use homeopathic approaches to plant nutrition and disease and pest control. Biodynamic farming, as compared to normative organic farming, is more sophisticated and yet more subtle. It derives an understanding of planting cycles and processes from an observation of formative forces, not just terrestrial weather."

Balliett explained why he made this commitment to a more rigorous and detailed type of farming. "It seemed it was a more conscious farming process, thus giving the humans doing the work a more awakened sense of their actions. One of the things that is paramount is the tremendously increased sense of reverence. It's what native people infer when they speak about the Earth. It's being aware that we are in processes that are sustaining and pro-life and far more complex than anything I had to wonder about. Things like preparing the soil for receiving seeds is done with such great care, as though tending to the Earth's body in proper fashion and assisting in her ability to produce living foods."

He spoke of farming the way a lover does the body of the beloved, adding that "your intentions in biodynamic farming will take root, so it is very important to be very clear why you are planting a seed and what the purpose of the food is. It doesn't have to be a dominant thing, but it is why earlier societies had rituals before they entered the garden or yard; they entered with a sense of focus. . . . In proper biodynamic practice, we don't break the crust of the soil unless the celestial aspects are correct. . . . At that point you really change what the influences in the soils are. The day of breaking ground is selected by the calendar." Among biodynamic farmers one finds the science of agriculture both spiritually and physically at its greatest integration producing nutritional food.

In addition to recommending planting by the calendar, "Steiner was an advocate of raised beds for row crops because he felt that the celestial influences penetrated deeper into loose soil," continued Balliett. "We also use compost preparation and homeopathic herbal preparations. Valerian, chamomile, stinging nettle, the bark of white oak tree, dandelion flowers, and yarrows . . . go through the composting process before they are incorporated into the pile. . . . We also make preparations in a cow horn."

It's this last example that has always been one of my favorite things about biodynamic farming: Rudolph Steiner, a mystic visionary, was shown how to enhance the life force in plants in a fashion reminiscent of the Hindu's reverence for the holy cow and their use of ghee butter made from cow's milk. This is performed in certain healing and purifying fire rituals such as agnihotra, an ancient Vedic practice performed today in Orthodox Hindu communities and by others as well. The great Egyptian and Greek rituals also worshipped the holiness of the cow for the fecundity of the Earth.

"But today," I suggested, "one would be hard-pressed to believe the effectiveness of this spiritual process without seeing it for oneself."

"That's true," said Balliett. "This is one of those times where you have to put away your little logic machine and experience it out. Preceding my peas conversion I told you about, I went to a biodynamic class in South Carolina taught by Hugh Cortney, [Founder of the Josephine Porter Institute of Biodynamics]. He passed around this primary biodynamic preparation, which is called BD500. It is made by packing cow manure into a cow horn, and then burying it in the topsoil through the six months of winter. Now, I had it in my head exactly what cow manure would look like when stuffed into a cow horn and left in the ground through the winter, but Hugh passed around what actually happened. It was essentially pure humus. Very light, good smelling, and pleasant to handle. . . . I then realized there was a level of transubstantiation that was occurring outside of my logic or experience."

To me, biodynamic farming seems to be a type of applied alchemy. It is gentle but rigorous in scientific attention. It is natural and yet highly creative, spiritually integrating the cosmic forces with human intention.

It is magical because it uses dynamic forces, both terrestrial and celestial, in a harmonic and observant pattern. It is scientific in the sense that it is repeatable and its outcomes can be measured and quantified. Biodynamic farming is agricultural alchemy applied to the Earth body directly to benefit the food chain, the entire ecosystem, and all sentient life. This is what I would call win-win science and why biodynamic farming could be the best model and practice for restoring and sustaining the Earth through agriculture worldwide.

Allan Balliett describes the cycle of biodynamic farming like someone describing a beautiful piece of art. With great reverence and a certain engaged awareness at every step of the process, he marks a clear and precise delineation of the various forces working in nature at every stage of a plant's development. It is a dance of steward and nature, of nurturing and birthing, of preparing and sharing. It puts agriculture where it belongs, as the bridge between the cosmic and physical worlds. We eat the cosmic forces in our food as well as the vital mineral nutrients the Earth herself provides. Our consciousness reflects what we eat. Biodynamic farming is yet another demonstration of resonance as the key to life.

Detailing the importance of incorporating biodynamic compost into the soil, Balliett said, "leaving some of it visible on the surface brings the earthworms closer to the top. They break the compost down and distribute it as it passes through their bodies, making it . . . easier for the plant to assimilate. The earthworm, more than anything else in the soil, works to keep it full of air, allowing the water to penetrate. Other biological and chemical actions that result from our earthworms also help decompose matter. The worm's manure is easily assimilated by both plants and bacteria when using a spading machine," something he was quick to differentiate from a common tractor. Where a tractor will disturb the Earth, biodynamic farmers use a tillage machine "because it works up the soil, but doesn't invert the layers of the soil, which is as damaging to the biological life as a plow can be. Also, it moves at a speed of only ¾ of a mile an hour."

Another methodology used in biodynamic farming is the utilization of quartz crystals to enhance the life of the soil. In this practice a small amount of BD501, a preparation of quartz crystal finely ground to almost a talc, is stirred into three gallons of water for about an hour then sprayed on crops in the very early morning just after sunrise. "It tremendously enhances the plants' ability to photosynthesize," Balliett explained, "and this is evidenced in the Brix test, which measures the sugar in plants and is a measurement of the quality in the plant that nourishes our life, our bodies. An application of the quartz crystal homeopathic mixture will measurably boost the sugar levels in the plant."

Balliett described how a biodynamic farmer working a three-acre farm will begin the day by walking through each row of crop, looking at them on an individual plant basis. "It doesn't take a lot of time, but after years of observation, a skilled eye is looking for the way the plant stands, what their attitude is, and on a grosser level looking for any fungus or insect damage." From that they will decide to use herbal tea, compost, or other remedies that biodynamic farmers use to restore the vitality of a plant. This is something that usually happens only in the development stage of a biodynamic garden, during the first couple of years.

"Any of us who are doing biodynamic farming on any scale and applying the preparations with any regularity start to realize that there are more birds. Birds are the first thing we notice more diversity of, a lot more singing birds, but also a larger variety of insects and more benign insects, ones that are nice to be in the garden. The whole sense of balance occurs in a way that you can actually feel; but realize that this takes until about the third year of biodynamic farming, if you use the preparations regularly."

With an appreciation that one has for a great teacher, Balliett recounted that "Steiner said that biodynamics was medicine for the Earth. He said it was essential for the spirit of the Earth that these preparations be applied. . . . It uses nature's forces for the world's benefit." Steiner's biodynamics, developed almost a century ago, show that as we honor the Earth as a living being and by giving her what she needs, she is able to sustain our lives as well. We know there are gentle ways of farming that enhance nature's qualities and use cosmic forces in a scientific and beneficial fashion. It is time to farm with reverence for life.

Allan Balliett's mention of songbirds made me think of Dan Carlson's Sonic Bloom procedure and how all these pioneers are working together in a kind of great and natural symphony. This dynamic of relationships showed an amazing and complex diversity of life, an integration that could be entered into just like any kingdom. The more we attend to nature, the more natural it becomes to cognize nature and feel her. We must appreciate the power of the songbird's song: powerful enough to open the plant's very cellular makeup in a blossoming, an unfolding partnership to life. I felt as Chris Bird must have felt decades earlier when he first recognized that there was a communication occurring between bird and plant. It is more than just the mechanics of frequency. It is a type of beauty that one appreciates aesthetically and deeply in one's bones and heart. It is a spiritual process as well as a physical one and supports an underlying philosophy of harmony among all life systems, in body, mind, and soul.

THE SONIC BLOOM OF DAN CARLSON

Along with everyone else discussed in this chapter, Dan Carlson, the inventor and developer of Sonic Bloom, is an Earth lover: they are all modern-era Westerners who have a sense of reverence for nature that is customary throughout the world's indigenous cultures. Carlson was inspired to find another approach to farming in order to pursue his goal of arresting famine. He wanted to enhance the way plants grow. "I was a kid out of high school," he told us on one of my broadcasts, "and I went into the service—ended up in Korea where I saw some very drastic events. I watched people starve to death. Actually, 45 percent of the farmers starved on the DMZ [demilitarized zone] where I was."

He remembers being obliged to watch a starving Korean mother lay the legs of her small child beneath the rear wheel of an army truck, as crushed legs created an authentic cripple and entitled the family to a food subsidy. "I decided to dedicate my life to solving the problems of world hunger." Back home on the G.I. Bill, he attended the University of Minnesota and studied horticulture and agriculture. "One of the first things I found was a plant growth stimulant that made three out of a hundred plants grow ten times their normal scale. I thought, if we could make all plants grow ten times their normal, we could end world hunger. I used this first product that affected 2–3 percent of the plants and studied plant physiology to find a way to make the other 97 percent of the plants accept this. The 3 percent, I reasoned, were doing something out of time."

Carlson studied plant physiology for about five years, he continued. "I was looking for a way to enhance the way plants grow and I thought that there must be something to the issue of resonance. I came across a frequency of sound that helps plants breath better. I just stood up in the library and shouted 'I found it, I found it!' And my reward was [being told to] shut up."

With the help of an audioengineer, Carlson found one range that was consonant with the early morning birds chirping that helps plants open wider their stomata, or mouthlike microscopic pores. "It took about a week of working with a sound engineer," remembered Carlson, "to create this frequency that was said to help plants breathe better." He noted that a frequency something like what is heard in natural birdsong, in the 5,000 hertz range, helped plants breathe with at least a 2 percent increase. He then provided an organic gibberellic acid, a plant growth stimulant, which is in every plant but its extract comes from the root of the rice plant. "I had a sound engineer help me create this particular frequency and I figured if they could breathe better they could absorb better. We played this frequency and applied this first product to a simple purple passion plant that I bought for eighty-eight cents. Within about four and a half months it had grown to 18 inches long, which is almost five times quicker than the [usual] time period."

Carlson's passion has led to many Jack and the Beanstalk experiences, beginning with that eighty-eight-cent purple passion plant, a harbinger of what his Sonic Bloom process has made available for the world. This plant was listed at 668 feet in the *Guinness Book of World Records* as the world's largest indoor plant—but it eventually grew to be 1,300 feet! "I put tea cup hooks in the ceilings," Carlson says, adding that his wife was "kind enough to let me do it. It ran through three rooms in our home and grew 2–3 feet a day." He credits the plant's extraordinary growth to the beautiful songbird's frequency that literally opens up the plant's cell walls, making them more capable of absorbing the proper nutrients.

When Carlson called the universities with his extraordinary news, he was told that no one cared about purple passion plants. "They said something interesting like, 'Why don't you grow something that we eat, like a vegetable?' It was a good idea. I got anyone who had a garden to take part. We made cassettes of this oscillating wave and with our spray bottle we got 600–700 tomatoes per plant, 40–50 peppers on pepper plants. Of course, we called the university guys again and said, 'Come on out and look.' And they said, 'Oh that's just backyard garden stuff. Why don't you try it on commercial farming?'"

Carlson was experiencing the familiar stonewalling technique applied by the status quo to most creators who step outside the conventional box of their fields. Finally in 1974 he succeeded in convincing a university agriculture tree Extension Service official to visit his garden. He remembers, "The man said, 'If you give me a chair and glass of lemonade, I'll come out and see ya.'"

The results of a series of tests proved that the combination of the oscillating wave and the foliar nutrient spray treatment created a dynamic relationship of events that enhanced the growing process and nutrient uptake process in the plant organism. "We were routine enough to have some good chromo-photograph work, which at 800 power enhancement showed the stomata of treated plants. That's the breathing apparatus. You can see these larger, much more complex cells and physiological units of the plant; you can see the treated and the untreated. It's very graphic. We were also able to do major radioactive isotope uptake studies with a major university in Utah, proving that the sound aids in the absorption translocation up and down the plant by 400 percent. The spray aids in absorption and translocation up and down the plant by 300 percent. The sound, which is sonic, and the spray, which is the nutrient or bloom, [together provide a] 700 percent improvement in absorption translocation—hence, Dan Carlson's Sonic Bloom."

Some of the most remarkable results with it have been in places like the Sudan where Sonic Bloom has been used with 130 degree temperatures and only 2½ inches of rain. "We had great success. I believe that with open pollinated seed treated with Sonic Bloom that we will raise some of the most nutrient-rich fruit, grains, and vegetables. Any child that is malnourished in the first eight months of life will be forever limited. Nutrition is fundamental to development and this would be a tremendous help in the third world."

After having done this work for almost thirty years when Carlson and I spoke in 2002, I asked him how this odyssey has shaped him. "I may not be a good businessman," he replied, "but I am a really good plant scientist. My reward is the twinkle in the farmer's eye when he has the best yield of his life. When I go all over the world and spend time with farmers who are nurturers, when farmers send their crops off to market [it's like] they are sending their children off and when their children become valedictorians they are proud. . . . I get to spend time with people all over the world, even those who don't speak the same language. We look at the plants, we do something together, we share some meals, we twinkle, and that's it." In September 2001 Carlson's name was submitted for the Nobel Prize in Science.

These amazing farmers and others like them really do offer us hope. They show us that we can grow enough food to support the planet and do it in such a way that even the growing systems are improved. We can do it in such a way that the Earth herself is nurtured by the growing, not stripped of any of her precious resources. Just as the ancients saw the cosmos in man, biodynamic and other healing agricultural methods see the cosmos also in the Earth. It is time to transform our current death economy into a life economy.

The Earth herself is a being with natural cycles, which can be enhanced to benefit all kingdoms. What better way is there to live upon the Earth than when all systems benefit by a process? Acting in a just and sustainable fashion is right stewardship. Any other approach to growing food seems wrong-sighted to me. The way we farm, grow foods, tend to livestock, use energy, create inventions, and apply technologies should lead to an increase in health—not just animal and consumer health, but also the health of the ecosystem. For most of the latter half of the twentieth century, agribusiness farming has decidedly not contributed to the health of the ecosystem. A life economy would place such a reverence on life as to make it the center of our societal axis, from politics to the economy, rather than having quality of life trivialized and battled for constantly as though an aberration, when it should be the standard operating procedure. *Choose life* is a fundamental teaching in all sacred society lineages. This must be reflected in our earthly activities as well.

CHARLES WALTERS AND ACRES U.S.A.

To understand how such a drastic reversal from natural and sustainable farming to chemical agriculture had happened, I called on Charlie Walters (1926–2009). In 1970, Charles Walters, Jr. founded the finest ecoagriculture paper in the country if not the world, *Acres U.S.A.*, attempting to reverse the dire consequences of chemical farming, factory farming, and agri-giant husbandry practices.

In one of several radio interviews, he began by explaining, "I wrote a book about thirty [now forty] years ago called *Unforgiven: The American Economic System Sold for Debt and War* examining [the effects of chemical] agriculture. When working out the statistics, the details, and the history, it was clear then that we were increasing inputs geometrically, but we were only increasing production arithmetically. We were destroying our resources, our landed resources. When we started *Acres U.S.A.*, we were taking on the change in public policy, starting in 1949, that installed into the university system these false premises—partial and unbalanced fertilization and toxic rescue chemistry. Those are not my words but those of Sir Albert Howard (1873–1947), the British scientist [considered by many the founder of the organic farming movement] who decried what was happening. What he said was that we're eclipsing all of the lessons we have learned up until then and refusing to learn any beyond them.

"So *Acres* took on the chore of not only reporting on biologically correct systems, including biodynamics and organic farming, but also the new developments in science that are taking place outside the umbrella of the university." One gets a sense from talking with Walters that the majority of problems we struggle to address and correct today were all preventable.

Walters' view is a long one. He has studied the problems and the solutions. *Acres U.S.A.* has made it possible for farmers and backyard gardeners to make a positive impact on the planet by building up their own soil and plant life, even while much of the world continues in the dangerous and unproductive chemical industry style of farming and the creation of genetically modified foods. With a degree of hopeful enthusiasm, he noted, "In recent times some university people and people from the USDA have picked up on the trend that *Acres U.S.A.* helped establish since that time." The USDA's little soil biology primer is but one example of this evident change. "Whoever would have thought that the USDA would be talking about something like that," marveled Walters. "So, perhaps the whole outlook is shifting. What we know is that toxic technology is sunset technology; it has to pass from the scene. The question is how much damage are we going to let it do before we change?"

It is obvious that economics—and specifically the drive for profit by the agribusiness suppliers and their duplicitous promises of greater yields to farmers—has had more to do with the direction farming has taken this century than any concern for producing healthful products and animals for the community. This is another aspect of the death economy's impact on the Earth. Like an acceptable risk strategy in war, which calculates unnecessary casualties such as civilian deaths, the toxic agricultural practices have destroyed the soil of millions and millions of acres on Earth, undermining the health of animals and people in the process. "We superimposed on agriculture an industrial procedure rather than a biological procedure," said Walters. "This leads to soil mining and farm units being consolidated, closed down, and recast into bigger models. The super farms can't operate without the government's cooperation, with continuing loans to be serviced if not paid." He told us of a Texas rancher in the panhandle area with maybe "eight or nine sections of ground with irrigation to grow corn. But he can't sustain his farm. And so the government issues some sort of relief loan, but it doesn't improve the farm's chances of doing better next time." All it does, in fact, is further indebt the farmer to the bank. Government subsidies and controls are not designed to benefit the land. As Walters stated flatly, "Farm subsidies see to it that the banker gets paid and the water supply gets ruined." Overfarming and particularly giant cattle farms are drawing down our nation's aquifers, our natural supply of water, much in the same way the U.S. government's policy of subsidizing failed farms draws down the natural resources of the people's labor.

"What will happen when we run out of good water?" asks Walters. "What's going to happen in forty or fifty years as the cattle pens with this kind of process suck the water dry? First we will run out of potable water, and then we could run out of food if we continue to depend on this type of industrialized agriculture. This is not just hyperbole. . . . As early as the 1930s, it was clear from studies of the Middle East that thousands of cities no longer exist. Land is desert because of poor agricultural practices that mine the soil rather than farm the soil. . . . It's a difference in the attitude that we have [particularly] run into on the farm in the last forty years. The old farmer, like my dad, figured it was his job to leave the soil in better condition than when he found it. That's not the concept or the vision that people have today. They move in and get what they can out of the soil and after they leave it goes down the drink, down the Mississippi, because there is nothing there to it any longer. The topsoil is being eroded, washed away by wind and water. We are bringing subsoil up and calling it topsoil and it's not able to produce quality crops that are able to nourish minds capable of thought and reason."

Particularly damaging are the processes currently in vogue in animal husbandry. Walters reminded us that most big dairies in this country are French-owned, and the majority "do confinement feeding, meaning they don't let those animals out for a mouthful of grass, ever. They give them rations that are figured out by the university. As a consequence of this type of husbandry, we have almost 300,000 cases of Para T [referring to paratuberculosis], which is passed through the milk, surviving the pasteurization process, creating bowel disease and Crohn's disease in human beings. There is a proposal in Congress that these animals be taken out of the milking industry with the government picking up the tab to the tune of $1.2 billion." Meanwhile, (at the time of our discussion before Charlie's death in 2009) the media blitz had us all worrying about hoof and mouth disease, which is not even transmissible to human beings. "They are ready to take Draconian measures worldwide, to imitate England, and send out SWAT teams to kill the animals if they get the fever blister. Hoof and mouth disease is treatable and most recover. The serious strain hasn't shown up since 1929."

And don't even get him started on milk. "What we have done to the milk industry in the United States is really criminal," Walters exclaimed. "We are feeding the people a product that is called milk, but it isn't really milk at all. The butter fat is removed, and other fats inserted. It is cooked, and other things like pharmaceuticals and hormones are added. It's not a healthful product."

He is right, of course. Field trials already show us that it's not right to fool with Mother Nature. "No one knows the consequences of genetically engineered food," he added. "It is so reckless as to be unbelievable. The most sensitive creatures are showing the effects already; such as the monarch butterfly becoming a victim to genetically modified corn. Extrapolate and you can see what we have done here. Europe, India, Russia, and a lot of civilized nations are rejecting this genetically modified grain," and as a consequence a lot of American farmers can no longer export much of their grain. Not to mention the genetic drift associated with genetically modified grain, which is worse than the chemical drift from pesticides, contaminating organic farmland and destroying it. It is yet another octave of that arrogance we humans demonstrate when we believe we can use natural and man-made resources without reverent regard. Again, this is a symptom of our death economy, which chooses short-term profit of the few over long-term welfare for all.

According to Walters, there are only a few thousand people in the United States who are doing correct agriculture work. They are making a living at it, but they are an apparition, he explained, because the U.S. Department of Agriculture doesn't fully count them. "Some are into it on a commercial agricultural scale, but many are quite small. They are producing a quality product. What we've done to help them over the years is examine all the different aspects of what it takes to make that soil system work, to make the natural nitrogen cycle work. About fifteen years ago we introduced something that is becoming quite popular. It's a refractometer, something used by the grape industry to measure the sugar level in grapes. We found that it could be used for any crop and it tells you if it has enough of the natural defense systems to ward off fungal and insect attacks." He described how any crop can be monitored in this way "making chemical resource superfluous." Cattle that are fed this type of healthful feed will have no diseases that are passed on to humans. "Now this is being done out there, but it goes unrecognized by the Department of Agriculture and universities. So this is what we do at *Acres U.S.A.* We bring [to the farmer] whatever is happening, from whatever part of the world, that will assist our right way of stewarding the Earth—from research of the beginning of the century, to something developed last week by a local farmer or a laboratory in the United States."

I asked for an overview of the new trends in farming, and Walters told us of a significant but unrecognized change taking place on the landscape. "Thousands, if not millions, of people are going out and getting themselves a few acres. A few of them are sinking their teeth in and making the small farm work and most of it is being done by forging direct links with the consumer. This is happening almost totally unrecognized by the agencies." Co-operative farms, for example, enable buyers to purchase the farmer's produce before he has even planted it. These CSAs, like the one Allan Balliett owns and operates in the Maryland area, guarantee the farmer will have cash for planting and harvesting and that the consumer will receive healthful produce. It's a collaboration that is predicated on faith. This is an example of the life economy at work.

Walters then told us about the benchmarks in his years of work. "The day we started is one," was his immediate answer. "When Dr. William A. Albrecht [(1888–1994), the pioneer in connecting soil and nutrition] of the University of Missouri made a gift of about 830 papers that he had written in his lifetime. He told me to run with them. He insisted weed and insect control was a function of fertility management. So, we have to show what fertility management is. How do you manage the biotic life in the soil? How do you manage the calcium, the magnesium, the sodium, the basic nutrients, the phosphorous, and so on? One of the other most important things we uncovered," he continued, "was the discovery made by Dr. Phil Callahan [who found that war zones on Earth correlate to places where the Earth's resonant magnetic field is cut off and that the stone towers of Ireland amplify and receive microwaves beneficial to agriculture,] that shows what attracts an insect to any particular plant. The sick plant puts out a wavelength in the infrared that calls in the insect. It is the function of the insect to remove a plant that is not fit to be passed through the food chain to the head of the biotic pyramid. This, I think, was really landmark stuff and confirmed by the refractometer we talked about earlier."

BIODYNAMIC BEEKEEPING AND THE SECRET LIFE OF BEES

Gunther Hauk of Spikenard Farm Honeybee Sanctuary in the Blue Ridge Mountains of Floyd, Virginia, which he and his wife Vivian cofounded in 2006, teaches biodynamic beekeeping and they offer workshops, publications, and resources for biodynamic Earth care and gardening as well. Joining me in 2012, we focused on the serious diminishment of the honeybee population worldwide, a topic Hauk had addressed in his book *Toward Saving the Honeybee.*

Hauk referenced colony collapse disorder by saying, "More than we can imagine depends on our ability to turn the crisis into an opportunity for change."

As a biodynamic gardener he is rooted in the integrated and tended ecosystem built on respect for what each natural system prospers the most by. He has practiced biodynamic gardening his whole life and was a teacher of the subject in German Waldorf schools and elsewhere, where the subject has been taught since the 1920s. In 1996 Hauk returned to the Unites States and cofounded the Pfeiffer Center for Biodynamic Agriculture and Environmental Studies. "I got so inspired and captivated by the biodynamic method that this has been a lifelong passion. It has

Fig. 5.1. Honeybees and their hive. Image courtesy of Waugsberg.

been a lifelong love affair." He attests that biodynamic farming "is the most holistic way of farming or gardening, whose quality is unsurpassed." He has made a special focus on the honeybee since reading an article in the *New York Times* called the "Hush of the Hives" in 1996. At that point he realized, "Oh my, it's that bad already."

"We've lost already 96 percent of four major bumble bees. If the honeybees go and the other pollinators go, of course this brings on a food crisis. From 30–70 percent plus of all that we eat is pollinated by the honeybee." But this, Hauk pointed out, was only one aspect of the situation. The other, which Rudolph Steiner was able to see clairvoyantly, was that the poison that bees, wasps, ants, and others put out is "formic acid and formic acid is the great invigorator of all of plant life. All plants, in the spring especially, need this formic acid in order to grow in healthy ways. We need the formic acid too." Hauk says when we see a decline in this formic acid, we will also see a decline in the health of plant life, "which is already happening."

He pointed out that even our DNA is acid and that all kinds of acids in dilute amounts are essential to our life as well. The crisis is "quite a bit deeper than most people realize, even beekeepers." It is a wake-up call that whatever animal we husband or insect we foster, that we must do so in more "appropriate ways, appropriate to their being." Reverence, yet another guest points out, is the foundation of proper action. "For pigs to be running about and rolling in the mud and eating some grass is appropriate. Chickens want to scratch and peck and not be cooped up."

One theme I spent countless years exploring was the pain and suffering caused by scientific animal experiments and factory farming of animals for food or food by-products. The suffering and exploitation of animals held captive in zoos, entertainment facilities, and aquariums worldwide is another problematic situation. Neither the animals, nor their human keepers, consumers, or audiences are engaging nature in anything like a healthy and natural manner. I pray that the suffering caused to other sentient life and that we inflict on one another is a phase of human behavior that is finite and will one day end. Evidence of this imbalance is the fact that the bee, the center of the ecosystem, is suffering from catastrophic colony collapse.

"I think," continued Hauk, "the dying off of certain animals, and others that are near extinction like the polar bear or the penguin and so on, does touch our heart, but it's the honeybee who most people feel [intuitively] is very precious." Just as the Native Americans were aware of the great Buffalo Spirit or the great Bear Spirit, "there is," says Hauk, "a great Bee Spirit as well. Operating as a group soul, like the ant, the bee colony is a combination of instinct in each part. The bee's status is our wake-up call."

The industrialization of beekeeping has had the greatest impact on hive instability. Hauk explained how and what can be done to change this. "Historically, keeping beehives was not a profession but a valued companion in every garden. The first unnatural thing that has to be instituted to factory farm bees is to prevent their swarming, a natural phenomenon of a hive. . . . In addition to creating things that prevent this natural migration of a hive, they also now artificially create queens. The use of plastics, corn syrup, and other artificial methods of breeding and feeding the bees has deprived them of their natural habitats, breeding cycles, and sustainable purpose as the pollinators on the planet. Like dairy cows who become milk producers—utilities for a by-product originally designed for nursing its young—bees are farmed for their honey and their natural habitats are artificially manufactured and natural systems and processes violated."

Describing how the bee industry raises millions of queen bees only to kill them on their eighth day of life as part of the manufacturing of what is called royal jelly, this "is something that should be stopped altogether," Hauk remarked. Some bees travel in trucks over a thousand miles away from their birthplace to California crop fields and elsewhere. The hives that are manufactured to breed these honeybees, which will be put in agricultural fields, are made of plastic foundations and the honey in the hive (which the bees would normally feed off of) is extracted for sale and corn syrup put in its place. Their natural habitat is a general area in which they have a hive and plantings to feed off of, like dandelion, eyebright, and other weeds people tend to spray away. Describing the misuse of pesticides, herbicides, and fungicides in agriculture, which is an issue I have been active in highlighting since adolescence, Hauk said, "They are using things that cause death in the field of life."

Once again, the death economy paradigm is self-evident in the normative big farming industry and unfortunately on many small farms as well. Describing the ease with which anyone can raise bees for the benefit of their garden, the ecosystem at large, and human health as well, Hauk reminds us that by planting flowering plants and bushes we can support the bee colonies in every community. Due to chemical pesticides and fertilizers, open fields no longer offer pollination benefits; rather, unsprayed suburban backyards can do more to restore the immediate bee population than waiting for agriculture to adopt more natural systems of nurturance. Noting that bee colonies have dwindled from 7.5 million to 2.5 million, "that is a lot of formic acid missing in nature and our lives depend upon formic acid," said Hauk.

The importance of formic acid was highlighted when Hauk spoke of a forester in Germany. He said, "wherever the ants are disappearing in the forest, the forests are dying more quickly. They are putting ant colonies back into the forests." The missing ingredient—"formic acid."

"You know Zoh, you mentioned the magic word and that is reverence. That is the reverence for all that lives; for every being has its role and it is important. I think the only way forward is that we rediscover the awe and reverence and wonder [for what's] beneath our very feet."

THE SECRET LIFE OF PLANTS

Indeed, just as the bees support life on Earth and have a communication system, plants also put out information—it is even accurate to say they talk. That is the secret life of plants. In fact, one of the most revolutionary books in the world of science in the past four decades is titled just that, *The Secret Life of Plants* (1973). A collaboration of Peter Tompkins (1919–2007) and our dear friend Christopher Bird (1928–1996) (the best man at my wedding in 1980), *The Secret Life of Plants* stood the world of science on its head by showing us that plants not only respond when humans talk to them, but they can talk back.

Bird and Tompkins collected the work of researchers from around the world and established that there is intelligence in all life that is perceptible and accessible. Their magnum opus, *Secrets of the Soil* published in 1989, and *The Secret Life of Plants* would have been followed up by *The Secret Life of Water,* which unfortunately was not completed before Bird's death on May 2, 1996.

Bird was responsible for many things, but one of his most important gifts was his ability to connect researchers from around the world. He loved to introduce people who were searching for answers and asking great questions. Because of his vital sense of independence as a thinker, he helped many others to find their own paths. He would underwrite their workshops and research needs or host them for weeks on end in his own home. With his wife, Lois, they provided a safe wayfarer station for hundreds of like-minded people: a place to discuss ideas that were too heretical for the universities and too threatening for the economists and corporations.

Over the thousands of hours of conversations we had over the years in his home or at ours, Chris made it clear that the Earth was ailing.

His overarching concern was that we would wait too long to do anything vital, always doing "too little too late." In our 1989 interview about his book *Secrets of the Soil,* Bird said, "in 1985 I became quite alarmed about what was happening. One could look at the conifers in the forests of Germany and Switzerland and see the fantastic decimation. In Germany at that time, the forest was already 40 percent gone, with trees looking like telephone poles . . . and we see this now all up and down the Appalachian chain in the United States. In Vermont, for example, if you look at Camel's Hump from the air, the whole south of the mountain is filled with dead trees. The same goes for Mt. Mitchell in North Carolina. You can talk to forestry experts at the University of Vermont, Duke University, and the University of North Carolina and the story is the same everywhere."

Bird always said that the soil is the foundation of our lives and that without healthy soil we eventually have famine. Remineralization efforts, tree planting campaigns, biomass rescue efforts, and organic and biodynamic farming are all actions taken against a relentless force that is destroying the natural equilibrium on Earth. With great gusto he said, "billions and billions of micro-organisms inhabit healthy soil. And above them, in terms of the organic interaction between soil and other life-forms, you get the earthworms. But artificial pesticides, herbicides, and insecticides have completely depleted the soil where they have been applied year after year. You will barely find an earthworm in them. It's the microlife that breaks down the original rocky constituents and can turn them into humus. So the more activity of the microbe, the more humus in the soil and that's what a healthy plant thrives on. The greatest challenge facing mankind is malnutrition. The quality of what we are raising in the soil is so depleted. Nutrition begins in the soil and this is the basis of the whole pyramid of life. . . . Fruits and vegetables from the general grocery store don't taste like they did thirty to forty years ago. That's a good indication that something is wrong with the produce coming out of the ground. . . . We have quantity but we don't have quality."

Bird was a wonderful storyteller. He had a way of making you feel like you were in the story, but he couldn't stand it when someone tried to rush him. With a sense of having fought a long war with no end in sight, he began by talking about the large mechanical manufacturers that have existed for the past eighty years. "It's a very interesting story, where it all came from. What happened was that after WWI, the chemical companies who made munitions for the war . . . had to get into something that would pay well. They got the idea of making artificial fertilizers based on the doctrine of a German chemist. The same thing happened after WWII, but raised to another power. So if you look at the production line schedule [of those fertilizers] on a graph, it has just been going up like a rocket since WWI. Along with that came the advertising, or propaganda, to persuade the farmers that they couldn't do without these new chemical products. Now, most of them are so hooked, like a drug addict, they can't get off the stuff." This presents a real dilemma for the farmer. "To turn it around and go back to healthy soil requires a transition period that could take one to three years, and during that transition the income of the farm is impacted. So once they're hooked," he said with a sigh, "most stay hooked for the life of their farming practice."

I asked Bird to tell us about major soil restoration areas, and he referred to Alex Podolinsky who introduced biodynamic farming on a million and a half acres in Australia more than thirty-five years ago. "This is what I call a *ground up* system," said Bird. "It starts with the soil and the preparation of it and, thus, everything will be an expression of that foundation." Dan Carlson's Sonic Bloom system of harmonics and foliar feeding through the leaves, as discussed earlier, is what Bird would refer to as a *top down* system.

It bothers me to no end to know that I listened to Bird saying all of these things for over twenty years, and even back in the 1920s Rudolph Steiner was warning against the same predicaments we find ourselves in today—almost one hundred years later. Unfortunately, most Americans remain ignorant of the high degree of science that validates biodynamic, organic, and other ways of growing food and raising livestock. Meanwhile, the use of destructive chemicals continues to increase worldwide. While we have purchased or grown our own organic vegetables and eggs for the past thirty years, most consumers, in subtle ways through our power of purchase, are still supporting a failed and disastrous agricultural system. One of the best reasons to buy organic is to minimize your contributions to an industrial war that has ravaged our landscape, our bodies, our health, and nature.

Another discovery of Bird's, which he reported on in *The Secret Life of Plants,* was the conclusion that demineralized soil seems to be what tips the scale prematurely toward a glacial age. He showed evidence collected across Siberia indicating that the climate in a large part of the world is cooling, but there is also a simultaneous warming trend that is going on. There is no question that we are currently experiencing inordinate weather changes globally.

John Hamaker (1914–1994) and Don Weaver, in their book *The Survival of Civilization,* found that demineralized soil can be replenished by spraying mineral rock dust ground from glacial stream rock on the affected area. Spraying this finely ground rock as a powder over dying forests has consistently proved that the trees that were sprayed were able to recover. Some of the most remarkable results have been seen in Germany's Black Forest, where the decimated trees actually recovered over a period of years. After visiting Hawaii I thought it would be great to pulverize the lava rock there into mineral dust for use in gardens, farms, and forests.

I often wonder what strategy Bird would devise for stopping today's revolution in agriculture, which is even more reckless than the last century's chemical disaster. Today's corporate giants in agribusiness manufacture genetically engineered products or GMOs. Monsanto is not alone in trying to promote their patented, genetically designed agricultural products. As mentioned earlier, in chapter 3, their Roundup Ready soybean is genetically engineered to withstand their poisonous chemical Roundup, which is used on crops to kill weeds. Over time farmers will tell you, as did Eric Herm, an organic Texas cotton farmer and author of *Son of a Farmer, Child of the Earth,* "the weeds come back and become immune to it."

Herm, like many farmers, learned the hard way that chemical agriculture and the more high tech genetic agriculture is neither prosperous for the farmer, the land, or the livestock. Since eliminating chemicals and GMO products on his farm, Herm has joined others in a national campaign against these dangerous practices. Two examples are enough to explain why this is being called genetic roulette by activists like Herm.

The Dow Corporation is hoping to sell its genetically engineered Enlist corn, which as discussed in chapter 3 is designed to withstand the herbicide 2,4-D, a main ingredient in Agent Orange. The production of wheat (for making bread, corn chips, cereals, etc.) that can survive this substance, which typically destroys whatever it touches, is nothing short of genetic and chemical warfare being waged on "we the people" by publicly held companies. It's important as well to keep in mind that it's not just the farmer and migrant workers who will be breathing in these disease-producing chemicals, sprayed acre after acre on the GMO and other crops, it's wildlife too, and anyone impacted by the wind that carries these deadly substances, some of them formerly outlawed in chemical warfare. I often feel like every farmer should be handed a gas mask and a hazmat suit before entering their own fields, as should every neighbor within radius of a few miles and every bird and every dog and every deer! You get my point: the wind blows everything around and this chemical drift is toxic, not to mention that its residue remains in the plant life we and the animals consume, and it resides in the soil and runoff that flows into our streams.

As for what's already known about the dangers of GMOs themselves, the International Journal of Biological Sciences reported that three products that were tested by Monsanto were poisonous to animals, in which it manifested as kidney and liver damage. The Institute for Responsible Technology and the American Academy of Environmental Medicine have reported that animal studies reveal autoimmune disorders, infertility, accelerated aging, and changes in organ systems including the gastrointestinal system, and this is why they assert that humans should avoid GMO foods and their by-products entirely. However, because GMOs are not labeled and are in snack foods, cereals, and even baby food, consumers don't realize what they're eating. So, even though genetically engineered plants haven't been found safe or fit for human or animal consumption, and in fact have been shown to cause birth defects, cancer, sterility, and other disorders, American multinational corporations continue to lobby the U.S. Congress for exemption from safety testing and labeling laws. If a food isn't labeled "organic," there's no way of knowing what's in it.

Another serious problem is that often the GMO seeds themselves contaminate adjacent organic farmers' crops, which Monsanto, as one example, then claims to own. Piracy by the contamination of organic farmland is a new "robber baron" business, and it's no different from when villages are seized by terrorists in other parts of the world. I encourage the reader to research this blatant raiding and destruction process online. It's not hyperbole to claim that this is a new form of biowarfare. GMOs and the politics and court proceedings that support the reckless use of disease-inducing products for short-term profit at the expense of long-term well-being are an obscene addition to the battle for our Earth and our health. It's a battle that so many of us have fought our entire lives and new generations are called upon to fight now.

These illicit gambles, along with the over grazing of land for increased meat consumption and crop land that is utilized for fuel production are an extension of an already failed corporatized agricultural industry, which has eroded topsoil, drained down aquifers, and depleted grain stock worldwide, leaving the world with only a seventy-four day reserve, while simultaneously doubling grain prices. For the most complete overview of our planetary situation, read the comprehensive and fact-filled book *Full Planet, Empty Plates: The New Geopolitics of Food Scarcity* by Lester R. Brown, founder and president of the Earth Policy Institute. Destructive agricultural and farming husbandry policies and practices must be stopped, and we are the people being asked to do just that. This is also one reason I have always supported the movement of organic farming and is why we plant our Dogwood Farm garden every spring. We should teach our children how to grow healthful food and save precious seeds, something Bird promoted. His own organic Georgetown garden boasted tomatoes the size of small cantaloupes.

It is obviously true that remedies exist for each of our problems on Earth, no matter how chronic they seem. It's a question of applying our talent, imagination, will, and resources to the task. So the question we might ask is: What prevents us from caring for our Earth, the very planet on which our lives and all Earth life depends? Why is it that in the status quo of today the industries of agriculture, the military, what is called health care, politics, and banking seem to be guided by a shared economic model of exploitation and experimentation, interlocked in the corporate framework whose current values of profit without respect for the world diminishes the life of humanity and the planet itself?

GREEN PSYCHOLOGY

Another Earth lover in this chapter is devoted to healing and harmonizing the relations between humanity and the Earth. Ralph Metzner, Ph.D., is a psychotherapist and professor at the California Institute of Integral Studies, where he teaches courses on ecopsychology and ecological worldviews. He speaks of ecology as a theology, a psychology, an entry way to the preserved Earth wisdom of the first people. Metzner has authored several books, including *Green Psychology: Transforming Our Relationship to the Earth* in which he eloquently translates the feelings that so many of us have wherein we regard the Earth with a sense of sacredness and holiness. Earth is a divine creation. It is every bit as divine as the heaven we imagine we may inhabit or as the angels sometimes seen in our midst. He calls our divorce from nature a spiritual aberration and I heartily agree.

Explaining how he came to view the Earth as a sacred, living being, Metzner told us, "My field in psychology originally was consciousness studies. In the sixties I worked at Harvard University with Tim Leary and Richard Alpert (who later became Ram Dass) researching . . . consciousness-expanding drugs and substances. Through that I became interested in consciousness expansion through nondrug means like yoga, meditation, spiritual practices of various cultures, and East/West psychology, which is the area I teach in at the Institute for Integral Studies in San Francisco. Then I became interested in shamanism, which is really the oldest spiritual and healing tradition on the planet. Shamanic practitioners enter into an altered state of consciousness, which may be induced by certain plants and substances or through various other means such as rhythmic drumming, dance, vision quests, and various modalities with various spiritual and healing purposes. . . . Then it dawned on me that these shamanic traditions and practices were based on an entirely different worldview than the one that I, and many others, had been brought up in—that of the worldview of science, mechanism, and materialism. A world that focuses on the material, physical world of objects as being the only true reality and everything else, consciousness, subjectivity, spirit, quality, is merely subjective and has a lesser role." I see it as a modern-era schism that has stripped the inherent value of life and replaced it with a utilitarian perspective, where nothing has meaning unto itself unless we can exploit it for some other gain.

James Olson, author of *The Whole-Brain Path to Peace: The Role of Left- and Right-Brain Dominance in the Polarization and Reunification of America,* would describe this schism as one that exists between the two hemispheres of the brain. While the right brain behaves as most women do—holistically, inclusively, concerned for how everything relates to the whole—the left brain isolates, using domination, violence, and separation as its modus operandi, which is how a patriarchal culture behaves. The modern western culture and its Republican body politic is dominated by the left brain, whereas native traditions and the Democratic party remain dominated by the right brain. The goal, however, for a balanced psychological, physical, and spiritual world is the integration of both parts of our brain, hence, whole-brain thinking, which, I joke, is why I became a Libertarian.

"The question that began to intrigue me," continued Metzner, "is what has led to our civilization feeling that we are above nature? This idea that humans are the superior animal is part of the mainstream scientific view [left-brain dominance]. Somehow or other we assumed that we own the place, we own the planet, and we have the right to whatever it is we want to do."

"Indigenous people's attitude is completely different. Their position is humble. They regard animals, human beings, and plants as all interweaving [right-brain dominance]. It is a consciousness that says these are all our relations. We are to find our place. We are not the inheritors. We are not the owners. We have one piece in the web of life and it is our job to be as conscious as we can be, to be conscious of our impact, and to consider our ancestors, our previous generations before, future generations, and those that come after us down to the seventh generation."

Metzner's ability to integrate the ancient and modern ways of approaching the world and the inner and outer disciplines makes for a green psychology that is reminiscent in many ways of the green traditions of the Celts of Europe before the eighth century CE. Those and many other ancient peoples believed that Earth is a Goddess, a holy mother.

"All nature is imbued with an energy field and a consciousness field that allows one to tune into not just animals, but rocks and rivers and clouds," said Metzner. There is no split between science and the mainstream of concepts or religion and spirituality ethics [whole-brain balance]. There is not a split at all. Everything is in one integrated worldview. "As above, so below. Everything you can see outside, you see inside." You obtain this knowledge of all reality, he continued, "by going within yourself. It's not self-absorbed navel gazing; it's realizing that we are all in this vast network of life. All connected to all." As another radio guest, Vedic astrologer Jeffrey Armstrong, puts it: "we are all a cell in God's body."

Matthew Fox, Ph.D., a spiritual theologian and Episcopal priest, is a pioneer in the renewal of the ancient mystical tradition of creation spirituality, which he described in a 2012 interview "as the oldest tradition in the Bible, which is a tradition not of original sin . . . but of original blessings . . . that creation is fundamentally good. It is really the mirror opposite of fundamentalism."

The task at hand is one of integration. With great fervor and integrity, we are being asked to address the Earth's specific needs. To ignore the fact that we and the Earth are one is to relieve oneself of the role as sacred guardian. Earth's natural laws, when observed and followed, create just and sustainable systems through which all life prospers. This is why I call these approaches an expression of a life economy. One of the great challenges we face is dealing with the impact globalization is having on local economies. We all must transform the forces of globalization that destroy natural habitats and guide them to support those cultural values and best practices that sustain the natural world.

JAMES DEMEO AND THE USE OF SOFT TECHNOLOGY

One such example of this way of acting in nature is Wilhelm Reich's cloud-busting techniques for drought eradication. James DeMeo, Ph.D., of the Orgone Biophysical Research Lab he founded 1978, is a pioneer in the use of soft technology to harmonize the natural elements, to amplify natural qualities rather than suppressing energies. Researching specifically the works of Dr. Wilhelm Reich (1897–1957) since the early 1970s, DeMeo formally studied the Earth, atmospheric, and environmental/social sciences at Florida International University and the University of Kansas, where he earned his Ph.D. in 1986. He openly undertook graduate-level natural scientific research specifically focused upon Reich's controversial discoveries, subjecting those ideas to rigorous testing with positive verification of Reich's original findings; this work was peer-reviewed and accepted as the first-ever graduate thesis and dissertation on these subjects.

DeMeo joined me on air several times to discuss his book *Saharasia: The 4000 BCE Origins of Child Abuse, Sex Repression, Warfare and Social Violence in the Deserts of the Old World,* which demonstrates conclusively that changes in the environment are reflected in human conditions and human actions impact the environment in ways we may be unconscious of. The way Phil Callahan (mentioned earlier in this chapter) put it is that when the natural magnetic resonance is cut off or interrupted, war dominates the land. Might this be reflected, he postulated, in the soil itself, which is meant to be paramagnetic? Might this also be related to what Wilhelm Reich understood?

DeMeo is continuing the work of the late Dr. Reich, who understood that the energetic matrix we inhabit is full of life-enhancing energy. Reich recognized that repressive human conditions energetically create a type of bodily armoring and psychological neurosis, which in turn affects our behavior and how we treat each other and the environment. Reich's genius and discovery earned him the wrath of the federal government of the United States and sabotage by some in the press. His life's work was confiscated, his interstate shipments of Orgone Accumulators that people would sit in to regain health, were stopped by court order. Six tons of his writings and publications were burned, and he died in prison of heart failure. All of this occurred because of his experiments and healings with a real subtle energy, which he called orgone, derived from the word orgasm and organism, which is naturally found in a healthy environment and a healthy person. It charges the human body and can be excited through nurturing touch and loving sexuality. In the natural world it is amplified through healthy electrical storms and rainfall. For those interested in seeing some of Reich's instruments, the Reich Museum in Rangely, Maine, features many of them.

Two diametric aspects of this orgone phenomenon are greening and desertification. "Individuals lacking in mother's love when they are little or sexual, romantic love in later adolescence and adulthood," observed DeMeo about cultures where people lack this kind of love, "tend to be very violent. They often organize themselves into fascist systems and they make a lot of trouble for their neighbors and the rest of the world." It's amazing that sexual brutality, repression, and abuse enable torture and it all comes as part of a cultural package. DeMeo agreed that sexual repression is "part of the mechanism that creates . . . dictatorships and other types of totalitarian forms of government. They have to suppress women because if they allowed for free sexual expression, their power base would evaporate over time." We see this brutality in the damming of rivers and the creation of earthquakes from underground nuclear detonations.

From a biophysical perspective, the environmental condition influences the social situation and biological conditions. DeMeo explained: "Reich talked about the emotions and sexual excitation being an expression of an energy of the body. He measured this energy in very fascinating psychic experiments. It is a life energy he [Reich] pointed out that was life enhancing, moving freely in the body as an expression of health. The key to natural ecosystems is that the energy that exists in the body also exists in nature. One can talk about the movement of energy in ecosystems, simultaneous and pulsing and moving, versus being stagnated. Under the stagnated and immobilized condition, one gets the expression of drought. There is a correlation between the deserts and the emotional deserts of the people who live there. When there is brutality, genital mutilation, there is an armoring, which impacts the entire society. Reich called this *emotional armoring*. When threatened or beaten, children naturally contract to protect themselves. If one is constantly being attacked, there is a tendency for that contraction to become permanent. You can see it in the way they hold themselves, their separation, their limited capacity for emotional experiences."

DeMeo conducted the largest cross-cultural study on human behavior ever undertaken. "I did this more than fifteen [now twenty-seven] years ago when I was at the University of Kansas. Basically, I made the discovery that among the cultures that existed around the world before the period of European colonials spreading, the most harsh, patriarchal, authoritarian, warlike cultures existed in the big desert belts of the world. These included North Africa, the Middle East, and Central Asia and I call that *Saharasia*. The further you get away from that area, the gentler you find that culture is—to a point where you come to Oceana and North and South America. [Those areas] had the largest percentage of gentle cultures as compared to the desertlike world, which was dominated by warrior kingdoms. This showed a geographical pattern to human behavior [and perhaps] how human social violence got started in the first instance."

DeMeo's work is what I refer to as soft technology, as it relies on love, tenderness, and genuine care for the world. He maintains that enhancing tenderness can enhance health and this will lead to a greener environment. But the Reich method for creating rain, or cloudbusting, is also soft in its simplicity and noninvasiveness. DeMeo says, "I like to call it a passive technique and compare it to a lightning rod in a sense. We basically have a long tube that is pointed to the atmosphere above and it is grounded with a line into a fresh body of water. This process seems to remove stagnant energy from the atmosphere, oftentimes leading to the necessary rainfall. . . . It's more of an antenna that has directional capability. When you work it correctly and the natural energetic

Fig. 5.2. James DeMeo with a cloudbuster in Eritrea, Africa, at the edge of the Sahara Desert. Image courtesy of James DeMeo.

pulsations start and you begin to see the clouds come in, at that point your work is finished." That means the stagnation in the atmosphere has been removed. Interestingly, Phillip Callahan also spoke of antennas both in the round towers of Ireland and in the paramagnetic elements in healthy soil.

DeMeo's greening projects have been implemented in Africa, Israel, South America, and in the United States. These simple tubes, or Reich's cloudbusters, show that when the energy flow is restored, cloud cover and rainfall usually ensue. "We had a project with the nation of Eritrea for five years, over five summers. Using this method we were able to increase rainfall . . . by 36 percent. That is just one example."

DeMeo and others like him exploring etheric rain engineering suggest that future solutions to global problems do not have to be high tech. In fact, DeMeo expresses his work much like an acupuncturist does, in terms of moving Chi or life energy. He is a new breed of scientist who understands that enhancing natural systems impacts all life-forms and creates an integrative, energetic relationship between nature and humanity. A type of loving engagement of nature's mystery and motions, as an act of reverence rather than debasement, will unlock the doors to wisdom and restoration.

THE SANCTUARY OF LIFE

When developing new technologies, stopping to ask *why* we are doing certain things is far more important than asking if we are able. Chemical and other forms of weather engineering are taking place and will continue to be used for economic gain in its applications to remove rain clouds from sporting events or produce low cloud cover for military maneuvers or to create drought, as some research suggests was done for three years prior to the entry of the U.S. military into Afghanistan.

As well, the rush to genetically engineer foods for short-term profit poses serious long-term risks on the Earth, including the loss of heirloom and other seeds that can reproduce themselves. GMOs cannot do this, meaning that one cannot save seed from each year's garden, but rather one becomes entirely dependent on the giant corporations in order to grow any food at all, which is an almost sinister recipe for corporate world domination.

We need to be mindful that other beings and life-forms inhabit our world, such as the animal kingdom, and are at our mercy. They are real beings with real intelligence even if they don't look like us. The more we can honor this reality, the more likely we will be to sustain the Earth to support habitation. As another guest of mine, Alden Meyer, director of policy and strategy for the Union of Concerned Scientists, put it, "saving the Earth is good business." And while that may be true in one regard, on the other hand the Earth doesn't really need saving; we just need to stop injuring our planet, to stop assaulting and abusing what is on loan to each one of us. The Earth, like the portion of the population who are brutalized and raped, has fared no better. The drive to conquer and dominate needs to be transformed to a need to protect and support *all* life, a higher aspect of human consciousness, a more noble awareness.

Being an Earth lover is not only reserved for our respect of agriculture, the bees, and earthworms. Since writing the first draft of this book at the opening of the twenty-first century, I have continued to pursue interviews with extraordinary men and women who one could easily refer to as Earth lovers. For me this has meant working on behalf of the animals. For decades I focused on the abuse and misuse of animals, especially in experimentation and factory farming because so many billions of animals' lives are impacted.

John Robbins is one of many people I have interviewed over the decades who have focused on the suffering of farm animals. His book *No Happy Cows: Dispatches from the Frontlines of the Food Revolution* focuses on this topic. "Contrary to the propaganda," he explained, "that comes from the dairy industry, there are no happy cows in industrialized agriculture today." All of the animals are treated with a great deal of cruelty. "It's mercenary," he pointed out, and "it's predatory, designed to just get as much out of each animal as you can," regardless of what their natural life cycle or habitat should be like, "or what kind of pain and suffering we cause to the animals along the way." There are no prohibitions to the kind of misery we create in bringing animals to our table as food, in part because there are no laws to protect farm animals from abuse (as there are for certain domestic animals). This divorce from ourselves is seen in our separation from nature, our ability to destroy habitats without concern, to imprison people, to abuse women and children, to torture humans and animals—all of these actions come from the same heart of darkness, from a humanity out of touch with its own holiness, its own divinity. This is a humanity dominated by the left hemisphere of the brain without the development of a naturally balanced whole-brain function. As neuroscientists posit, if each person is born with one side of the brain more dominant than the other, then it is up to each family, each educational facility, each culture, to balance the society by using an integrated whole-brain approach to learning and life, as James Olson (mentioned earlier), articulates so beautifully in his work.

In the same way that DeMeo's study of Saharasia showed the impacts of patriarchal brutality and its relationship to desertification, the abuse of so many sentient animal lives has created a similar desert in the hearts of human beings—desertification can be personal as well as geographical.

Since 2002 I have turned some of my broadcast attention to the sanctuary movement in the United States and elsewhere, where people are doing their best to provide food, shelter, and autonomy to species that have been abused by humans in the labs, on the farms, in circuses, zoos, aquatic and mammal entertainment facilities, and abusive domestic situations worldwide. Among the leaders in this field is Gay Bradshaw, Ph.D., author of *Elephants on the Edge: What Animals Teach Us about Humanity.* She is also the founder and executive director of the Kerulos Center in Jacksonville, Oregon, which is an educational nonprofit organization as well as being a small domestic and wildlife animal sanctuary. Her pioneering scientific work establishes sentient consciousness in animals that, like humans, have family, culture, and personal stories. They undergo suffering and trauma and likewise joy and pleasure. Her scientific breakthrough in transspecies psychology shows conclusively that elephants, like other sentient beings, suffer from post-traumatic stress disorder (PTSD). The ongoing slaughtering of these majestic animals for their tusks has led to a dissimilation in the herds, in their matriarchal hierarchies, in their sense of being, belonging, and education. All of this trauma and displacement is having an impact on their psychological and physical well-being.

"Traditional psychology," Bradshaw said, "has been based on a two-tiered system. You have one theory about how the human brain and mind works and another model for other animals. Transspecies psychology, which is a field I founded, really integrates data and theory from neuroscience, psychology, and mythology that speaks to the fact that we share pretty much the same things. In other words, you don't need two different ways of looking at human and animal minds. It takes the same theory, the same perspective to really understand what animals are thinking and feeling just as we do with humans."

Bradshaw continued, "We tend to forget that animal cultures like the elephants' really have a vast civilization. So to really understand the elephant [and any other species] and the elephants' lives, you have to study them in an historical way. Elephants used to create in humans a feeling of awe but today they are merely objects of the trade in ivory, poaching, habitat destruction, and culling, which are orchestrated killings, capture for zoos, and so on. What has happened is that elephant society has been broken up into small pieces. It's been dismembered, Zoh, as you put it. Therefore many of the young elephants are motherless." It's horrifying to know that eleven thousand elephants have been killed since 2004 in Gabon, Africa, by ivory poachers who hack off elephant's tusks often while they are still alive, leaving babies in traumatic terror and their victims left to die painful, brutal deaths. The business in ivory should be made illegal worldwide, as should the trade in all animal parts.

Bradshaw makes clear that as we see in human society, the loss of parenting has tremendous impact on the elephants' matriarchal system, where learning is passed on to the calves through the female elephants in every clan. "The science that we have," she said, "that talks about animals having feelings and ways of thinking like we do, and having cultures and all sorts of experiences we humans have [in community], is a huge ethical and psychological challenge to humanity. The right to do what we do to other animals, to make these assumptions that we can have a law that says we can kill wolves, have a law that says its legal to kill a bear, to make the presumption that a bear doesn't have a life of value in the way a human life has its own value, is no longer valid by science and social standards."

The science supporting the sentience of animals, Bradshaw makes clear, has been built over hundreds of years. All indigenous peoples have recognized this, as have animal rights activists and sanctuary caregivers. Ordinary people have realized this as well, if only in relation to their own dogs and cats. Even our own scientific experiments on animals have shown us of their awareness and their experience of pain and the pain of others. We also know they share with purpose and protect others. Observation of animals in their own environments proves this as well. We know animals have belonging, personality, differences in intellect, styles of play, family, food preferences, and experience the loss of their own kin and other kinds of animals with grief.

"The whole scientific point is that animals share in having feelings and emotions like we do," Bradshaw continued, "and the difference is almost like the difference in cultures between people." She shows us that the space between animals and us is a lot smaller than some people would like to believe. "Science is really calling us and saying, 'Well, if that's the case, then we need to have the same kinds of consideration that we have in respect for ourselves, for other species.'"

In fact, the experience of nonlocality of consciousness that humans experience can be seen clearly in the natural use of telepathy by elephants or by dogs, bears, birds, and between species as well.

When Lawrence Anthony, author of *The Elephant Whisperer,* died in his sleep on March 5, 2012, at his home in the Thula Thula Game reserve he co-owned in South Africa, more than twenty elephants came to pay their respects, demonstrating not only their feelings and their community rituals for a lost friend but also their telepathic capacity. They came to Anthony's home before an announcement had been made about his death. This telepathy is well known in the literature of animal communication, and as Rupert Sheldrake, Ph.D., articulated in his book *Dogs That Know When Their Owners Are Coming Home,* animals can communicate, like humans can, telepathically at a distance. I have had hundreds of such conversations with animals and do so today as part of my own volunteer service in speaking for animal beings—communications that not all humans can hear.

Whether someone's lost cat is stuck under a deck and unable to return home when called, or a deceased dog is visiting to say thank you, whether it's a bonobo matriarch telling me of the time of the land of the giants, all species can communicate with humans, other animal species, and their own kin. Animals have maintained their transspecies capacities and transdimensional awareness. It is we humans in which this capacity has been diminished.

In J. Allen Boone's (1882–1965) 1954 work *Kinship with All Life,* he and others discuss how this nonverbal communication between animals and humans has been a constant theme in popular culture throughout humanity's history. Throughout the ages, animals have been given places

Fig. 5.3. An elephant community in Africa. Image courtesy of www.sxc.hu.

of position and importance, trusted and loved as companions and guides, helpers and friends, viewed by native traditions as custodians of animal wisdom. Just as Metzner speaks of a green psychology to improve our relationship with the Earth, Bradshaw speaks of a transspecies psychology as another addition we need to properly understand. Add to that Sardello's spiritual psychology, discussed in chapter 3, and we begin to see how multidimensional human beings really are and how disconnected our civilization has become from nature, especially in the industrialized nations.

"Psychiatrists and psychologists," Bradshaw added, "are making another point: that you can't evaluate human suffering by traumatizing other species and studying them. The modern mind has created a very profound ability for disassociation," an issue Bradshaw often addresses in her work. Being able to say one thing and do another, to cause harm in another species and not feel that suffering in oneself through compassion or empathy is a statement about human beings, not animals. These are imbalances in the human being that are becoming very clear when we do an honest self-evaluation of our conduct on Earth.

"We need to be more connected with other species and ourselves, know that we are already connected," Bradshaw insisted. "This is a very profound phenomenon that really marks our culture. . . . Their suffering is no different than our own. To heal nature," she advised, "we must heal ourselves—heal that part of us that causes so much violence and harm." Whether it's rats and rabbits in labs, monkeys or mice, cows and their calves, hens and their broods, steer and their herds that are abused on their way to becoming table food commodities or food by-products, they all suffer from the appalling practices of the industrialized factory farm, which bears little resemblance to the peasant farm and its more humane practices that include natural feeding and allowing healthy play among the animals it oversees.

The pharmaceutical, biological, and other corporatized university- and government-sponsored industrial abuses of animals using systematic exploitation and pain-inducing methodologies, passed off as necessary for the advancement of science or consumption, are insidiously destructive to our own human natures. How can inflicting pain or trauma in one species produce positive outcomes either in science or life? A better question is: Why are human beings able to justify brutality as a methodology for studying behavior, mental and emotional development, medicine, robotics, genetics, food production, warfare, and so on? This comes at the expense of other sentient life-forms.

Again, the death economy on Earth today is a pervasive paradigm of destruction and avarice. It is rooted in a selfishness that is preventing the soul of humanity from blossoming on the world stage. A death economy treats all of life as a utility, having no value of its own. By contrast, a life economy honors the role all life-forms play in a balanced ecosystem. Attending to the Earth requires that we tend to her bounty and the species that coinhabit the Earth with us. The human ultimately benefits by humility and reverence, and from these attitudes one is aligned with nature and divine right order.

When we bring alchemical concepts into this equation of human activities on Earth, we become aware of the interplay of elements within us: water, fire, Earth, air, and ether. Seeing the elements as great forces that are part of us and other sentient life, we begin to appreciate that the consciousness with which we attend to the Earth, each other, and to our daily lives is the essence of the shamanic path that has been followed for millennia. In all wisdom traditions the elements have correspondences in our organ systems. In Chinese acupuncture, for instance, fire is found in the heart and small intestine, metal in the lungs and colon. Correspondences such as these exist in every culture of the world.

In Kabbalah one speaks of learning to overcome certain aspects of various emotions or actions that are partnered with certain organs: anger

THE COSMIC MAN.

Head and face - ARIES, The Ram

Arm	Neck
GEMINI	TAURUS
The Twins	The Bull
Heart	Breast
LEO	CANCER
The Lion	The Crab
Reins	Bowels
LIBRA	VIRGO
The Balance	The Virgin
Thighs	Secrets
SAGITTARIUS	SCORPIO
The Bowman	The Scorpion
Legs	Knees
AQUARIUS	CAPRICORN
The Waterman	The Goat

Feet - PISCES, The Fisher

Fig. 5.4. The cosmic man depicts how planetary influences are ascribed to the human organ systems.

arises from fire in the heart; melancholy or frivolous pleasures from the water element in our digestive system; pride arises from the Earth element in the limbs; and idle talk from the air in our lungs. Such hermetic systems of correspondence pervade all wisdom teachings. They point to the universal need and ability of the human being to discover the cosmic or divine presence in the human body, the holy soul incarnate.

Seeing ourselves and the Earth as one engages the whole mind, body, and soul in appreciating right relations and living on the Earth as lightly as possible. It is an ancient tradition that invites us of the modern era to become fully aware of our rightful inheritance as Earth healers, as Earth lovers, and to remember always that what we do to the Earth, we do to ourselves; what we do to the animal kingdom, we do to each other; what we do to the world, we also do to the cosmos.

6

KNOWING THE
DIVINE BODY AND THE
SACRED HEART

*God is our highest instinct to know ourselves; we are more
than our bodies. Though life works through our brains
and bodies, the bottom line of the story is that we are
nonlocal, we are infinite in time, we are infinite in space,
we are immortal . . . our consciousness is simply eternal.*

LARRY DOSSEY, M.D.

When humans look skyward we are essentially looking at our roots, like
an inverted tree. When we look within we are looking at divinity, as
though heaven is stretching downward with a certain balance between
levity and gravity. "As above, so below" and "as within, so without" are
well-known and vital axioms concerning the way the material and immaterial find correspondence in each other. These precepts of spiritual science express another fundamental reality: "We are spirits having a physical
experience," a favorite phrase of world-renowned scientist William Tiller
of Stanford University. Tiller is among the brave few, like his friend the

late, world-renowned creator of scientific remote viewing, Ingo Swann, who have pointed to what the future of the scientific community will entail, much of which relates to developing capacities beyond our five senses. They describe a science facilitating nonlocal, remote communication, the improved use of telepathy, healing from afar, and other latent talents that we all have.

This new science is built upon observation of the reciprocal universe, which—like our own consciousness—is multidimensional and unrestricted by time (as we currently define it). Frontier scientists are pursuing the edge between the material and immaterial worlds, where creation is both visible and invisible, present and remote. It is as though in each human a heavenly and earthly kingdom collaborate for a purpose. I suggest that the purpose is for each human to become conscious of our destiny, to realize our reasons for incarnating, and to pursue life with purposeful meaning and clarity. Incarnating helps us accept and practice our godly status as fully embodied creators. To some this would simply be called consciousness. So how is the consciousness engaged in healing?

The body is the vehicle through which we animate matter with spirit. Our very breath acts as a carrier of this energizing, physical, and ethereal formative force. Some would say that when we breathe, the Creator breathes too. When we experience love, love is experienced in God's body or in the universal sea. These are no longer metaphors, nor perhaps were they ever, but exact descriptions of real scientific processes regarding the way in which light materializes in the physical world as particle and wave, and which take form because we engage the immaterial world with our awareness, bringing *it* into manifestation.

I suspect the future of energy medicine will be based on several pillars:

1. There will be a complete acceptance that all life is part of an integral whole, differentiated yet interconnected.
2. All life is a state of frequency, both in material and immaterial realms. Learning how to manipulate these frequencies will enable healing as well as dematerialization.

3. The axiom of life on Earth is love. Love is an energy that is inclusive, nurturing, expansive, beautiful, even noble, but most of all, unifying and harmonizing. We are all capacitors for receiving and giving light. Furthermore, it seems clear that all life on Earth is regulated by this fact in some way.

If we accept the model of the human being as a spiritual vessel designed with bioenergetic capacities to utilize and reflect cosmic influences (the very thing that ultimately makes us immortal), what will happen if the vessel gets mechanized, programmed, and controlled by mathematical formula rather than love? For instance, as we move toward the use of artificial organs, especially the replacement of our hearts, will we unknowingly be stripping the human being of the opportunity to be entirely a soul-inhabited vessel? Will an artificial heart be able to reflect this cosmic oneness through it? Can love be programmed? Is love the active presence of spirit or light energy moving through the hearts and beings of everything on Earth in a harmonic way? Or is consciousness the receiver and amplifier of every emotional and intellectual impulse? Is it subject to something even subtler, to every vibration from all realms of existence?

In pointing out that we are essentially more like a river than anything else because of the 60,000 miles of veins in our bodies, author William (Marks) Waterway says we are water beings. "Blood is approximately 90 percent water. We each drink about 6,600 gallons of water in a lifetime and about five times our body weight each year. And the brain is 85 percent water." When he joined me to discuss his book *The Holy Order of Water: Healing the Earth's Waters and Ourselves,* he emphasized "that we are to learn the secrets of life from water. Water endows life. Protoplasm is mostly water and without it, there is no life. Our own blood and seawater are comparable liquids."

If water in our own bodies helps to create the right conditions for conduction of thoughts and impulses, what happens when the Earth's water body is prevented from freely flowing in and out? "When we damn up the rivers, we are cutting off the Earth body's natural energy—

a great energy. It puts pressure on the plates and it encourages separation of that which is to generate life through the ecosystems." We fail to believe that nature is holy and that we are holy as well. "The dams on the Earth," Waterway said (there are more than 75,000 dams in America alone), "as unbelievable as it seems, can be seen to have caused a change in the Earth's axis, contributing to its now-noted wobble. Recent presentations show that the moon, in fact, causes the Earth to bulge at every full moon." What came to my mind when he said this was the fact that more women give birth on full moons, just as I did, than during any other moon phase worldwide.

THE DIVINE BODY AND NATURE

As we have already seen, consciousness has many ways of expressing itself. In our bodies we have begun to understand how our minds impact matter. Ancient medical arts like acupuncture and Vedic medicine rely heavily on an observation of the natural world in the human being and the human being's place in the cosmos. Our organs have relationships to the seasons and elements; and they, in turn, have qualities that we experience as emotions. "The body has an amazing capacity to heal itself; we just have to facilitate that," says Dr. Brian Berman, medical director and founder of the complementary medicine program at the University of Maryland School of Medicine. "Whether it's acupuncture, homeopathy, or some other energy-related therapeutic, the whole system is a balance of energy. In Chinese medicine [the balance is] between the yin and the yang; the yin being more female, more receptive, and the yang being more male, more penetrating. A person is a reflection of the outer, larger world. Just as the seasons impact our health, our personhood affects the outer world. We know there is a dense physical body but we also know there is a subtler energetic body. Seeing them as integrally one is what future medicine will address, as has been done for centuries. Trying to explain it seems to be, in part, what the Western medical research component is about."

Beverly Rubik, Ph.D., founder of the Institute for Frontier Science puts it simply: "The theater of activity is a biofield. It has certain properties. It can be measured. We can see it increase and decrease and from it gauge with some degree of awareness the quality of health of the person."

As director of the Cardiovascular Institute at New York Presbyterian Hospital and author of *Healing from the Heart: A Leading Surgeon Combines Eastern and Western Traditions to Create the Medicine of the Future,* Dr. Mehmet Oz described in one of our interviews why he began using complementary medicine in his practice. "One of the most fantastic advances in science is how we can do tremendously complex operations on people who should be dead. . . . My specialty happens to be heart transplant with patients who have mechanical hearts and bypass surgeries—the big operations that patients sometimes don't survive from. As good as the science is, many times patients will undergo these operations and still not feel healed. That is very undermining to the confidence of physicians like myself. We go to medical school to learn how to do these high technique interventions. When they don't make the patient better, even though they *do* make the heart better, we need to look a little deeper. This is what inspired us to really look into other pathways of healing and to really take a holistic approach." Though Dr. Oz focuses on the heart, he teaches us lessons for our entire being by showing how fantastically sensitive and intelligent the heart really is.

If we are vessels for the Holy Spirit, or what some might term cosmic forces, then healing the body must be a holy art, not just a chemical or even just a physical process. Optimal recovery and well-being require both the patient and the healer to hold sacred thoughts in their minds. Increasingly, science is showing us how our thoughts and feelings not only impact our own well-being, but also how they affect others and even the environment around us.

Dr. Oz told me that holding a reverential attitude toward all of life has always made sense to him and that this type of approach to the process of healing is beneficial to both the patient and the doctor. "We have not yet really gathered data to try and quantify what kind of impact that has, but we know it has effect. . . . If you think about the whole process of surgery, it really is a spiritual endeavor and has many of the relics of other kinds of sacred rituals. For example, the patient is separated from their family . . . cleansed, and they lie naked, in a way alone. They are joined by a healer who is scrubbed, in other words we cleanse ourselves. During those processes there is a meditative approach, in that we start to plan and choreograph in our minds what we are going to do. Then the medical team gathers around that patient. . . . The operation itself is a dance where two experienced individuals work together without even speaking, in complete harmony, to accomplish the goal of the operation. We do this at the physical level and sometimes people forget there is a spiritual aspect to this as well. And when we begin to quantify what that is, we find that depression and pessimism are huge predictors of success. The reverence that you speak of, Zoh," he concluded, "is vital to our understanding and to the healing itself."

Many pioneering healers without the cardiovascular training of Dr. Oz have also focused their healing work on the heart, but in a less technical way. Modern electronic gem therapy is being pursued in Britain by Jon Whale who calls the region of the heart chakra "the assemblage point," describing it as a vortex that is relatively midline in the chest cavity where the energetic being is centralized.

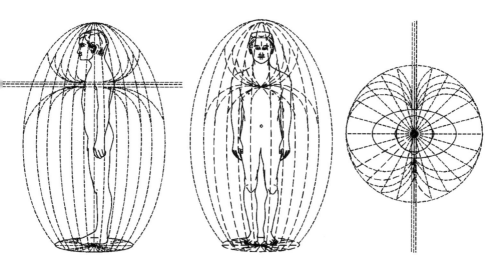

Fig. 6.1. Jon Whale's assemblage point, where the energetic being is focused and concentrated. Image courtesy of Jon Whale.

"This assemblage point determines the health of the organs, the attitude of the person, and their general way of life and experience. It can be moved out of position by trauma, accident, aggression, and can be changed through subtle manipulation." Whale attempts to transmit the energy of the gems to the skin of the patient and then to the organs themselves, saying he "treats the body like a particle and wave. It looks for frequencies that can be utilized in and around the body to set things in right wavelengths. You actually see jaundiced patients change skin color before your eyes."

The Institute of HeartMath in Boulder Creek, California, a nonprofit research/development and public education organization, specializes in creating exercises to make one's consciousness more heart centered. As Howard Martin, the executive vice president of strategic development, explained, "any person can perform these exercises and access and support the heart to become more vital, less stressed, and more able to contribute to and benefit from life." Martin also reminds us that we may not be conscious of it, but as soon as we get within a few feet of any person, our heart fields interact. So part of their Institute's goal is to further the research on the role of the heart in learning, cognitive performance, health, organizational effectiveness, and stress reduction.

So often we treat the body like a machine. Our love affair with machines and their increasing role in our lives is dangerous when we divorce ourselves from the life force that inhabits us—our soul. The Vedas call this life force *nous,* the Chinese call it *Chi,* in Judaism it's called God's spirit or *ruach,* but it is all the same force that animates each and every one of us. Dr. Oz said that almost every time a doctor operates there is the experience of moving past the world around us and entering the moment, so I asked him for a case study that illustrated this moment. He described patients whose bodies required extraordinary effort to pull them back from the brink of death.

"When you quiz them about what went on," he said, "you are reminded of how little we understand the whole process of life and death. One individual was a Vietnam War veteran who insisted that I operate on him even though *I* insisted there was nothing I could do for him. I thought he would die during surgery. The man said 'I have been through worse than what you are offering and I know I am not dying today on the table.' He convinced me. I thought he was wrong and, in fact, several times during the procedure I thought I could not save him. Each time he miraculously pulled back. The end of the story is that after thirty-six hours he awakened spontaneously when no one really expected him to. So I asked him what happened. He said, 'I saw myself under a bright white light and I was lying on my back. I felt like I was in an ether, heavy sludge, where I had to swim back and forth under the light to stay alive. I knew that if I lost sight of that light that I would be dead. I wasn't scared. I wasn't happy either, but I realized I had a role, that I had a partnership with you.' That is really the lesson," Dr. Oz emphasized. "I try to explain to the patients that this is a group experience; we are going through it together."

Pointing out that "the immunological response is deeply tied to the emotional qualities of the person's inner life," Dr. Oz related that "depressed people tend to get more infected after surgery than those who are optimistic. Cellular memory, which is a concept that memory is not just in the brain, but in every cell of the body, is true." Some recipients of transplants even experience their donor's life content as a conscious factor.

Other transplant patients are held back from full recovery by feelings of inadequacy. (I thought to myself, how interesting that so many healthy people are also held back in life by such feelings). "Many patients have a sense that when they lose their heart that they have been rejected by their heart. I have had numerous patients who, when they have had rejection episodes, complain they do not know why they are being victimized by their own heart or the new heart. They lament that they are unable to hold this precious muscle, which personifies so much of what a human being is. They speak of it in the literature continually. They feel inadequate and unworthy of maintaining a heart. So for many patients it takes not just recovering from long months or years of suffering from heart-related ailments and pain, but spiritual recovery before they obtain true health.

"When you take out the heart, the organ that has been the internal metronome since the eighth week of gestation . . . it doesn't stop beating," explained Dr. Oz. "It keeps loping away futilely, with no blood to pump, outside the person it came from. That invariably makes people quizzical. As I look at this picture, here is this organ that most humans have never seen outside of the body, pumping air instead of blood. It's like a snake that has had its head cut off, it's still moving. It clucks," he said, "desperately trying to find out what's happened. It's almost asking you a question while it's beating its last few beats. 'What's going on, what's going on?'"

Apparently, the spiritual intelligence of the heart has a life outside the brain. Continuing with his description of the actual surgical procedure, Dr. Oz explained that the heart comes out of an Igloo cooler "looking like an old piece of steak. It's gray, cadaveric, and ashen. You take this thing out and you trust that it was harvested properly. You don't know for sure. So along with the process of sewing it into the patient, there is the thought that, perhaps, it is a futile effort and the heart will never start. . . . You don't know until it is sewn in, attached, and the blood allowed to flow through it. . . . You take off the clamp that holds the gateway to the flood of blood and you watch the heart change color. . . . As you watch it reprofuse with blood and regenerate pathways in the muscle, it changes from the ashen, cadaveric color to the dark red, tick color, which is the healthy color of the heart. Then, like a fish that has recently been caught and put in a bucket of water, completely out of the blue . . . the heart will go flip flop and then it is something that's awkward. . . . You want the heart to start beating. Then a few seconds later, if you're lucky, it will generate back that same rhythm that it left its donor with. Flip flop, flip flop and you know you are done."

What an amazing story to hear! "You watch life be rekindled," he continued. "It's a tremendous feeling. It sends goose bumps up the spine every time you see it and then this tremendous warmth rushes up to your head. Everyone in the room senses that. There is very little said during that period of time when you take the clamp off and allow the blood to return."

I commented that as a heart surgeon, he was the connector between two lives, the lives of the donor and recipient, and that to my mind this was very much like being a high priest. But I wondered if the recipient felt different with the new heart. Dr. Oz responded by pointing out that the heart is central to so much. "The heart can be light, heavy, hopeful, big, brave, open, cold, crooked, straight, tainted, pure, mighty, or meek. People have all kinds of words to express various qualities of the heart. Bleeding hearts, in my case, and there are also broken hearts." So when one's heart fails and one receives someone else's heart instead, or an artificial heart, "if your heart has left you, you should feel abandoned and you should feel comfortable addressing that, in fact you should want others to help you address that.

"For the heart transplant patient who feels a real separation between their spirit and their body," Dr. Oz continued, "the first thing we have to acknowledge is that these are real feelings that are justified and that there is nothing to be ashamed of. . . . Once a patient can get past the feeling of abandonment by their heart, then the issue of regeneration or rebirth is possible. That's really what the transplant ritual is about."

I was particularly interested in transplant patients who have received the new plastic or artificial hearts that have no pumping action, no pulsing rhythm to the blood. From my own experience in healing through hands and prayer, it is clear to me that we are all made of the same universal materials. We breathe in time and space together. My body and your bodies are all interconnected. Just as our soul comes from the same great creator stream, our bodies, too, come from the same pool of atoms that will take shape, have purpose, and then recirculate back into energy to return and be reused again in reshaping matter. How, I queried, would a person without a heartbeat be different from the rest of us who are literally, physiologically entrained to one another by having one?

Dr. Oz believes the challenge is greater for the patient who receives the mechanical heart because "they always know they don't have their heart in there. For one thing, the mechanical heart makes noise and has a pounding to it or a whir to it that is very different from your own active heart. . . . In fact, the newest generation pumps don't generate any pulse. They are continuous flow pumps, like jet engines. You can't measure a blood pressure because you need a pulse to do that. So these patients are walking around without the usual kinds of ups and downs that most human beings experience." Not to mention that most human heartbeats are entrained to the Schumann resonance, the vibration of the Earth at approximately 7.6 hertz frequency; that in itself must make for a greatly different type of inner life experience.

Dr. Oz wonders whether the pulseless heart "changes your appreciation for things like music, smell, and love? What role does pulse play? Now we have a human population that can help us answer these questions. We can compare the experiences of those with a normal human heart with those who live, but have no pulse. . . . We have gotten really good at taking care of the biology of human illness. We've gotten pretty good at engineering devices that can replace human organs. We know the man and we know the machine, but we don't know that man and machine interface."

ARTIFICIAL ORGANS, ARTIFICIAL INTELLIGENCE

With all the leaders in the fields of artificial intelligence and artificial replacement of body parts I've interviewed, including inventors, robotic designers, software creators, and surgeons, the future is commonly described as a post-human era. While enthusiastic to support and increase longevity, I wonder what will become of our souls in an era when mankind will be partially replaced or augmented by machines. What will a civilization be like when humans are outfitted with neural implants with bioports for downloading or uploading information, all of which are being designed today? Medicine has been pushed into mechanics, and at the same time there has been a concerted effort to invest healing with love. It is as though two worlds, the ancient and frontier, are on parallel paths that are converging inside of our bodies.

First we applied our machinery to the land and now we are applying it to our bodies. This concerns me to think that it took less than a hundred years to denude the soil of her bounty. How many decades of robotics, bionics, and cloning will it take to find that we have denuded the divine body, thereby creating something akin to a human, but perhaps not a natural human? Indeed, the future is now and the divine body is being used as a testing ground for new inventions. There are even nanorobots so small that they can be put into a person's bloodstream and programmed to help the body overcome a disability or disease. I know I am not alone in my concern that this stretching for immortality via mechanical means might cause us to overlook our authentic natures.

As I listened to Dr. Oz that day, I was struck by the way in which our entire world seems to have forgotten its heart. We have become so caught up in the mechanistic accomplishments in the world that we have forgotten the pulse, the current of life behind the pulse, and the current of deity behind the current of life. The heart, no doubt, holds the keys to much of the divine body's purpose, capacities, and needs. Just as biodynamic farmer Allan Balliett describes walking the fields to get a sense of the plants, so too do the best health care providers walk the patient's "field"—his body, emotions, mind, and spirit—which provides insight into the patient's attitude. A healer allows their hands, eyes, heart, mind, and soul to show them what part of the person may need support, seeking to balance the life force evenly between all organ systems. "In the case of heart patients," Dr. Oz concluded, "each of them has the potential to become heroes like we read about in mythology. They are tested in ways most humans do not have the ability to be tested in."

DEEPAK CHOPRA ON THE DIVINE BODIES

During the decade of 1992–2002, I held an ongoing dialogue with Dr. Deepak Chopra, a Vedic medical practitioner and world-renowned educator. Speaking on radio with me from the Chopra Center for Wellbeing in Carlsbad, California, which he founded, Chopra wanted to make something clear. "The physical body is a microcosm of the universal body. Each of us has a personal body, but we also have a universal body. The personal body comes and goes; the universal body is always there. When we look at the environment we see it as part of our extended body. We are part of the ecosystem; we are part of the web of life." Chopra has a way of igniting images in the mind as he speaks. "The trees are our lungs. The earth is our physical body. The waters, the rivers, are our circulation and the air is our breath."

Chopra speaks with such a reverence for the environment that he says, "it is not called the environment, it is called the universal body. Both the personal body and the universal body are made up of the same stuff, the same material: space, air, fire, water, and Earth. Your metabolic fire and the fire of the sun are the same thing. The air that you breathe and the atmosphere are the same thing. So the five elements go to create the physical body, but behind that there is a subtle operation at work. Both the universal body and personal body have a subtle body and that subtle body is what we today would call the body of information and energy." Chopra's way of seamlessly integrating ancient and modern sciences and arts shows there is no differentiation between ancient worldviews and modern expressions of them in science. "In our personal body it is reflected as our mind, our intellect, and as our emotions. And then beyond the subtle body is the causal body, which is the soul and spirit. This is the domain of nonlocality. This is where we are, in fact, beyond space and time."

What he is describing are classic ageless wisdom teachings from the East and the West. In this case the Vedic scriptures from his native India "say that the subtle body and the causal body are actually in the realm that is not apparent to us. Fire cannot burn and weapons cannot shatter the causal body; it is without beginning and without end. Water cannot wet it and wind cannot make it dry. It is eternal. It is immortal. Today, scientists would call that nonlocal domain. You can have disparate subatomic particles in different locations of space-time communicate with each other without the exchange of energy or information. This is a very counterintuitive idea. Nothing moves faster than the speed of light, yet according to nonlocality it can happen simultaneously." We had moved from the realm of the natural elements to our natural invisibility and fundamental connectivity. As Chopra made it easy to understand, this is part of the physical body's anatomy as well.

"Now when we look at our physical body," he began, "it is an expression of nonlocality. It is a projection of your soul. In our physical body there are a hundred trillion cells and each has to know what the other cells are doing, otherwise your body would fall apart. Your body can have thoughts, kill germs, and play the piano at the same time. And while it's doing that, it tracks the movement of stars. The intelligence that orchestrates all that is the intelligence of the nonlocal part of yourself. In the Vedic tradition it is atmic, or soul, which is one with Brahman."

How important is *intention* to the unfolding of our humanity, or even in the healing of a person? With his deep understanding of the natural dynamics in our bodies and how they reflect the natural laws of the planet, Chopra clarified that "both attention and intention are triggers for transformation. Consciousness works through both attention and intention. In the eight limbs of yoga these qualities of attention and absorption lead into unity consciousness where the observer and the observed are one, the physical body is the object of our observation, a process of observation. In reality, they are the same field of consciousness, which is beginning to observe itself. In reality, there is no separation."

"The body is a field of molecules and the mind is a field of ideas; one is experienced objectively, the other is experienced subjectively, but they are essentially the same. Physicists might say this is a tangled hierarchy. The consciousness and the observation of consciousness simultaneously co-create each other. The principle is: Before you can view a subatomic particle, it is a virtual particle. You, the observer, are essential to its manifestation, that is, to making visible the actual particle from the virtual body. Similarly, before you have a thought, it's there, it exists as a virtual thought; or before you manifest a memory, it's there. Where do these virtual memories . . . and desires reside? They reside in our soul. Where are the laws of thermodynamics or Einstein's relativity written? These which are so essential to the workings of the universe," Chopra said, "these are the thoughts of God."

We both agreed that humans are awakening to our purpose of serving the divine order or being in harmony. Chopra went on to point out the qualities you see in those who have accepted their role as co-creator:

"Once you get in touch with that part of yourself that is inseparable from everyone else, it has to be experiential, not intellectual. Once it is experiential, there are certain symptoms such as spontaneous joy and the ability to share it with others, the progressive expansion of happiness, the ability to love and have compassion, and a sense of connection to the creator of all the universe. There is a sense that one's life has meaning and purpose that ultimately overcomes the fear of death, the fear of the mortality of the physical body. . . . These are progressive stages of awakening that happen spontaneously once you get in touch with that part of yourself that is immortal."

We tend to think of karma, the law of cause and effect, as very linear. However, according to Chopra, "It's an approximation of a phenomenon that is immensely complex because every action is the result of the entire universe. The fact that we are talking on the phone is a conspiracy of the entire universe. Every space-time event orchestrates the activity of the whole universe, and not in a minimum manner. Since we are part of the universe—and a complex part of the package— when we change, the whole changes. So, the best way to change the world is to change ourselves. When the electron vibrates, the universe shakes. So yes, every act of ours has good and bad [effects], and that's a judgment anyway. But every act has an effect on the entire universe. Every time we act from selflessness it comes from a more expanded level of pure awareness. We are not acting from our skin-encapsulated ego. The more it comes from the nonpersonal domain, the more impact it will have on the universal domain. In the tradition of karma yoga, or in a person who has an internal dialogue, everything they do, every thought, every breath, and every movement is a divine moment of the eternal, being established in light before action. Thus one experiences spontaneous right action. It removes the anxiety of the action, for you are not doing it personally and it creates the law of least effort. You accomplish a lot more by doing less: again, acting from a universal domain of awareness."

Many of us believe the body can be a vehicle to an expanded awareness and thus to improving the world. Used wisely, pleasures that are life enhancing and use energy consciously can also be spiritually enabling. No matter what training one turns to, these energies are always described in natural terms—of fire and water, positive and negative, male and female, in and out. It is as tidal as the ocean and as delicate as the snow melting when it is touched by the warm sunlit Earth.

A discussion of the human body inevitably returns to discussion of the elements, as Chopra and others point out. He is certainly one of our best spokespersons today to describe the domain of the divine human body. Love is not just a sentiment, nor is it just an emotion. "Love is the ultimate truth, the heart of creation," he says, "and the truth at the heart of creation is unity consciousness. We are the same divine spirit in different sizes. As you peel away the layers of the souls, you ultimately have the creation of knowing that there is no such thing as a person. There is only the universe manifesting in all these portions. It is the same being. And when we have that experience, then we cannot help but be in love. And love becomes our essence . . . which permeates the atmosphere and creates peace, harmony, and laughter. It becomes an experience of belongingness."

In the modern era, when exploring the multidimensional qualities of healing, we find that love has played an enormous role (as already examined in terms of agriculture and divination). Love comports with it an essential truth about the divine human, the divine body, and the divine Earth. They are all expressions of love. Love is a natural trait of the right hemisphere of our brains, while fear originates in the left hemisphere of the brain. Together, working in harmony, they enable us to protect what is holy. In the Judaic tradition it is said that the Divine Creator withdrew himself in order to create life out of nothing and did so out of his great love for the created—so that the many could all become godlike and express oneness. Each one of us, as divine sparks of the Godhead, expresses the potential divinity in our own incarnations, or at least we have the opportunity to become conscious of this aspect of our lives and to make the awareness an expansive influence in our own communities.

LARRY DOSSEY'S RESEARCH
YIELDS THIS TRUTH:
WE ARE IMMORTAL BEINGS

Another of America's true pioneers in integrative medicine is Larry Dossey, M.D., who has also joined me frequently on the radio for more than two decades. As the modern laboratory begins to express the tenets of the ageless wisdom teachings (that we are immortal souls in potentially immortal bodies), Dossey is able to assert "that mind affects matter. Thought begets energy, begets matter." Dossey and Chopra are among many who are suggesting that the body has its own type of cellular memory beyond the brain. Every cell carries water and thus within it a signature of an emotion, an experience, a thought, or a stimulus that could have originated from the self or another. "Our bodies are not machines," says Dossey. "They are special vehicles of consciousness that enable us to experience the physical plane." The reality is, and lab experience is now able to show us, "that we are infinite beings in finite bodies. We are infinite mind, always a part of the universal mind."

While Chopra's ayurvedic tradition sees the realm of nature within our bodies, Dossey has made a special study of the power of loving prayer in healing, just as the Spindrift Institute, mentioned earlier in chapter 3, has done. The success of these orientations makes it readily apparent that we are, like it or not, creating the world every single moment. As we build or deconstruct events by the power of free will, orientation, and our thoughtful intent, we are utilizing the invisible life energy or Chi that circulates in the body and that has a correspondence to nature. That we are carbon-based water beings makes us part of the natural world and its elements. From acupuncture and homeopathy to herbal therapeutics, the practitioners of complementary medicine have been applying ancient understandings for decades. Finding correspondences within the body's organ systems to the harmony and changes of the seasons makes it possible for human beings to reach greater inner potential and generate more refined and integral outer acts. These holistic modalities have been the foundation of my own health care since

1972. Their positive impact in overcoming the ill effects of Crohn's disease, which I was diagnosed with in 1970, was the reason for my founding the Ruscombe Mansion Community Health Center in Baltimore, Maryland, in 1985.

In terms of human health and human evolution, some suggest we are moving into a period of post-humanism, when man and machine will become more and more intertwined as biotic creations. Ray Kurzweil, a leading inventor of our times and principal creator of the first CCD flatbed scanner, sees this development of the human machine as inevitable to humanity's evolution. I'm not sure how inevitable it is, but I am certain of one thing and that is if we don't come to these technologies with spiritual and ethical precepts, we may fail to safeguard ourselves as divine spiritual beings. We could risk further diminishment of spiritual aptitudes if we don't constantly double check our technological advances with the right questions. Terry Ross, dowser extraordinaire, always said one should ask: "Should I, could I, may I?" rather than simply asserting, "I can."

During the first twenty years of Dossey's internal medicine practice in Dallas, he began to focus on mind/body healing and took an interest in spirituality. "About ten [now twenty] years ago there was a profusion of studies looking at prayer, distant healing, spirituality, and the health care outcome. It is a matter of good science and I feel like I have been tugged along by the data and by the evidence that these things really do matter." Prior to discovering biofeedback and other options, Dossey suffered from such severe migraine headaches accompanied by blindness that he actually tried to drop out of medical school. As I have always said, if you want to make a believer of someone, let them experience it for themselves. "I stumbled onto biofeedback," continued Dossey, "which most of your listeners know is a way of changing your body by changing your thoughts. This was career saving for me. It really explained the powers of consciousness. That opened me up to the fact that we can use our own minds to affect our own bodies. From there it was not a huge step to ask: If we can use our minds to affect our own bodies, can we use our minds to affect other people's bodies? I discovered that this was indeed the case, as shown in the studies on distant intercessory prayer."

Dossey believes that these breakthroughs will lead to a whole new era in medicine. "A way of helping make sense of different therapies that crop up across history," he explained, "is to start back in the middle of the 1800s, which I call *era one*. We had scientific medicine as we see it today with mechanical procedures such as drugs and surgical procedures. One hundred years later, about the 1950s, mind/body medicine began to crop up, which I call *era two*. People were looking at the effect of hypnosis, meditation, visualization, and so on. Now we have entered *era three*, where we look not at the ability of our minds to change our own body, but to affect . . . other bodies from a distance, which we see from the many studies on distant healing and prayer does work."

We can't understand health and healing unless we make a place for consciousness. "We've given consciousness away in the past century," Dossey continued. "We not only said that it didn't matter, we said that it didn't exist. I think this will go down historically as one of the strangest periods in human thought where we have absolutely disowned the most essential part of what human beings sense themselves to be. . . . We all, in our innermost hearts, believe that consciousness really does matter. The situation we are in now in medical science is that science is coming up to where we've been, in terms of intuition, for an awfully long time. We have to make a place for consciousness. We can't be true to our own deepest intuition and wisdom if we don't. What is so exciting now is that science is affirming that consciousness is fundamental. It can do things in the world and it can certainly get involved in healing and recovery from illness."

In 1986 Dr. Randolph C. Byrd, a cardioligst in San Francisco at the time he conducted his now famous study on *intercessory prayer* (IC) showed a correlation between prayer and effectiveness in healing. Dossey explained that Byrd's study, the largest ever conducted on IC, examined 393 patients experiencing heart attacks or severe chest pain who were admitted to San Francisco General's Coronary Care Unit. "One of the reasons I adore these randomized and double-blind studies on prayer," Dossey explained, "is because they speak the language of science. . . . Byrd then farmed out half these names to prayer groups around the country.

He simply asked that they pray for these hospitalized heart patients in the way that they thought they should. As a double-blind study, no one knew who was receiving the prayer and who wasn't. There were fewer deaths in the prayed-for group. They had lower incidence of the need for CPR and being hooked up to a mechanical ventilator. They needed fewer potent medications. It looked like a great leap forward."

And yet it will take a great deal more to sway many Western scientists. "After looking at the distant mental influence studies," Dossey said one doctor told him, "this is the sort of thing I wouldn't believe even if it were true." The politics, belief systems, and economics of science too often take precedence over the data. Sir Winston Churchill (1874–1965), prime minister of the United Kingdom, put it this way: "Once in a while you will stumble upon the truth but most of us manage to pick ourselves up and hurry along as though nothing happened."

Dossey continued our discussion on IC by explaining, "The highest profile study to be published in the *American Journal of Cardiology,* the most influential cardiology magazine in the world, is a study at Duke Medical Center. Again, it is heart patients who need an angioplasty or coronary catheterization, who may or may not be prayed for. Prayer groups from around the world are being used from as far away as Nepal and Tibet. Patients who are prayed for have 50–100 percent fewer side effects from these invasive cardiac procedures when compared to people who are just treated conventionally. . . . So here you have, in the language of science, a randomized, double-blind, perspective-controlled study. It is going to be increasingly difficult for skeptics and cynics to say they need more evidence."

Dossey is credited with coining the term *nonlocal mind* in 1989. He said, "I created the term to be able to capture what it is when we talk about remote manifestations of consciousness." The word *telesomatic,* Dossey pointed out, "comes from a Greek word meaning 'the distant body.' These are very, very common experiences where one person is empathetic, emotionally close, and involved with a distant person so what they are feeling, even though they are far away . . . is related to that distant person or distant event. Usually, these telesomatic events occur in times of crisis and danger. In one case, Dr. Ian Stevenson (1918–2007), former chairman of the Department of Psychiatry at the University of Virginia School of Medicine, writes about a woman who felt that her sister had been hit in the chest. At that moment her sister had a fatal auto accident and her chest was crushed by the steering wheel. This demonstrates that human consciousness acts as though [and we sometimes behave as though] we had a single body shared among us all."

The fascinating thing is the shared contexts in which these experiences occur. "These phenomena happen between family members, lovers, friends, associates who like each other, siblings, and particularly identical twins." As a twin himself, Dossey admits he's had a natural interest in these sorts of things all of his life.

I asked Dr. Dossey to take a moment to examine what happens when people ignore their senses, hunches, or intuitions about something dire. "There is a great survey about children who died of SIDS," he stated, talking about the tragic sudden infant death syndrome that kills babies in their cribs. "The Southwest SIDS Center in Lake Jackson, Texas, interviewed parents whose babies had actually died of SIDS and asked them if they had ever had a hunch or intuition that their baby was headed for trouble. Twenty-one percent said, 'Yes, we knew it was coming, and it was so real to us that we put the concern forward to our pediatrician.' So the researchers looked into whether this was just a normal fear that 21 percent of average parents have. They pooled a population that had not lost children to SIDS and only 2 percent reported having any such fears. . . . What is so important here is that when the parents in the 21 percent bracket took their concerns to their pediatricians, saying they know something bad is coming and to take precautions, in every instance, without exception, the doctor responded by developing a condescending attitude or actual outrage. They said things like, 'How dare you tell me how to practice pediatrics on the basis of a hunch?' Had some of those doctors had a worldview that could embrace this type of knowing [that the mind is nonlocal and can function outside of space and time], some of those babies would probably still be alive."

Dossey is pointing us to the future in medicine. "There's no question in my mind that this acceptance of nonlocality is the most important fundamental change we can have in our current civilization. It will impact everything." Dossey believes making the shift will be difficult for current health care providers and he explained how he had brought it into his own healing practice. "This is what I said to myself. I have this data. If I don't use what it is saying, this puts me in a very difficult moral and ethical bind. How can you deny your patients a therapy that evidence shows is very helpful and may be life saving? It really turned my whole practice upside down. It got so I thought I could not deny my patients prayer.

"So I began my day earlier. I would go and have my own prayer ritual and pray for all the people I would see in rounds and at my office. I don't think you can do this without it affecting you at profoundly deep levels. . . . If nonlocal mind cannot be confined to the present moment, we never lose touch with each other when our bodies die. We are immortal, eternal. If we could really appreciate this, it would help us take death a lot more lightly. We would not see it as the annihilation of who we are, but simply a transition. Something that's immortal doesn't die. This is the most majestic implication of this research. Death is a transition. The most essential part of who we are couldn't die even if we tried to. This, to me, is the greatest contribution of this material to human welfare."

THE TRANSCENDENCE THEORY OF
JOSEPH CHILTON PEARCE

Over the decades Joseph Chilton Pearce has joined me to talk about his amazing books *Crack in the Cosmic Egg: Challenging Constructs of Mind and Reality* and, more recently, *The Biology of Transcendence: A Blueprint of the Human Spirit* and *Spiritual Initiation and the Breakthrough of Consciousness* in which he makes perfectly clear, as he said in one interview, that "intelligence is based in consciousness." It's the compassionate mind, an innate process that's a function of the brain and heart, he explained, that links us all to each other and the world and this is why imaginative play in children is fundamental to their healthy development as loving people. Through imaginative play they learn to master their environment, strengthening both sides of the brain's capacities such as intuition (right hemispheric) and deductive logic (left hemispheric). Like other guests of mine, he asks with an obvious concern whether or not machines, computers, and the new social media are weakening rather than strengthening an individual's ability to interact with others in a more meaningful way.

In the same way that Thomas Moore showed how our films are not stories but artifacts of story, might the social media that deliver messages instantaneously worldwide be something that looks like a shared relationship, but instead is information that lacks the presence of soul? Children today grow up with computers from infancy—I recall the day I watched a young boy about the age of ten who was riding his bike in a neighborhood I was driving through. He was paying most of his attention to his phone, busy texting someone on the other end of the data stream as he pedaled. This boy had no ability at that time to see the sun as it illuminated the tree he rode under, nor did he likely see the two dogs playing on the opposite side of the street. He was absorbed by what seems to be a lesser form of communion with life.

As Pearce pointed out, "some sort of spiritual discipline is necessary to allow growth to take place" in terms of consciousness and greater awareness. The imagination needs to be nurtured for creativity to blossom. Being in a transition age from the industrial to the information age, he creates a beautiful characterization of the future when he says that "even our biology is designed for transcendence and that while some aptitudes may be diminishing, others are rising—we have children who can see the dead or predict things," but we also have an inordinate illiteracy rate.

Pearce reminded me of Frank Tipler, Ph.D., a mathematical physicist and cosmologist who wrote *The Physics of Immortality: Modern Cosmology, God, and the Resurrection of the Dead*. After his own inquiry as an atheist into the nature of life and death, he discovered that we are in fact designed for transcendence, immortality, and even bodily resurrection. He shared all of this one day in a wonderful interview I hosted. What he had to say really resonated with me because I had come to the same conclusion from my decades of studying the Kabbalah, long an oral tradition, on the hidden mystery teachings of Judaism.

What each of these creative thinkers describes is a process of spiritual and physical transformation, one where spirit and matter and science and spiritual traditions intertwine to make us who we are: immortal light beings. Everything that exists or has existed or will exist is present now in some manner and we are each receivers and amplifiers of these influences—be they cosmic or personal.

7

EXAMINING SCIENCE
AND TECHNOLOGY

BRAVE NEW TOOLS

Once a person can accept that all is one and one is all, that they and the tree, the star, and the atom are varying states of frequency, then we can see that the powers utilized in creation are always available to us. The question is: What will we do with them as we learn about them? As we humans begin to dissect DNA and delve into the study of the elements that contribute to the various traits and qualities in a species, we are learning how to insert our will into their design and our imagination into their expression.

Does that not mean we are expressing a great power of creation? Are we always practicing wisdom in the utilization of these natural secrets? Are our deeds full of compassion for all life-forms? Do our technological acts reflect a spiritual reverence for all life, not as a utility for our use but as a natural expression of the created world? Many scientists worry that humankind's quest to dominate and manipulate nature as a commodity will lead to unimaginable difficulties for the planet and all that reside on it, as we are now beginning to see with GMOs (as discussed in chapters 3 and 5), with the impacts of global warming (and cooling) and sea level changes.

Some of the greatest scientists in human history like John Dee (1527–1608), Johannes Kepler (1571–1630), Sir Francis Bacon (1561–1626), and Albert Einstein (1879–1955) have realized the importance of love to unlocking the secrets of nature. Peter Pesic, Ph.D., author of *Labyrinth: A Search for the Hidden Meaning of Science,* wonders, "When did we start thinking about nature as having secrets? . . . The leading thinkers [mentioned in his book] all realized there were secrets beneath the surface. The language of love wove itself in and out of early scientific writing. It certainly finds its expression in Greek and Roman discussions." Exploring the science of magnetism, the physician William Gilbert (1544–1603) "wasn't just going to observe magnets. He was going to try to enter into the inner life of them to understand the heart and soul of the magnet. Francis Bacon used the tale of Prometheus, the Greek and Roman God of forethought who stole fire from the Gods, as a metaphor for the danger scientists had to face in order to secret out the powers of nature." Pesic was reminding us that there is inherent danger in finding the deeper secrets of nature.

"This had a lot to do with the moral agonies of what they were doing, a kind of price for the power they are offered," Pesic continued. "Sir Francis Bacon understood that previously held beliefs might turn out to be false. . . . The danger to the scientist erupts when these new ways upset the comfort zones of the status quo." As the sixteenth century's greatest genius, mathematician, astrologer, alchemist, navigator, and hermetic philosopher, John Dee found this out. Even though he was under the protection of Queen Elizabeth herself, his laboratory was ransacked by an angry mob.

The search for the hidden meaning of nature is a human activity, as Dee and others throughout history have made certain, and is accomplished best by a basic reverence for nature as something to be honored, loved, and even seduced, as Pesic writes. All the seekers in this chapter would probably agree with this, although their approaches to that same truth are significantly different.

Ray Kurzweil, a futurist, scientist, inventor, and champion of accelerating intelligence by our interface with machines, would have us believe that we'll all be better off as semibionic hybrids, an integrated "machine-human." Hans Moravec, another futurist and adjunct professor at the Robotics Institute of Carnegie Mellon University and creator of mobile robots since 1963, told us of his conviction that we will engineer ourselves out of our bodily existence. According to him, we just won't need them anymore. On one level he is right, as our consciousness doesn't need a body to exist, but we do need them in order to inhabit the physical plane. Nick Begich, Ph.D., is working on educating the public about the health and environmental dangers of some of the new technological advances, while the late Eugene Mallove, Ph.D., (1947–2004) pursued cold fusion and other energy options as answers to our energy needs. Looking at what each has to say about the frontier edge of science, we see a pattern that begs the question: What are we trying to accomplish and in so doing what are our obligations?

RAY KURZWEIL ON MACHINERY'S IMPACT ON CIVILIZATION

Inventor Ray Kurzweil, Ph.D., believes in the predestination of technology in humanity's development as a species. Kurzweil is a well-known inventor and advocate of artificial intelligence. He was the principal developer of the first omnifont optical character recognition (OCR), the first print-to-speech reading machine for the blind, the first CCD flatbed scanner, and the first text-to-speech synthesizer, among many other inventions.

Author of several books, he joined me several times on my broadcasts to discuss *The Age of Spiritual Machines: When Computers Exceed Human Intelligence*. Addressing the evolutionary course of machinery's impact on civilization, Kurzweil told us, "If you compare human life today to two hundred years ago, our life span is more than doubled. Most humans lived labor-intensive, precarious, disaster-prone lives subject to many diseases. Very few people had jobs that gave them any fulfillment. So, we have liberated ourselves from many of these things. . . . As we move forward we'll have technology that may heal or may be harnessed for destructive purposes. Technology will continue to be a double-edged sword . . . [while] accelerating and doubling every ten years."

Kurzweil suggests that by 2020 numerous implants will be inside a new bionic human. "This process doesn't just happen overnight, it happens through thousands of little steps. . . . There is tremendous economic imperative to keep technology going. No one can stop technological development. I do think, though, that we need to devote specific resources against the possible misuse of these new technologies that are developing. The Internet is an example of a relatively stable system, because it is decentralized; when a portion is taken down, the whole is not brought down. Technology like this is a very intelligent way to build systems."

Speaking about how we can augment biological intelligence with machine intelligence, Kurzweil continued, "In about thirty [now twenty] years we will be able to send microscopic robots—nanobots—into our brains and communicate with our neurons. We could have billions of these in our brains, communicating with each other, communicating with our biological neurons. We could be online and augment real intelligence with artificial intelligence, and go into virtual reality . . . integrating all of the senses."

Kurzweil's conviction of the future of humanity's interaction with technology reminded me of another guest's apologia or endorsement of the modern process of genetic engineering. This was Gregory Stock, Ph.D., a pioneer in the entire field of human genome engineering and human enhancement. He suggested to me off air that genetic engineering is as much a gift to our future as clean air is for our lungs. According to Stock, we have to venture into genetic engineering as a way to preserve our species. He maintains that "without this capacity, we may not survive." His 2002 book *Redesigning Humans: Our Inevitable Genetic Future* further develops this worldview.

Not everyone is as enthusiastically optimistic about technological advances as Kurzweil, that's for sure. And when he predicts a technological facilitation of abilities that are already available to many shamans who utilize their astral and causal bodies to connect to other planes of reality in a nonlocal way, I am struck by the effort of humanity to manifest in the material realm what can already be accessed in the immaterial realms through techniques of applied consciousness. As an example, cell phones express the basic reality of our interconnectedness etherically, given our ability to call each other's cells and share information.

Kurzweil's vision shows a time when we will pick virtual sexual partners and have virtual relations. He suggests that people talking on the telephone are presently experiencing virtual reality, using the auditory sense. We already value the ability to communicate with people at a distance, and Kurzweil makes an educated guess that in a few short years we will have full immersion virtual reality. The electronics will be in our eyeglasses and our clothing, meaning that we can be online all the time. I for one am not convinced that this will enhance our lives, but rather distract people from a deeper and more meaningful communion with life. For certain it will change the way that we interact with each other and the world.

By 2030 we will be able to replace, he says, the body's and brain's signals with these virtual images, incorporating all of the senses. While I can share in this interest, I can't help but be deeply concerned that the technocratic materialism being described ignores the spiritual capacities that human beings already have. As demonstrated in the labs of Tiller and others, these exceptional abilities inherent in all of us are part of our nature, they just remain undeveloped in most of us.

But Kurzweil insists that we aren't going to stop the integration of technology inside the human body. In fact, he suggests that our bodies might change in a revolutionary way as a result of human neurology and computer technology becoming integrated. It seems that "big science" may be turning its attention now to dominating the human body, after testing its prowess on dominating the environment with both positive and terribly destructive outcomes.

So what does all of this mean to our souls? "This is all part of technological evolution," Kurzweil says. "Evolution, even though it involves creation and destruction of what we perceive as good and evil, is spiritual progress. Evolution creates more and more intelligent and more and more beautiful entities. It moves us closer to the ideas that we associate with the spiritual life and God, what we call infinite intelligence and . . . beauty. So in the future that I see, we become more intelligent, more beautiful, and more creative as we go through the evolutionary process. Evolution is moving in a spiritual direction which is why I see [the evolution of] robotic and artificial intelligence as a spiritual process."

THE FUTURISTIC VISION OF HANS MORAVEC

Hans Moravec, Ph.D., former director of the Carnegie Institute Robotics Lab and author of *Robot: Mere Machine to Transcendent Mind,* has the same sincere attitude about the ultimate importance of robotic and artificial intelligence. He states, "robots will outthink us and outperform us in the future. We are already creating robots that can improve themselves. . . . It's not that we will become slaves to machines, but that machines will replace much of what we think of as human activities. They will eventually be viewed as children of our minds and by 2040 they will reason even better than humans do."

Moravec began childhood with the belief that robots were our future. "My father was a robotic engineer, so from a very early age I was building things. Some of the things we were building were very much like animals, though built with inanimate parts. So the idea that we could build animate-looking things out of inanimate parts really intrigued me from a very young age. The rapidity of change today affects our planet in numerous ways. The development in machinery can be put on a scale similar to vertebrate and invertebrate intelligence."

Like many great revolutionary ideas, the pioneers in robotics modeled their inventions on what they observed in nature. "In 1950," Moravec said, giving us a short time line of robotic evolution, "the first light-sensitive robotics were based on the complexity of bacterial behavior. In 1960, a machine at Johns Hopkins University, called the Beast, could work its way down the hallways using sonar and was able to plug itself into a wall socket. It had more sophisticated sequences of directive behavior, like recharging itself when it needed to. In 1970, two large mobile robots were built and were controlled by computers built by Grey Walter [1910–1977]. These robots could, albeit crudely, interpret images. In 1980, we had robots that could run obstacle courses, making millions of decisions a second. By 1990 we were building systems of two-dimensional mappings that enabled robots to run around all day: not quite practical, though there are still many running in research situations. Now we are designing three-dimensional, statistical mappings which look almost like virtual reality."

Moravec believes this will give the machines enough understanding so that they will be able to move to places for months at a time on their own. He even described a car that drove itself 98 percent of the time from Washington, D.C., to San Francisco, California. "It was really good at staying in a line, which was almost its sole skill, and that was enough for its success."

"At the moment," Moravec continued, "robot intelligence is still very insectlike, which means they can't really be used in most places. We are just at the threshold, now, of having machines that can freely navigate so that they can begin to transport things from place to place just about anywhere." I wanted to know what the first broad scale application of robotics in the consumer market would be and Moravec promptly said, "Robotic vacuum cleaners—something quite small. Within ten years we will have machines that we can carry into our house, turn it on and it will explore the house, build a comprehensive map of it, and find its docking station where it can recharge and regulate its dust load. It will know where things are and what surfaces to avoid. It will work when you aren't at home and we will trust it to run for months without attendance." The road signs that show these times are coming are "basic economics. When it's cheaper to use a robot versus a human, we will see robots taking away human jobs."

Indeed, Moravec was right when we spoke a decade ago: Minirobotic vacuum cleaners are on the market today. One manufacturer alone plans to bring one million robots into their electronics assembly line in the next three years, saving untold amounts of money in labor costs. Analysts add that there will be no international cries of inhumane factory conditions.

Already the United States, Japan, and South Korea use robotics in the manufacturing of automobiles. Indeed, the factory worker may be phased out over time.

"When the field of artificial intelligence got started in the 1950s, it was natural to look at what human beings do and to put at the top of the lists those things that not very many people do very well that involved really deep, hard thinking—like proving mathematical theorems or like Deep Blue playing excellent chess." But as the field developed, it turned out that the activities that most humans do with ease, like picking something up and putting it away, were not so simple for a robot to do. "Our ancestors evolved and the most important thing was that they could find their food, avoid predators, and raise a family and so on and all of that involved perception and the ability to move well. Evolution has been making that better and better with more and more active neural tissue. Much of this is done by the human retina, which is worth a billion calculations a second."

Over the next two decades Moravec predicts a rapid expansion in the industrial utilization of robotics. "The computational speed in programming is accelerating so quickly," he explained, "doubling about every twelve months, that we can now program for a billion calculations per second in a desktop computer. . . . In a few decades we will have machines that will be able to do computations that humans, currently, do most efficiently."

A first generation robot, Moravec explained, like a robot vacuum cleaner, is a slave to its program. It moves around and picks things up. It's programmed to do lots of useful tasks. A second generation robot can, if something goes wrong, learn from that and adapt to the new situation. By 2030 we will have the third generation robot, which represents an evolutionary path for robots ten million times faster than our first robots. By the third generation, robots will model and rehearse applications before doing them. They will be able to watch an action externally, build a model of it, and use that model to simulate its own behavior.

This will be followed by a fourth generation robot, which will add a reasoning layer, so that by 2040 the robots will be most humanlike. "By 2050," Moravec suggests, "robot brains, based on computers, will be able to execute a hundred trillion instructions per second and will start to rival human intelligence." Applications such as off-planet colonization will be dependent on such robotic helpers to prepare places for humans to inhabit and do tasks humans are incapable of doing without great risk to their lives.

Moravec and Kurzweil and other robotic enthusiasts share a passionate conviction that this is simply a natural evolutionary aspect of humanity. We don't have to worry about robots taking over the world. Rather, we can change the world and our tasks in it by using robots, which will free us up for other kinds of activities and occupations. By the year 3000, they say, the boundaries between what is human and what is machine may not be so clear. We will be supported by a machine economy. "The robotic evolution will end capitalism," said Moravec. "Economic competitiveness will continue, but corporations will be more and more fully automated to not involve human beings. Human beings will be squeezed out of the rat race. The machine's goals, desires, likes, and dislikes are programmed in. . . . They are built to do the job they are supposed to do." Moravec suggests that unlike humans who have an individuated free will, robots will have a limited range of free will because they can only desire what they are programmed to desire. The exception will be a type of future robot Moravec predicts as the *wild ones,* or those that will evolve past their original programming. Just like we've seen in countless science fiction films, that could indeed be an issue and a future wild card.

HUMANS STILL SUPERIOR TO MACHINES

James Martin, Ph.D., is a former rocket scientist, internationally recognized computer scientist often referred to as the "father of CASE" (Computer-Aided Systems Engineering), futurist, and the author of over 105 textbooks. In his book *After the Internet: Alien Intelligence,* he eloquently focuses on the many-faceted problems artificial intelligence will require us to address. "It's pretty important to say that, while computers are going to be a million times faster, humans are superior in many ways because we have the ability to associate together an enormous diversity of different knowledge; whereas computers can do relatively simple things but at incredibly high speed. And so with computers you're going to have the capability for machines that can learn automatically and they'll learn millions of times faster than we do and they'll be able to recognize patterns. And they can recognize patterns that humans can't possibly recognize."

It is for this reason Martin refers to computer and artificial intelligence as *alien intelligence*. It does not function as human intelligence does. As an example Martin explained the work of "legendary commodity trader Monroe Trout in Bermuda who has an amazingly good track record in trading commodities. It doesn't matter whether the market's bad or the market's good he seems to get about the same high return on investment every year. And he's got a computer that is watching all of the trading patterns and analyzing them in a very sophisticated way indeed. And amazingly, although he sits in Bermuda, he's got a link to the States so if the computer detects a very sharp downtrend he can be out of the market in seconds. And there was one interesting day when his position dropped 4 percent, about $9.5 million dollars, and all of that loss occurred in nine seconds. The reason for it was that the U.S. secretary of state started a press announcement with the word *regrettably*. As soon as he said it everybody pressed the panic button. So what he's done is to program his computers so that when that happens, they can sell faster than anybody else. They're going to be out in two seconds."

This example highlights one of the reasons many futurists express concern about the division between technologically wealthy nations and the lesser developed ones. Martin called it a planetary correctness model, in which ethics are the defining source by which creative impulses are checked. "It's a complex term because it involves many things," he explained. "It obviously involves ecological correctness but it also concerns what do we do about the rich getting outrageously rich and the poor getting poorer? What do we do about the destitute nations in Africa? We can't go on like this. What do we do about the fact that we've got enough nuclear warheads to cause nuclear winter and they're in a sense, completely out of control of ordinary human beings? We have got command and control systems that are very dangerous indeed. Now there are many other issues like that, some of which are more subtle, and adding all these together there's the term planetary correctness."

Martin acknowledged the impact of [His Holiness the fourteenth] Dalai Lama [Tenzin Gyatso] to the discussion of ethics in future speculation. "He's got a sort of different description of ethics which seems . . . to apply very effectively to the super high tech with ultraintelligent computers that we're going to have in the future. And basically he's saying that if you behave ethically you're trying to make everybody else improve their happiness or quality of life and you've got to avoid doing things which damage the happiness or quality of life of other people. And that translates into a whole elaborate pattern of behavior. Now if that is the pattern of behavior that we're talking about, we could train and program ultrapowerful computers to behave in an ethical fashion."

NICK BEGICH'S TAKE ON HAARP

Though not everyone is enthusiastic about the amazing advances in technology, most would agree that ethics should be a foundational part of the discussion. Coming from both a political and scientific background, Nick Begich, Ph.D., author of *Earth Rising: The Revolution; Toward a Thousand Years of Peace,* has dedicated himself to educating the layperson about the applications of technology to world affairs. In recent years he's focused especially on the HAARP (High Frequency Active Auroral Research Program) in Alaska, one of many current trends he warns is suggesting a different kind of future.

"The HAARP is [mainly] a large radio frequency transmitter," said Begich on one of our many interviews, "or field of transmitters that when fired in a certain way and in a certain sequence can get a focusing effect similar to the light coming off a flashlight that spreads out very rapidly. [This is] opposed to a laser, which focuses on a relatively small area. . . . Radio frequency energy dissipates very rapidly as it spreads out. But if that energy is focused, it triggers events in the ionosphere, the layer [of our atmosphere] that begins about 30 miles above the Earth's surface. This can create a number of effects, such as communication enhancement, missile interference (like ICBM), missile defense applications in surveillance and offensive utilization.

"The other issue, and an important one, is that any change in one part of the natural system will affect all parts. Heating of the ionosphere causes the ionosphere to lift. You can push it out from its lower elevation, about 30 miles up, to about 230 miles up. When you push it up, the lower atmosphere rises to fill the void. Now when it fills that void, supposedly it changes the relative pressure systems of the weather systems below. Or it can be used to divert jet streams, having a profound effect downline on weather fronts." Begich made clear that the HAARP was just one example of a growing effort to utilize the natural energies of the planet for greater and greater control, with potentially harmful outcomes.

"There are arrays in Canada, Europe, and here in Alaska. [The HAARP] appears to be [a part of] an integrated system for missile defense. Alaska is where they are preparing the base for interceptors. . . . By manipulating the ionosphere you can change its character so it acts as a broadcasting center. It can send energy back to the Earth in the form of ELF, extremely low frequencies, so it can be used for communication with submarines and for Earth-penetrating tomography . . . like x-raying the Earth several miles deep underground." These ELF signals also have grave impacts on the human physiology. "It can interfere with brain function and research shows that external oscillations in the ELF range can have profound effects on human emotions and human behavior."

Our government is not the only one exploring frequency for crowd control and mind control. We should all be seriously concerned about further developments that manipulate subtler and subtler energy states because they have a corresponding effect on living systems.

HAARP was a starting point for Begich; from there he began to look at the use of energy as a weapon. What is referred to as the revolution in military affairs, or the RMA, is a change in technology that is so dramatic that it will alter the way in which wars are fought in the future. Begich provided several examples of the use of frequency in modern warfare. "In the Gulf War we used a signal embedded on the radio broadcast, so that when people tuned in all day long to prayers and music [they also subliminally heard] a signal that created fear and panic. We saw that when the fourth largest army in the world surrendered en masse. Compare that to the bombings in WWII [where] we didn't see that kind of reaction. Surrender on this level was inordinate."

These so-called nonlethal weapons are a high priority in the United States, causing grave concern for Begich and other activists. He described technologies being deployed or about to be deployed that render entire groups of people incapable of motion. These crowd-control weapons prevent one from being able to move one's limbs. Certainly, the public has seen the impact of an energy weapon called a Taser used by law enforcement, which is said to have caused over five hundred recorded deaths in the United States in the last decade. Though it's called a nonlethal weapon, it obviously can kill. During the spring uprising of 2011 all along the Mediterranean rim, I had the feeling that that some kind of an "excitory" wave (one that overstimulates the nervous system) had been deployed. People took to the streets en masse to overthrow oppressive regimes one nation after another as though under the influence of a domino effect: first Tunisia, then Egypt, Yemen, and Syria. These uprisings continue to this day.

While I have made no effort to prove that such a device was deployed, or a signal beamed into these areas from a remote location, it is now within technological capability to do so, as well as to superheat the skin of enemies with a simple portable device that will cause them to quickly surrender or retreat. The Long Range Acoustic Device (LRAD) currently deployed in various settings can create permanent auditory damage, as well as headaches, in those subjected to its signal. Reportedly used in several crowd-control situations in the United States, such as the G-20 Summit in Pittsburgh in 2009, it has been sold to China and deployed in Canada, Brazil, Honduras, and elsewhere.

Some other technologies utilize currents of energy that create something akin to an electric shock severe enough to momentarily disable someone, and supposedly without long-term impact. But when you remember that all life is vibration, anything that changes one state of energy to another is going to have a long-term impact; though we may not yet know how to measure it or even recognize what we are observing in people or nature.

"Using these types of technologies domestically can go both ways, I mean for things like riot control or crowd agitation," Begich said. The intention to develop some of these new weapons reminds me of the tales of Atlantis and its death rays, matrix blankets, and mind-manipulation tones. In 2012 the Laboratory of Applied Optics of ENSTA Paris Tech found that lasers can direct lightning; this is just one example of the growing interest and application of weather engineering through technology.

A growing awareness of how all life energies work will hopefully also lead to the development of positive technologies such as healing with sound or the ability to heal illness by adjusting the body's vibration. The choice is ours whether to use the abilities we have, and those we are developing, for harmonizing and sustaining life or for harming or taking life. Still somewhere between science fiction and science fact, the ability to manipulate energy is, in my opinion, at the heart of our twenty-first-century future.

COLD FUSION IS HOT NOW!

No discussion of science and technology would be complete without an examination of our energy consumption. Obviously our planet needs to shift to a sustainable energy plan with renewable resources, but as Alden Meyer of the Union of Concerned Scientists explained, "it takes sixty years for one fuel-based economy to transition into another." Germany is one of the few western nations that has consciously and deliberately begun this transition with the implementation of a thirty-year plan.

For many of us, nonpolluting energy ideas have been a passion for the past forty years. Together we have promoted wind, hydrothermal, solar, hydrogen, and other natural, renewable energy options. Today it is even considered good business to preserve the planet and many more scientists have come to the task with great interest. Despite the economics of research and development that remain in the hands of the status quo whose vested interests retard the speed at which progress and collaboration can be made, smaller laboratories and individuals toil on—sometimes in obscurity and sometimes in the limelight of opposition.

The perseverance of those involved in cold fusion is one such example. Regardless of intensively ridiculing media coverage that dismissed it as a fluke in 1989, hundreds of small labs and curious scientists have pursued the experiments with astonishing results. One of the best known cold fusion supporters was science writer Sir Arthur C. Clarke (1917–2008), who said in a 1998 *Science Magazine* article titled "Presidents, Experts, and Asteroids," "My guess is that large-scale industrial application will begin around the turn of the century, at which point one can imagine the end of the fossil-fuel-nuclear age, making concerns about global warming irrelevant, as oil-and-coal-burning systems are phased out . . ."

Clarke is not alone in criticizing the world media and the scientific community for the blinders and personal prejudices based on vested interests that keep them from seeing cold fusion as a scientific reality. The late Eugene Mallove, Ph.D., (1947–2004) faced the battle to redeem cold fusion head-on to bring this vital advance to the marketplace. For his effort he was murdered in 2004. Mallove was editor in chief of a remarkable scientific magazine called *Infinite Energy* and in 2000 was selected to brief President Clinton's staff on the subject of cold fusion.

On one of Mallove's many visits to the Hieronimus & Co. radio programs (*The Zoh Show, Future Talk,* and *21stCentury Radio*), he discussed one of his incisive editorials entitled "Science, Scientism, and Meaning." As Mallove noted, a vital commentary to the question of cold fusion includes questioning what is real science, what is political science, and what is junk science. "Well, certainly on the matter of cold fusion, I agree with Arthur C. Clarke entirely," he said. "There has been a virtual blackout in most general media circles regarding the ongoing cold fusion research and development.

"The term cold fusion, by the way, needs to be clarified a little bit. This began at the amazing news conference at the University of Utah, March 23, 1989, ironically only about twelve hours before the *Exxon*

Valdez ran aground off the coast of Alaska. There we had world-class chemists Drs. Martin Fleischmann and Stanley Pons stating that in a small glass of ethyl with heavy water (which is in all water) they passed the current in a so-called electrical chemical reaction. They said that in that particular kind of cell that they created with heavy hydrogen and palladium as one of the electrodes, that they were able to get more heat out of it than electricity going into the cell—so much heat that, when you added it up over time, it turned out that they could find no other explanation other than a nuclear reaction of some kind." He continued to explain that although they didn't have the definitive reaction then, and there are still questions about exactly what or how many different reactions are occurring, there is no question about the phenomenon of the excess heat. "The energy generation in these types of cells, and others that followed, there is absolutely no doubt about it at this point. It is 100 percent certain, and I agree with Clarke that it is a disgrace that world media outlets are ignoring it and, in fact, ridiculing it in many cases as a nonissue."

Since the average citizen does not have personal knowledge about how fusion works—either hot or cold—I asked Mallove to explain the difference. "Today, we have power plants that generate electricity using nuclear power. This power is so-called fission nuclear power. It came out in the late 1930s and early '40s and is the same type of nuclear reaction, in a controlled fashion, as were the bombs dropped on Hiroshima and Nagasaki that ended World War II. This is the splitting of heavy uranium atoms. Uranium is much heavier than hydrogen. Now in the case of cold fusion, we believe that what is going on is the joining together of hydrogen—a particular kind of hydrogen, in water, called heavy hydrogen. It's very abundant. This creates a new element called helium, which is absolutely nontoxic. You find it in children's party balloons."

If helium is the only by-product from this electrochemical reaction, then this was, in fact, a revolution in energy. You would think the scientific community would get excited, or at least view it as a starting point!

With our planet comprised primarily of water that is constantly being replenished, it is the obvious choice as a source of fuel. "Here is the bottom line on the total story," continued Mallove. "If cold fusion is real, which it is, and when it is commercialized what will happen is this: the amount of heavy water in just one cubic kilometer of ocean, a small portion of the Earth's oceans, a tiny insignificant fraction, just one cubic kilometer of ocean, has enough heavy hydrogen in it, such that when the cold fusion creates that helium for nontoxic energy it is equal to all the energy of all the known oil reserves on Earth. It is a water-fueled age that is about to happen once this technology is made reliable, repeatable, and scalable, which hasn't occurred yet."

The history of cold fusion is one of the most blatant examples of how scientific progress is so often obstructed and how society suffers as a result. Mallove explains how it happened in this case. "The first shock troops against cold fusion were the people in the vested interest program called hot fusion. They get hundreds of millions of dollars a year [from the Federal Government], even to this day. They say their large machines are destined to possibly give us football field–size power plants in the year 2050. That is no joke. That's what they say. They could possibly give us such a plant if the spending could be increased more. For these people, when they first heard that there was a possibility of a new phenomenon that they had overlooked, that it would be easier to generate electricity without deadly radiation (which their reactions still would produce even if successful), they were the ones who didn't believe it, denied it, conducted experiments such as those done at MIT, my alma mater, in which data was manipulated, not because they believed it, but because they saw a result that was positive and they had killed cold fusion off to the press anyway, and why bring out any embarrassing positive results six months after the cold fusion announcement in March of 1989? So, basically, those were the shock troops against it. The Department of Energy convened a kangaroo court of scientists who signed off, within months, just months, on a difficult scientific issue, dismissed the whole thing and got rid of it. At least they thought they had gotten rid of it. The good scientists, those who continued investigating and sharpening up the investigation of this miraculous energy from water, they persevered and today there are thousands of papers written on the subject. Many of them are in peer review journals, and there can be no doubt about this at all. There has been virtual blackout in most general media circles regarding the ongoing cold fusion research and development."

Since 1989 my husband and I have tried to do what the rest of the media refused to do and have reported on the many advances in this field. Hundreds of labs around the world have modified and improved on the original Pons and Fleischmann experiments. "The contrast between cold fusion and current forms of nuclear power is like night and day," continued Mallove. "One is large, major installations producing radioactive waste. The other offers the promise of small compact units that will go in your home, your car, your plane, your boat, whatever. Virtually zero cost as far as the fuel cost. There may be replacement parts, but the actual fuel, which is nothing but water, very tiny fractions of water at that, the heavy hydrogen costs for example, this is the only requirement. So therefore, it is in effect free, safe, clean energy that no one has to fight wars over because it is not localized in one spot like oil. No one has to worry about explosions of nuclear power plants or disbursement of radioactive waste, burying radioactive waste. It is like night and day. As far as the infamous hot fusion, which Uncle Sam continues to drop hundreds of billions of dollars per year into, that's also like night and day. Hot fusion has never achieved more energy out than in. When Pons and Fleischmann made their announcement, they already had a positive ratio."

As Mallove lamented, the ideal of the scientific community and the reality of the scientific community are two entirely different matters. "Ideally, scientists are completely open-minded, they are objective and they will explore any idea, but in reality that is not the way it works. The vested interests that [prevent that] would include not only vested financial interests, and hot fusion and high energy physics, but it would also include what I would call vested intellectual interests. That leads to a complete myopia, a blacklisting of creative work on the frontiers—and this is more, by the way, than just in cold fusion. It is in other areas of science, frontier science, too. But in an area as important as energy and abundant energy, clean energy, you know, this has reached almost the level of a crime. Almost the level of a crime against humanity where a real discovery has been made and the established interests in hot fusion, the American Physical Society, academicians of all kinds, and the journalists that go along with them, they virtually participated in this crime against humanity, because at the very least human beings need hope. And this is a hope." And I added, "and a vital solution."

Although more research grants would help grow this new science beyond the beginning phase, thanks to Mallove and hundreds like him who have refused to give up on this hope, cold fusion remains a viable source of energy for our future. Inventors like Randell Mills, Ph.D., of BlackLight Power are working on similar free-energy devices and many of them routinely experience patent rights interference or collegiate sabotage. These men and women continue to safeguard our future by dedicating their lives, talents, and resources, regardless of the opposition.

"Cold fusion is kind of like the transistor in its infancy," said Mallove. "Of course, transistors have revolutionized the world, but when they were first introduced, around 1947, it was a very finicky device. It didn't merit much space in the newspaper. Tube radios were not being threatened at the time, but the solid state materials had to be high purity and so forth and this caused many problems back then. There was a huge amount of money put in it by Bell Labs and others, and that's why we got the successful transistor. The same thing is occurring with cold fusion. Difficult material problems, difficult circumstances controlling the very subtle things that are going on—what we call catalytic action leading to nuclear reactions in the cold, which should never occur. The whole mystery of cold fusion is that there should never, ever be, by normal understanding of physics, nuclear reactions occurring anywhere near room temperature. You should require millions of degrees. It does occur; there are difficulties and that is holding it back. The problem is it has not been taken seriously, as Clarke so clearly states. There are blackouts. *Nature Magazine* and *Science Magazine* only accept technical articles on this subject. This is like going back to the Inquisition when certain things were literally on the index of the church. That is precisely what we are talking about."

A science devoted to the assertion that all life is sacred, not just our own, but the Earth itself, would eagerly explore what Pons and

Fleischmann gifted to the world in 1989. Once again in the science industry of energy we are dominated by the death economy, which exploits the world for oil and contaminates water, air, and land sources and which continues to promote nuclear plants whose waste obliterates life and remains radioactive for thousands of years. But the story of cold fusion as an example of scientific subterfuge shows that our challenges are not just ones of insight, but also must be met and fought on the political, institutional, and corporate playing fields of America.

As we approach the time when artificial intelligence collaborates with human intelligence to accomplish great advances—like space voyages once thought possible only in science fiction—some scientists are asking the deeper questions. They are looking for a deep technology, one that will exhibit respect for nature as a prerequisite for problem solving and technical enhancement. I personally believe that for our further positive evolution, we must become more engaged as partners and helpful participants than dominators or exploiters of natural resources and phenomena. In the race to the future, we must not forget to pause and reflect on what exactly science is, and we should constantly reassess—if one could dare to name it—what divine science *should* be.

8

BEING CONSCIOUSNESS

THE LINK BETWEEN
EVERYTHING

If archetypes come from our past origins, as some postulate, prototypes may come from our ability to envision a future. Being knowable, but as yet unmanifest, a prototype will be broad enough to facilitate a maximum potential: that potential being those things that might come into form if there is the environment of awareness to hold them. If there is a conditioning for their manifestation, they will manifest. We are divine beings with godly powers that are ours to develop; this determines what *does* come into being.

Many guests on *The Zoh Show* (1992–2002*), Future Talk* (2000–2008), and *21stCentury Radio* (1988–present) have shared their research into deciphering our divine potential, and this chapter looks at the work of Terry Ross, William Tiller, and Ingo Swann as three such pioneers in their fields. These three and many others have developed methods where one can learn to take part in shaping the world and the universe by conscious acts of cocreation. As we will learn, the conditioning of the environment is the result of paying attention. By paying attention, miracles can and do occur.

Technology is both material and immaterial. In addition to the systems we can and will design in the future that will enable us to do remarkable things—such as exploring places as diverse as Mars, underground habitats, or the cells of our own bodies—we have always had an innate capability of doing this work from a subtler or immaterial realm. Ingo Swann calls these operating potentials *biomind superpowers* and they include the ability to see at a distance, hear and see into other dimensions, and heal at a distance. It seems this nonlocal mind and our internal management of the biosystems are related, with consciousness in the driver's seat. This century will probably be characterized by the science of soul, as a spiritualizing of the sciences will be gained through an appreciation of the role played by consciousness, via intention and attention, in the creation of the manifest world.

Just as we began with ancient software, let us look at our own ancient hardware—our own biomind superpowers. Professor William Tiller joyfully declares, "We are spiritual beings having a physical experience." What is it about human beings that is godlike? What human attributes give evidence of the great creative force and the laws that seem to guide it?

Cosmic awareness is a big topic in my broadcast work and the majority if not all of the people presented in this book advocate that being in the moment is in fact being in eternity. We are light beings whose material existence is still the outcome of spiritual influences on physical matter. We represent and function within a biology of transcendence, as Joseph Chilton Pearce maintains. Candace Pert says, "we human beings are wired for bliss." Or as my friend the late Jeane Dixon (1904–1997), a world famous astrologer and visionary, confidante of presidents, the pope, and thousands of readers, put it, "it's all in the stars within us." It was Jeane who told me one day, when Bob and I were visiting her in Washington, D.C., "Never discount what you see with your mind's eye. Don't let anyone tell you that what you see about the future is wrong. Trust your divine talents." I met Jeane when I was in my late twenties and she was very supportive of me and my work. Given her support, I knew I was on the right path, which confirmed what my husband had always believed and told me, even when I doubted myself.

The consensus seems to be that we are entering the age of harmony. I am, as I like to say, a "cheerleader for paradise." In the paradise that I see, nonphysical and physical humans, nature and nature spirits, wildlife and animal spirits, plant life and plant spirits, and mineral life and mineral spirits coexist in total harmony.

The science of the spirit invigorating this harmonic life stream is being deciphered and codified through research into dowsing, remote viewing, instructing machines at a distance with our minds, and more.

THE MAGICAL ART OF DOWSING

World-renowned dowser and my old friend and teacher, the late T. Edward Ross (1921–2000) used to say that it is our ability to see "everywhere and everywhen" that makes it possible for us to do and see things that are hundreds or thousands of miles away.

He once did something so profound that it changed my worldview, even though I already had a pretty vast alternative compendium of unusual phenomena that I had experienced and believed in: I watched him move a water vein on our land. He accomplished this by asking permission of the water first and then, through a mutually responsive consciousness, collaborated with the water to cause it to move location. I am not the only person in the world who found in him the meaning of the word *magi*. Ross, or Terry as all his friends and students called him, began dowsing at the age of eleven and continued perfecting the art right up to his death, a total of sixty-eight years of practice.

In 1958 he took part in founding the American Society of Dowsers. In 1990 Inner Traditions published his book *The Divining Mind: A Guide to Dowsing and Self-Awareness*, written in collaboration with Richard Wright. (The history of dowsing has also been written about beautifully by my husband's and my cherished and beloved friend, the late Christopher Bird, whose work in soil and plants has been mentioned on a number of occasions throughout this book. Published in 1979, Bird's masterpiece on dowsing, *The Divining Hand: The 500-Year-Old Mystery of Dowsing* remains the most comprehensive book on the topic to this day.)

EPREUVE par la BAGUETTE.

Fig. 8.1. A dowser as depicted in an eighteenth-century French book about superstitions.

The publication of Ross's book gave me the opportunity to have him as a radio guest. He joined me on the air in February of 1991, one of the few times he shared with a radio audience his deep, personal love of dowsing. Ross guided the audience through the stages of the dowsing art, beginning with an effort to bring us up to date on dowsing. "The comic strip figure with a forked stick has given way to a normally active person just using their mind. Dowsing is a matter of consciousness rather than mechanics. It is being used on every continent to locate and to quantify all sorts of targets, both tangible and intangible. Dowsing is a function of the human biosystem. . . . It is as old as man. . . . The ancient Chinese were familiar with it. A dowser marched with the Roman legions. It fell into disuse during the start of the Industrial Revolution, but in Russia, for instance, they use dowsers in an interdepartmental way all across the land. They do a lot of natural resource dowsing, archaeological dowsing, and, as we say, water dowsing, too."

There are three basic devices that are commonly used today for dowsing. Ross explained, "If a dowser is still on a mechanical kick, a Y rod could be gotten from a tree or a plastic rod could be used. [The dowser holds the rod] with palms up and when he gets to a target that he has in mind the rod will snap down. The utility companies across the county still use bent pieces of steel or copper 18 inches long. They hold 6 inches of the rods pointed forward. When the operator walks across the target, holding it in his mind as precisely as he can, these two L rods, as they are called, will swing apart. The third device used for dowsing is nothing more than a weight suspended on string or small chain: a pendulum."

Ross then described the steps a dowser would take in looking for, for instance, the best place to dig a new well. Beginning with holding a pendulum in hand, "you use a map or a sketch of the site where you want to find water and mark it with your location. Then proceed to the site and confirm that X on the ground [by using a pendulum and walking over the spot.] Stake it for the driller and note the depth, the flow (flow per minute), and the quality. Ask the driller to plunge his bit so that he will pierce the narrow stream you are dowsing so you are dowsing from flowing water, not stagnate water, and make sure the driller stays in touch with you as he proceeds. This is really the natural sequence of events."

I asked Ross to explain the importance of requesting permission to do dowsing work before one begins. "I think that you are using higher levels of consciousness just to clear any obstacles or road blocks that might be in your own subconscious, as well as in those you are trying to help. It's just as well to ask for permission, not only from the people involved, but also from your concept of the higher source."

Always adamant about the simple fact that *the question contains the answer*, he and other world-renowned dowsers instruct their students in the art of question asking. "It is really quite simple," expounded Ross. "If you ask a general question you will get a general answer. As an example, if you say: 'I want a supply of water for this factory here,' that provides you with a different answer than [if you say] 'I want a supply of water exceeding five hundred gallons a minute that is perennial and is of such and such a quality.' That's the difference between asking in a general way and in a particular way. It is most important to ask precisely for what you seek. . . . The more precise the question, the closer you get to the precise answer. The question is a shadow of the answer and the answer is a shadow of the question. If you a get a close approximation in your question to the target, your device will respond because it is in sync, or in harmony. It is in resonance with the target."

It is not the instrument that is important, but the intention and the consciousness of the operator. We have the ability to do these things because of the nonlocal mind, or that part of consciousness that reads within and without simultaneously. The pendulum or the rods act as conduits through which the practitioner's consciousness is conducted and seen.

In fact, people can even dowse with what Ross called their "bobbed suit," meaning nothing but their own bodies. As he made so clear to thousands of students worldwide—the mind is a divining instrument itself. The mind can come into harmony with anything it reflects its focus on. What we attend to, we impact. What we intend is what gets communicated. Consciousness has effect because it focuses its attention. It is the attention itself that brings the observer into rapport with what is being observed. This is the realm of future sciences like dowsing, remote viewing, and other forms of communication, all of which operate outside of time and space. "The desire to serve selflessly is fundamental to a skilled dowser," repeated Ross time and again. "I think this opens up the pathways where the very subtle farseeing and far doing are functioning. I think it's very important that there be an element of altruism in this kind of art."

During our February 3, 1991, interview, Ross reported for the first time on a study that he was participating in that demonstrated how no tools beyond the focused mind are needed for this work. "We took a container of water and focused an electric eye on the meniscus [the curve of water that rises above the surface tension and makes an ellipse in the water, with the sides higher than the center]. It would act as a lens if the electric eye was focused on it. If we could change the hydrogen bond, the surface tension would be changed—the meniscus would be changed and flop down and the electric eye would lose its focus. The electric eye was hooked up to the circuitry in millivolts. After 10 seconds [of focusing my mind on the water] we had a significant change in the focus of the electric eye. This, to the scientists, was a very efficient effect achieved by mind operating at distance."

THE EXPLICATE ORDER

Quantum physicist David Bohm, Ph.D. (1917–1992), who explored theoretical physics, neuropsychology, and the philosophy of the mind was deemed a communist Jew by the FBI and in 1942 was refused clearance to work with Robert Oppenheimer on the Manhattan Project in Los Alamos. (I consider this to be a blessing in disguise for the life economy.) He did, however, contribute information on the collision of neutrons and deuterons, which later became classified information that was used by the Manhattan Project. In effect, Bohm was denied access to his own findings; however, other groundbreaking work that he shared publicly almost forty years later in the 1980s truly changed the world in a positive way. He was able to explain the operation of the nonlocal mind.

"Bohm reported that the life force comes out of an innate, unmanifest state," said Ross, "emerging from an enfolded state to an explicate or unfolded state; materiality, in short. . . . We can describe the process; we can describe the steps that the force takes on its pathway from the enfolded state to materiality. We see, for what it's worth, a four-step process in this unfolding. We see these steps and they are interrelated and they interpenetrate each other. It is my view that the dowser is able to journey into these realms of being, this chain of creative power, and pass into a state of timelessness and spacelessness and see the essence of his target there."

I asked him to explain the evidence revealing that a practitioner has definitive changes in brain wave activity when moving into these unmanifest realms. He began by identifying dowsing with a development of consciousness. "I agree with you, Zoh, there is a very good analogy in the electroencephalogram. Brain waves are measured in several categories: the beta condition, which is about 30 hertz; the alpha at 13 hertz; theta around 7 hertz; and the delta around 4 hertz, maybe a little slower. The ordinary consciousness, like the one we are in when we are talking back and forth, is the beta. Falling asleep is the alpha. The dream state is the theta and deep sleep is the delta. When you hook up a dowser to a machine that can measure these things, you can see it on a monitor screen. The dowser functions in beta, alpha, theta, and delta in equal amounts, which says to me that they are working with all of their potential in perfect balance."

What does dowsing reveal about human potential and our biominds? "I see everything in terms of that creative chain of being," he explained. "From the innate there were four different realms, all hitched together, but also interpenetrating. [These terms] we might loosely designate as spiritual, intellectual, emotional, and material (or physical). We find that this chain of being can be described as a double helix. There is a spin to it. There is a rate of spin. There's color and sound, but of course you can't hear the sound or see the color. Everything that is, from the smallest little part of a tree, is composed of and surrounded by an essence: Shakespeare's mortal coil. When you are seeking a target by a very precise question, you set up a double helix right in the midpart of your third eye and that, when you begin to scan, actually hones in and becomes one with the actual target.

"When you get near it and if you are using a device, it will go down. If you are not using a device, it will become very clear that, yes, this is the target. I think it's just a question of agreement between waveforms. [In advanced physics] people are working on the superstring theory. It approximates the double helix that we draw. This explanation of form has worked for me for years and years, not only in the 'quadrapart double helix,' which is a successful model or point of reference in the dowsing fraternity, but it has also been observed as the delivery system in nature and inherent in all things." Advanced dowsers are able to use it to co-create with nature, according to Ross. He explained that a beginning dowser would walk over the land to perform on-site dowsing to find a well, but that with some experience, a dowser can stand at the edge of the horizon and scan it for water flows. With a little more experience you can see beyond the horizon and then later even reach intangible and abstract targets. "When the onstage dowser addresses the rod and asks if this water will last season after season, that dowser is asking something intangible. He is going into the future," said Ross. "People get to the point that they can ask intangible and abstract things and be accurate about it. The first step is cooperation with nature. Now, we're getting into pretty rarefied things, but this does happen. You can take the chromosomal structure and rearrange it. Nature will co-create with you. The final stage of dowsing is the *reflexive state of dowsing*. I call it that because of Arthur Young's [(1905–1995) developer at Bell Helicopter] work in his book *The Reflexive Universe*." We met Arthur and shared lunch with him and Chris Bird. Terry continued, "It's reflexive when you are doing everything intuitively with nature, as she would have you do. Now, not many of us can do it for long, but some of us can do it for a moment or two."

Ross presented a concise worldview regarding the art of dowsing and using those aspects of our biosystems and immortal selves that work in an integrative way for specific purposes. "Dowsing," he continued, "is farseeing and far doing through the use of full consciousness, being a conduit for everywhere and everywhen. Prophetic power knows no time or space

Fig. 8.2. DNA double helix

limits. I think this way you can even read the future intent of the universe." We can read the spiritual realms as an imprinting of matter, both as an energetic form before it manifests into dense material atoms and as energetic qualities in the immaterial realm. What is it, then, that facilitates that ability to interface with all life? Certainly, this is a capacity of the divine human.

DELTRONS, EMOTIONS, AND THE DIVINE MIND

There are very few scientists in the world qualified to do what William A. Tiller, Ph.D., is doing. After nearly thirty years at the Department of Materials Science at Stanford University, and as its former department chair, he is devoting his time to the development of reliable instrumentation for the detection and study of subtle energy fields in nature.

Fellow of the American Association for the Advancement of Science, Tiller is an expert on the structure of matter and has been consultant to government and industry in the fields of metallurgy and solid state physics. His fields of specialization are crystal growth, surfaces and interfaces, physical metallurgy, semiconductor processing, thin film formation, and computer simulation. He has published more than 250 scientific papers, three technical books, and has had five patents issued to his credit.

More inspiring to me, however, is the fact that Professor Tiller has a long-term interest in anomalous and exceptional energies, psychotronics, Kirlian effects, healing, modes of consciousness, and psychoenergetics. He has developed theoretical modeling to understand these manifestations of subtle energy within a conceptual framework that incorporates the whole of conventional science.

In his book *Conscious Acts of Creation: The Emergence of a New Physics,* coauthored with Walter Dibble and Michael Kohane, they chart what can best be called the science of consciousness. As Tiller explained during one of our several interviews, they show us how subtle energies, a term he claims to have coined several decades ago (and which has always been a part of esoteric literature), are sustaining and animating life and predicating physical existence. Far from being simply things that communicate ideas and feelings, our thoughts are energy units, expressed in waves and particles—and as such they touch all life, even the immaterial domains of the universe. It is said all becomes one, yet is still differentiated. Being able to control one's mind and emotions is the goal of spiritual practices worldwide, the effect of which some call cosmic consciousness.

This type of bio-self-management leads to Ingo Swann's biomind superpowers, or what is shown in classical wisdom teachings and oral traditions to be the key to a type of teleportation or even time travel, bilocation, healing, and more. Traditions show us that having total control over the faculties of mind and feeling gives one the ability to consciously be in many realms at once. This may even explain accounts of multidimensional beings who seem to pass in and out of our physical dimension. Witnesses around the world have spoken of these beings, which may even include the creature known as Big Foot.

"The conventional paradigm says there is no place where any human quality of intention or consciousness can enter physics," said Tiller, explaining the problem of objectivity in science. Science is currently dominated by the belief that it is "not possible for humans to meaningfully interact with and change any aspect of physical reality, in particular, target experiments. My intuition said that was wrong, big-time . . . and my goal was to prove or disprove the supposition, to move the envelope."

Tiller, however, has done more than simply move it. It is as if the envelope has levitated—the envelope of science itself. He is able to describe in precise and technical ways how our consciousness conditions our environment through will, focused intent, and attention. It seems that our thoughts create an imprint in the etheric matrix. If we then apply our will to shaping this form, it will coalesce in the material realm. "Even the littlest of our conscious acts," stressed Tiller, "has an effect far beyond the range we are taught to believe is possible."

He has been working on a new model for over forty years, which he calls a *multidimensional simulator model*. This simulator shows the human reality surrounded by "lattices, or weblike structures that enable the interaction between the mind, the body, the soul—the material and immaterial domains." He says that in the course of his research almost immediately, "it was necessary to expand the number of dimensions of our physical reality beyond the four we normally talk about. It became very quickly a ten-dimensional model. As we ride the river of life together, the spirit aspect of self basically interacts with a ten-dimensional simulator, a device kind of like a teaching machine. The structure of that teaching machine at the highest level, the level of mind, is basically as a set of nodal networks, of consciousness/energy conversion points in space, which have an amazingly small spacing, like 10^{-25} meters. Within that close-packed network was a convertor of emanations from the mind domain to what, for the moment, we will call the etheric domain. And then there was another super lattice, which was yet again about ten orders of magnitude larger in scale than the etheric nodal network in another hexagonal pattern interfacing with what we were calling physical reality."

Tiller went on to describe the various interconnecting lattices and the mathematics by which to discuss them and make better use of our awareness. As noted on his website, although he writes and speaks clearly like the experienced professor that he is, his books do require a broad scientific background to grasp the full impact of his groundbreaking findings. Despite this, however, the average curious reader may be inspired by focusing on only a small part of Tiller's theory at a time. He is beginning to show how science can prove the correspondences between subtle energy and physical phenomena and his speculations are constructed upon the most solid theories of matter and electrodynamics.

"Human intention can be captured in a simple electronic device and then that device can meaningfully interact with a specific target experiment," said Tiller, describing how he and his research team began with three target experiments. Tiller demonstrated that human consciousness can alter the manifest world in chemical, biological, and living systems. "In one experiment," he explained, "we used two simple electrical devices, identical in all respects. We wrapped one in aluminum foil and put it in an electrically grounded Faraday cage, which shields the device from any static electricity or electromagnetic waves. That was the control. The other one was then set on a tabletop around which sat four very well-accomplished meditators, highly inner-self-managed individuals, who would go into a deep meditative state. Once they were in that deep state, first they would cleanse the environment, make it a kind of sacred space. Then one would state the particular imprint intention for this device and that was ultimately to influence the particular target experiment."

In what Tiller called a "thy will be done sort of thing," the participants held the imprint intention thought for ten to fifteen minutes and then just released it entirely. The results have demonstrated how information is transferred from the mind to a receptive environment through a field that interpenetrates the material and immaterial realms. Tiller and his team used these intentionally imprinted electrical devices (IIED) to affect the pH in water both up and down, activate liver enzymes, and reduce larval development time in fruit flies. "These were the three target experiments we started with and we were robustly successful with all three of those," explained Tiller. "There has been a large body of good data around, but the effect magnitude of it is very small. So, in that case, one has to use careful statistics to show that there is a real nonrandom signature, which is down close to the noise level. In our studies, the effect magnitude was large, often 100–1,000 times larger than our measurement accuracy."

As their team discovered, equally interesting was the effect their experiments were having on the very space in which they were being conducted. "When you use these intentionally imprinted electrical devices for three to four months, the electrodynamic symmetry state of the space is raised," he says. Repetition of the experiments in given locales can dramatically increase the power of the locales to reproduce the results, creating a sacred space, so to speak.

Work like theirs shows us that humans are like capacitors comprised of systems including those of our chakras and glands, which are circuit vehicles for the harmonization of our multidimensional aptitudes and our physical and spiritual organs. Thus, we are god simulators or little universes of creation, all interconnected. Our cells emit photons, coalesce as a light body, and constantly change and adapt in a sea of energy that all life is a part of. Tiller mentioned that qigong masters emit infrared radiation of up to four microns; the average person emits less than one micron. The healing magnetism of some healers' hands is the equivalent of a 20,000 gauss magnet. Our bodies are bioelectric and magnetic, but they are also subtle light bodies that are encoded by the power of thought and word and, obviously, deeds. The experiments of Masaru Emoto, author and doctor of alternative medicine, in Japan have included priests praying over polluted water and actually purifying it, demonstrating once again that thought is real energy and it impacts the material world. Where people gather with focused intention and a feeling of love, transformation can and does occur, as Dr. Larry Dossey and Bill Sweet and others have so successfully demonstrated with their study of the healing power of prayer.

"Any measurement you make" of this effect, continued Tiller, "has two parts. It has a part that is due to the distance-time frame of reference. That's the particulate part. And it has a part associated with reciprocal distance-time. That's the information wave part, or what I called the etheric part, or the magnetic part. It turns out that under normal conditions of our reality the second part, the wave part, is very, very small. It is real and it is what is involved in most parapsychology experiments, but the magnitude of that contribution, compared to the first contribution, is small. And yet, through careful measurements, it can be detected. When you take our kind of imprinted devices and you turn them on in space, it basically pumps the space to a higher level of symmetry in the universe. And it's at the higher symmetry level that the second contribution can become much larger."

They have interpreted this to mean "that some state of order is developing in the physical vacuum. If you have a higher symmetry state, then it is also a medium of higher free energy. And it's free energy that drives this world, sort of a chemical energy type thing; but more than chemical, it can be electrical, it can be magnetic, all aspects of substance." This makes God as an omnipresent, omniscient creator more understandable. God is a field supporting everything and being everything. We are godlike. There is no separation and thus no duality.

And still, interaction between the physical and etheric particles is not possible unless something additional is added to the picture. As Tiller explained, "in our particle world, relativity theory says that things have to go slower than the velocity of light. But in the reciprocal space, that wave space, everything goes faster than the velocity of light. So the magnetic monopole particles that can function in a vacuum are going faster than light and in order for them to interact, which they must do in order for there to be electromagnetism, I proposed a higher dimensional substance called *deltrons*. This is in the domain of emotions and [a deltron would act as a] coupler—it can couple between the electric substance and the magnetic substance." In other words, the deltron particles can interact with etheric particles traveling faster than light and also interact with physical particles traveling slower than light—and can thus bring about energy exchange between them.

"The deltron force is that which affects rapport," Tiller continued. "Our focused attention to something conditions its environment to receive it, an upholding at a higher order. By paying attention to something, we elevate it in all dimensions simultaneously. That coupler, which I call deltron, is really a key element. It does more than just couple. Human intentions can influence that substance. Here is how one sees the effects of intention on physical reality."

Tiller explained how in the realm between the manifest and unmanifest one finds a coupling of an image and its inverse. For every shape with density, there is a reflective frequency, a reciprocal wave dancing in the ethers. A fascinating look at the Shroud of Turin suggests that the resurrection event may be an expression of these little-known laws. Dr. Gilbert Lavoie, author of *Resurrected: Tangible Evidence That Jesus Rose from the Dead,* explained on one of our several interviews, that what is imprinted on the cloth is a "negative" image, the inverse of the physical person, much like a negative of a photograph. Lavoie and others suggest the image could have resulted from some low plasmic energy phenomena, a sudden great burst of light energy (which intriguingly is also described as a possible explanation of the energies forming crop circles). Could it be that the resurrection from the dead is a matter of manipulating the subtle energies that give matter shape and density and the light energy that invigorates it? Is this what is meant in the Hebrew scriptures regarding the eventual resurrection of souls by God's will, which will precede a thousand years of peace?

Tiller's "multidimensional simulator model" is really a wave diffraction model. The consciousness waves from the mind domain go through the lattice points of the etheric domain because of the reciprocal nature of the two lattices. When the intensity is high enough there is a conversion to a form of energy that is then refracted off the nodal network and through the space-time sublattice. These nodal network points are both convertors of consciousness/energy from mind to the etheric to the physical, but they also radiate out patterns of energy appropriate for that sublattice. "That's what feeds and nourishes us as physical bodies walking through this great grid of nodal networks," declares Tiller.

I wondered how water fit into this vision and, because we are primarily water beings and live on a planet chiefly composed of water molecules, it seemed reasonable to ask Tiller about the ability of water to carry or amplify vibration. In symbology water is not only the source of life, but it is often used to symbolize the emotional and intellectual life. Perhaps if water was connected to the deltrons, that might explain why emotions and thoughts can affect us so strongly, both individually and collectively.

Tiller revealed that indeed, "water is very high in deltron content. It is the easiest substance to activate of perhaps any other material. I don't have enough data to substantiate it, but [I believe] water is that sacred substance. Water seems to have a very high potential deltron content, which can be activated by intention." This realization led him to investigate the healing powers of homeopathy and prayer. My own hunch is that water—the water on Earth, in the oceans, and in cosmic space, like the water in our brains, hearts, organs, and cells—is the medium via which the supra-intelligence is facilitated.

Water lover and expert William (Marks) Waterway said in a 2012 discussion of the beautiful book he edited, which includes four hundred color photographs and is entitled *Water Voices from around the World,* "There is a mystery about water. Everything that water touches it imprints. The foundation of consciousness and intelligence, [the brain] carries the most water of any organ in our body. Water is a vehicle that allows knowledge to be imprinted and for creating intelligence. There are some belief systems that feel . . . like the Akashic Record, everything from the very beginning of the creation of the universe is created in the molecular structure of water. . . . It has inherent in it the ability to give us consciousness. But also water has an intelligence unto itself."

Waterway added, "The manifestation of water at the creation of the universe giving birth to intelligence was to allow us to be witness to creation to interact with it," to be, as I posit, co-creators. Whether a dowser, a healer, or a space traveler, water may be the very key to understanding life on Earth and in the cosmos and calls to us to repair the waters of the world, to enter what Waterway calls an age of water consciousness.

Some of these theories may also explain the efficacy of mind control, crowd manipulation, and other destructive or disintegrative methods used to impact free will. Creating fear, polarization, and intense states of emotional "charge" can be used to drive mass movements, hysteria, and even war. How? Perhaps the ability to control these causative forces comes from engaging the mental function of the higher mind and the astral or emotional bodies with the electromagnetic nature of the grounding apparatus—in this case our consciousness. Fear causes a contraction, a movement away from unity and balance. It exacerbates the left hemisphere of the brain into a state of division, or aggression. As Tiller's model demonstrates, the emotions nurture the ground in which the world will manifest. How we feel about something, or the way we are manipulated to feel about anything—a person, an idea, an action— has a great deal to do with what we are willing to see and, in fact, mind control can also be used for affirmative and unifying effects. It can be used to benefit healing and even create conditions for miracles to occur, as sacred traditions worldwide have taught for millennia, which in these

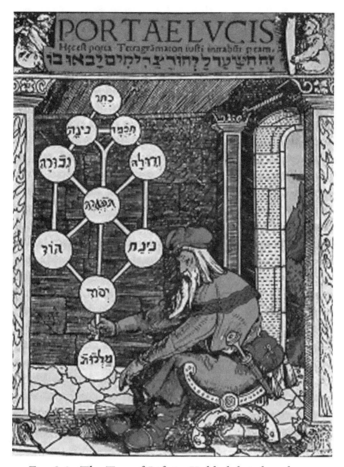

*Fig. 8.3. The Tree of Life in Kabbalah is based on a
ten-dimensional pattern.*

instances stimulate the power of the right hemisphere of the brain. Ideally, we need to become whole-brain humans, neither predominantly left nor right brained.

A major portion of our life force originates from the energy in the vacuum of space. Tiller's ten-dimensional world could be a modern, scientific understanding of the ancient Kabbalah.

Kabbalah's ten-dimensional cosmo-genesis shows us precisely how to refine our emotions and intellect in order to achieve divine revelation, to become godlike. This is the focus of one of my prior books

Sanctuary of the Divine Presence. What Tiller confirms in modern science is the ancient Judaic tradition's recognition that our lives, our collective and individual origins in the Tree of Life in the Garden of Eden, have ten different qualities or fields of light qualities. In the tradition of the Kabbalah, these are called sefirot; they emanate to us from the divine domain, but are also reflected in our physical anatomy as well as our emotional and spiritual makeup. This same ten-dimensional Tree of Life is contained in the Mayan calendar, which Carl J. Calleman explained in a 2012 interview as being the source of all life in the cosmos as well. This energy, which rises and falls in our bodies, is according to Hindu tradition called the kundalini life force. It is activated and controlled through the Vedic practices of yoga and meditation and it engages the double helix of our anatomy. In their deepest signature of pattern, these storied patterns are in our DNA.

Patrick Obissier's *Biogenealogy: Decoding the Psychic Roots of Illness* explains how this takes place—this passing on storied DNA from one generation to the next. Any given bloodline (gene line) has a historic events line recorded in it. Disease, suffering, emotional fears, hardships, and their counterpoints—relative ease, success, and love—come with a body made from an egg of a female Homo sapiens fertilized by the sperm of a male Homo sapiens, both bearing DNA informed by the past of its generational bloodline.

Tiller's ten-dimensional lattice system and Kabbalah's ten-dimensional system show us how we exist in the physical, emotional, intellectual, and spiritual domains of our being, just as other traditions reveal similar analogues in their own respective landscape of terminology. They all share the purpose of teaching us about our natures, which are as deeply intertwined with the cosmos as with the Earth.

Acquiring self-mastery of our emotions and our intellect applied to right intention, we are able to manifest the best choices for any situation—personal or global. We, through a divine alignment, are in divine harmony, unfolding the divine plan of peace and paradise as the archetype and eventual fulfillment of the human journey. Our story can be a success story of coming to divine awareness. In this, is it possible that the modern physicists have at last solved the riddles of the ancients' teachings? Is this the sixth sun of the Aztecs spoken of in chapter 4—the cross-pollination of all times, all cultures—the time humanity is taking a quantum leap, a leap that is outside the bounds of time and space and results in our shifting our entire perspective to a compassionate love affair between life and the divine? Did this not, in fact, break into the time line in March of 2012, as Carl J. Calleman said and as predicted thousands of years ago by the Mayan civilization and its calendrical timepiece?

In Tiller's ten-dimensional lattice structure and Kabbalah's ten sefirot are models of our consciousness as well as guidelines as to how to create from intention to action. Just as the creator field manifested the world from *mind,* so too do human beings. Our bodies, minds, spirits, and souls are interpenetrating, but at the same time they exhibit unique states. From Tiller's ideas about latticelike structures we learn about reciprocity in nature, that we can assemble or disassemble matter with our minds and that we are doing this all the time. In this sense, our consciousness contains the effects of the past as well as the potentials of the enfolded future. Tiller is on the way to proving that consciousness is nonlocal, how telepathic thought transference works, and how mind control can be facilitated. The qualities of emotions that people have and the ideas that inspire, beautify, and enrich our lives all condition the environment in which things become manifest. As a simple example we can all feel the energy differences in people's homes. Some feel and are full of love, while others feel empty or chaotic.

Looking at the way we view matter and spirit and their material and immaterial qualities helps us to understand the capacities of the divine human. The human soul interacts in the frequency of life, or the field of love, which is a nice way to see us all potentially existing in a sea of love.

INGO SWANN AND
THE SECRETS OF POWER

Ingo Swann (1933–2013) was a gifted artist and intuitive who had a wry sense of humor and a talent for teaching others how to do what he did. Like his dear friend Bill Tiller, to whom Swann introduced me, Swann was a pioneer in the effort to endow mankind with a doorway to our own capacities. In the 1960s, under the auspices of the U.S. government, he devised the protocols of the military's remote viewing program. He participated in many programs at prestigious universities like Stanford Research Institute, where he, Hal Puthoff, and Russell Targ and others tested the process of remote viewing. (Another of the early researchers to use remote viewing in archaeology in the late 1970s was Stephan A. Schwartz, author of *Opening to the Infinite: The Art and Science of Non-Local Awareness*. Together with his team of explorers, he was able to locate "Cleopatra's Palace, Marc Antony's Timonium, ruins of the Lighthouse of Pharos, and sunken ships along the California coast, and in the Bahamas.")

In Swann's book *Penetration: The Question of Extraterrestrial and Human Telepathy,* he describes one of the more astonishing experiences he had in the mid-1970s when he was essentially kidnapped and forced to remote view what was happening on the moon. Some kind of secret government outfit took him to an underground base where he was forced to perform his remote viewing and reported, to his ultimate surprise, that he saw evidence of a mining operation on the lunar surface being performed by humanoid-looking forms that were mostly naked. "It was very disturbing," he told us. "Can you imagine expecting to find some nice rocks and dust and such and instead seeing tracks of machinery and bare-butt humans carrying stuff around?"

But as exciting as this story is, in this chapter we are going to focus on a different Ingo Swann book, *Secrets of Power: Individual Empowerment versus the Societal Panorama of Power and Depowerment,* which is volume 1 of a trilogy that was in process at the time of our discussion. In this work Swann recounts his own youth growing up in a small Colorado town where his mother and aunts had regular discussions of who had "power" and what they could or couldn't do. "It fascinated me, even then," he said, "to realize that some people had power and others didn't. Why some . . . were powerless in the small community in which we lived, while others exerted great influence and control and affected other people's lives. So I made a study of it."

He went on to describe this small mountain town in Colorado that, during his youth, had a population of 210. "It's amazing to think," he remembered, "that all the old ladies, including my two little grandmothers, were always assessing who had power and who didn't have power, and why. So, my mother and aunts were great people watchers and they would sit and dissect these people and I would watch. And I was always fascinated about power. For many years, I accepted the conventional idea of power: that you look at people who have power and you say 'that's power.' But very few people have power of that kind. In the 1950s, in the Army I worked with a powerful general. But I noticed more profoundly all the soldiers, the many more who really had no power except to do what they were told. At that point, I began to realize that everything written about power takes note of the powerful, but pays no attention to the powerless. The reason for that became visible to me when I looked up the definition of power. It said power is the authority, influence, or control over others. Almost all power books, even if they are really good ones, talk about the powerful and they do not talk about the others that the powerful have authority, control, and influence over." Swann added with a laugh, "And those others included me! It really included just about everyone. Maybe only 5 percent of the world population can be thought of as having power and the other 95 percent of the world are the others that they have power over.

"So I began to look at why powerless people are powerless. I couldn't find anyone discussing that at all. . . . If we are an intelligent species then everyone with intelligence ought to have the rudiments of power. I began to notice that this is not nurtured amongst the powerless at all. The powerful prevent that, actually, by making it impossible to have such a simple thing as a school where you can go to study power. There aren't schools where one can go to study power and likewise there is no encyclopedia about the powers of the human species. I consider that a very egregious and terrible omission in our cultural framework."

In this he had seized on his most passionate topic. There are no schools, per se, that you can attend to learn to be telepathic or how to heal at a distance. Of course, there are systems that people are teaching and practicing around the world today that cultivate inherent powers within each human being, but as a whole the Western world does not provide an environment favorable to the development of these biomind superpowers.

Swann found his research into the powerful and the powerless to be a very rich experience, "because the more you see how people are powerless, the more you see it is a sociological effect that keeps them powerless. . . . If you go into the background of the term *power* you'll see that the English language existed for about a thousand years without a word for power. The rudiments of it, as we know it today, only began in the 1300s. . . . Largely, the balance between power and powerlessness is implicit in that definition which came into use about 1540 BCE. . . . Power was vested in a king, deified in a way, and everyone else was a functionary of that individual. Then [the concept of power] grew in scope with ideas of democracy—that those who weren't powerful should play some significant role in social power. So it began to include functionaries of the common person. The etymology can be followed through to see that certain concepts that belong with the term *power* began to be minimized, sort of pushed to the wayside. The important thing to understand is that if the definition of power is authority, control, and influence over others, then the others have to exist in order for the powerful to have power over them. If the others did not exist, then the power would not exist, because power can't be power unto itself in this context. It has to have something or someone to have power over."

Swann's historical examination of the word *power* showed how empowerment of the individual was effectively blocked. Instead, power and its development became a sociological tool of the few over the many. "In short," he said, "society has come to view power as that which you exercise over others rather than the truer reflection of power, which is the ability to exercise one's own innate potentials."

If our definition of power, Swann stressed, is influence and control over others, then you have to deny access to information about power.

Power is then a state of dominating. "It became apparent over the centuries," he explained, "that the best way to keep the masses powerless was to have no schools or philosophy that articulated what real inner power is or where manufactured, politically enforced power comes from. We don't even have an encyclopedia of human powers and human abilities!" he added incredulously. "We have them of sea slugs and stars, but not of our own potentials. We have encyclopedias of rocks and waters and dinosaurs, but there is not a trace of an effort to catalog and develop real human powers." The power system on Earth today is manufactured for people to take assigned positions within that framework, while the innate biomind superpowers are hidden away from the majority of people who don't know they have tools of personal power.

Paradise is ours, the tools are ours, all we need do is exercise them, says Swann. "If you deny information about power and what actually goes on in power systems, then you are creating a powerless class." In the case of global economics today, the infrastructure and capacity to assign the majority of humans to conscripted servitude with labor pools exists, with the conditions and rights of production being determined by fewer and fewer people through more international, rather than local, organizations. It's easy to understand why a global economic and political system that depends on taking the fruits of others' labor would rely on force for their power and be disinclined to support an individual discovering the source of his or her own inherent power. Swann and I even discussed the possibility that there may be forces, which are not indigenous to Earth, that do not want earthly humans to achieve telepathic excellence, for instance, or to become space voyagers. He described how, when he remote viewed the moon, he felt that a few of the beings there recognized his mental presence with some displeasure.

It is at this juncture that the challenge to paradise is most clear. We humans do not lack the ability to manifest harmony and abundance; rather, the vast majority of humanity is never shown the power of the inner self and the inherent power of communal effort. Nor are we mindful enough of the fact that our words, thoughts, and deeds literally shape the manifest world. While physics is expanding to show us the power of the mind, politics continues to suppress that reality. Human beings, when using focused intention, can discern truth from fiction, but we're being hypnotized by mindless materialism and purposeless consumption as well as violence and greed. Once again, a death economy benefits by keeping humans chained to a worldview that limits individual freedoms. A life economy would relish the creative power of a humanity wide awake to our multidimensionality.

The lack of discussion about power seems to me no different than the lack of a serious plan for sustainable development on this planet. Once we are able to come to terms with our great creative capacities and "god being," it will be clear that loving service enables authentic power. It will also be clear that our ability to create peace on Earth with our words, thoughts, and deeds is not a childish or naive sentiment, but a reflection of actual laws that rule matter and the immaterial realms. To what degree will we choose to develop and explore those realms of inner power that can enhance our capacity to know with conscious clarity what is asked of us? Which of us is ready to be honest enough with ourselves to take responsibility for what we think, say, and do? Which of us is willing to adopt a life framework that acknowledges our divine capacities, declares ourselves divine human beings, and says that we and the source of all life are one? Which of us is prepared to deliberately participate in creating the Good Earth Society now or, at the very least, to reverse the degeneration of our home planet? Which of us believes it is our birthright to do so and, as a birthright, also an obligation and a shared responsibility?

We are conditioned for powerlessness and vast numbers of people, even in family structures, adapt to a pyramidal power structure. They come away from this programming feeling inferior and powerless. "I began talking to homeless people here in New York," relayed Swann. "When they trust you, they give you a very clear understanding. They do believe they have powers that have not been nurtured. Either [because of the] educational system or because no one really knows how to empower people. There are no power schools anywhere in the world. So, if we are an intellectual species then we need information to work with. [If] the information is not available then we do not have what we need to work with. I believe we are a power species. Power is part of our makeup, so depowerment has to be a sociological artifact, but it is taught, not natural." As Swann says, it is because of these systems filters—these overlays of our personal, socioeconomic, religious, and social experiences—that we become blind even to our own powers, blind to the power to feel deeply and to see into the future.

Power structures limit the number of people that are assigned power, Swann reminds us. "The top of the pyramid determines the educational perimeters. . . . I looked and looked and looked for a power structure that says it is OK for individual empowerment to take place on a broad scale. There are none that say that. There are none that permit that. And the most effective way to prevent wholesale empowerment by the individual is to deny information in any form whatsoever as it applies to empowerment. If information is denied to the masses, then this equates to a kind of secrecy."

Using these innate powers and essential tools that humans are wired to access is in fact the kind of power that Swann spent his life developing, understanding, and teaching to others. His lifelong effort to create a way for human beings to tap into these abilities has enabled men, women, and children around the world to explore and develop the kind of power that is just and sustainable. That is the divine inheritance of each human being.

"You never hear anyone," Swann said with his customary chuckle, "talk about stealth power. You never hear that term used. I brought that into usage in order to broaden the awareness that there are stealth powers: powers that can be utilized in a way no one will recognize and therefore are almost certain to win in the end. . . . In fact, all power structures have learned to use their power in stealthy ways rather than in open, accessible ways." Global institutions like the World Bank, the International Monetary Fund, and the United Nations today are a clear example of such processes that remain secreted away from public view and public participation. They affect millions of people's lives directly and yet the individuals from every nation are effectively unrepresented by those who are political appointees or employees of the system.

Once one understands the pyramidal structure of power, one understands that this is a dramatic tragedy. But it can be changed and each one of us can contribute to that shift. "Awareness is primary power," Swann reminded me. "But we aren't taught how to develop our awareness. One easy way to keep people disempowered is to not nurture their awareness."

Swann's work to develop our biomind superpowers—such as an ability to see "everywhere and everywhen" as dowser Terry Ross taught—leads to being able to effect healing at a distance, to read someone's mind, or to engage in conversation with other galactic travelers. In short, it enables access to all talents once referred to as prophecy or divine insight. Like Bill Tiller and Terry Ross, Ingo Swann is a national treasure. His effort to endow mankind with a doorway to our own capacities is indeed the work of a pioneer.

As regards the wild card events discussed in chapter 2, might it be that the awakening of human powers, of nonlocal consciousness, is the greatest wild card of all—the answer to apocalypse and a key tool for creating balance on the Earth? I believe this to be so. Each one of us, through even a simple daily prayer (which we now know has a real effect in the world), can add to this eventuality. When we focus our will in this way and with the right intention, we are truly capable of elevating the world.

Up until this point in the book, we have outlined the many different ways we exhibit the capacity to heal ourselves and the planet. Fundamental to the basic teachings of most sacred societies is the ability to increase the student's awareness to understand the relationship between cause and effect. It requires exacting observation skills and entering the world of causative forces with a conscious and loving deliberateness. In Kabbalah the student learns that the act of manifesting anything—a city, a spaceship, a clean energy technology, a good relationship with someone—is made of emanation (atzilut), creation (beriyah), formation (yetzirah), and action (asiyah). Inherent powers are developed, not assigned, and real power is built from within, not from without.

We can with deliberateness entrain to one another, to other species, and to nature. Hence, a group of people focused with loving intent, holding hands in a circle, might be able to cure the lame, give the blind sight, and even raise the dead. Hasn't this been demonstrated worldwide and throughout history? What is it that takes place in miracles? What is accessed and expressed that is profound enough to alter our organs of perception, the limb of a person, or to create something out of nothing? What we are learning from Ingo Swann, Bill Tiller, Terry Ross, and others is that what some would call *nothing* is, in fact, the storehouse of cosmic, divine energy that floods our environment and is responsive to our presence. It may be the electrical volume of energy generated by the stars that we use in healing. It may be a magnetic field of healing power exhibited in our own bodies. However this presence of a unifying field shows itself, we are learning of the divinity in our capacities to be entrusted with accessing this holy power.

9

EXPERIENCING THE IMMORTAL SOUL

At some point in our lives most of us have asked ourselves, who am I? When we ask this question, are we not also suggesting other questions like, why am I here? What is my purpose? Why is my life the way it is? What will happen to me when I die? Who am I? What dies? Is there really a death of me, or just my body? Will I be able to continue communicating with my loved ones? What will the afterlife be like? Is there reincarnation? Who will I be and what does that have to do with now? And the list goes on. The questions within the big question of one's identity are what I think of as the colossal beingness questions. These are the eternal questions asked by every generation. We ask them because we are destined to realize that their answers lie in our experiences. We are wired for blissful immortality . . . and godliness.

Yes, it is true that we are immortal beings. In fact, most of the world believes in reincarnation or the afterlife and only a small fraction of people on this planet professes that we are no more than a physical entity that is born one time and eventually dies, nothing more, that's it. After years of study, my own personal inspection of past lives, and interviewing some of the brightest and most open-minded people on the planet, it is my conclusion that human beings are the accumulation of experiences one has in the journey from life to life. Our consciousness may change vessels, but it is still the same operator driving on the consciousness highways and byways.

As we have already discussed, consciousness is nonlocal and inside a framework where there is no time or place. There is only information that is accessible across all time from the past and into the future and from anywhere the mind can imagine or focus its attention. Over the millennia, oral and written records are evidence that much of our lives are spent focused on the more spiritual aspects of ourselves. To figure out what we are doing here, we use normative religion, revive rituals of ancient pasts, Earth devotions, or the spiritual quest in which we try to hear the inner voice of consciousness.

Howard Storm has written a great book called *My Descent into Death,* in which you get the feeling that the descriptions by Dante and others who wrote so graphically of the inner and underworlds of the afterlife are actual states of being or environs. But are they environs we create with our mind, words, and thoughts? Might the habitations we visit in the afterlife, like those we inhabit in the here and now, reflect our nature, our vibration, our likes and dislikes, strengths and weaknesses, fears and loves? Whether one is talking about near-death experiences, afterlife communication, or what happens between lives, it appears we remain unique identities that continue on an evolutionary course.

In the subtler fields or realms, perhaps we are better known to one another as energetic qualities or resonances, rather like notes in a musical performance. Some have said that soul recognition after life, between two different people, looks like merging fields of colored lights. It is also consistently said of our afterlife learning that we see how our consciousness has been directly engaged and continues to take part in shaping events and encounters. Just as Bill Tiller's research shows, our thoughts are changing things faster than the speed of light. While it can take years or even decades for ideas or plans to manifest in the material realm, they are in fact shaping matter instantaneously in the subtler realms.

When looking at the vast library of research into life consciousness outside the body, unity is the one trait categorically mentioned in practically all near-death experiences, afterlife communications, and other between-life accounts. It seems we are all learning the same lesson: We are one. We are an immaculate aspect of the unified field of life. We are made of and reflect the coherent light of the Creator. Every particle is the expression of that inner dynamic and it is this symbiosis between origination and manifestation that is described by all sacred traditions and great wisdom teachings. We are one and yet many. Or, as our own nation's obverse coat of arms or Great Seal proclaims, e pluribus unum, out of many, one. The simple is in the complex. The part reflects the whole. The whole is greater than the sum of its parts.

DR. RAYMOND MOODY AND THE BEGINNING OF THE NEAR-DEATH EXPERIENCE

Raymond Moody, Ph.D., M.D., is a licensed psychiatrist fully trained in the Western scientific approach to health care and mental health. He is also what can rightly be described as a spiritual scientist, one who studies the immaterial realms related to the manifest world. In the mid-1970s when he first became well known as the author of one of the first bestsellers about the near-death experience, he started a gale force hurricane that swept the academic world off its feet. He was a pioneer in the effort to shift the paradigm that held fast at the time and that promulgated the theory that death meant a complete extinction of consciousness. "I had always been very interested in philosophy," he told us during a live broadcast interview, explaining that he enrolled at the University of Virginia in 1962 as a philosophy student. "In 1965 I was an undergraduate student and was told by one of my professors about a Dr. Richie who, some years before, had a near-death experience. Years after I had heard his story, in 1969 or early 1970 when I was philosophy professor at North Carolina, a student came up and told me . . . a story that was identical to Dr. Richie's story. It was at this point that I realized there must be many of these stories. So when I entered medical school in 1972 I had a number of stories already, which gave me a great opportunity to talk to people who got resuscitated. Over time I talked with, literally, thousands of people from all over the world who have had really astonishing life-changing experiences while on the verge of death."

Moody said that it would have seemed that his background in philosophy, with a major in logic and a medical degree in psychiatry, would have stacked the deck against him ever desiring to investigate the ancient roots of life-after-death studies. "There is a difficulty in studying these realms so that we can have what we call scientific proof," he said. "In fact, the scientific method, as it is at the turn of this century, is just not adequate for establishing the great spiritual heritage that is ours." But we are trying!

On June 29, 2001, Reuters News reported on a study examining heart attack patients, which was performed by a British scientist who concluded that consciousness continues after the death of the body and death of the brain. This report demonstrates the tremendous positive impact that Raymond Moody and others like him have had on our world. Of course, the notion of an afterlife has been a part of the human experience from our beginnings. But as Moody said, "what has happened in the last few decades is that we have developed technologies to bring people back to life from states of being that a hundred years ago would have been called death." This has created more opportunities for patients to report the experience of their consciousness in the time when they were in limbo between life and death.

Although many ancient civilizations made a fine study of this state of consciousness and the passage in time from one state to the next, "modern" science and medicine, particularly of the past century, have worked hard to eradicate belief in anything that cannot be quantified and weighed and measured. Thanks to the courage of people like Dr. Moody, today these practices are being revived, much to the benefit of making our lives more understandable and complete.

In addition to pioneering the modern discussion and study of near-death experiences (NDEs), Dr. Moody tapped his great interest in ancient Greek philosophy to re-create an environment and the tools he believes were used by the Greeks in their psychomanteums, the place where they would go to make deliberate contact with the deceased. He paid the price for being honest with what he has learned about communication with those we call the dead, as he details in his 1999 book, *The Last Laugh: A New Philosophy of Near-Death Experiences, Apparitions, and the Paranormal,* in which he answers the criticism he's received from the religious right, professional skeptics, and parapsychologists. After several decades of research, he and others can demonstrate correlations and quite a bit about what appears to be life after death. What we still have a lot to learn about is how we go about this miraculous transformation each lifetime from immortal beings to material humans.

Moody's laboratory research in the psychomanteums he's designed once again demonstrates how the domains of the mystery traditions and of mysticism in general are finding confirmation in the laboratory. Using a reflecting pool of water for the person to look at while directing their thoughts to a deceased loved one, images and communication occur between the living and the deceased—reminding me once again of the deltron content in water that seems to facilitate this multidimensionality in consciousness. Like the ancient Greeks, we are creating experiences and machines to help us understand the immaterial nature of ourselves. The paradox wasn't lost to either of us as we laughed at this notion during his interview. Indeed, the last laugh may be our own when we see the beautiful symmetry and simplicity of an ongoing creation process that we are each part of and always have been part of.

CHILDREN AND PAST LIVES

Children often make the best subjects for researchers into near-death encounters since they have less conditioning than adults about what to expect. More relevant, perhaps, are the long-term and lasting effects that a near-death experience can have on a person. Dr. Melvin Morse, author of several books including *Closer to the Light: Learning from the Near-Death Experiences of Children,* is a pediatrician and neuroscientist who has made an intensive study of children who report near-death experiences. According to him, years after their own youthful encounters, these children "were more directed and more focused than their peers or even most adults. They tended to be more generous, kinder, and had a sense of certainty about their purpose in the world. Most all were involved in volunteer work and were very much focused on helping others. Another interesting thing was that, as a group, they tended to eat better, to like fruits and vegetables, and to want do good things for their bodies."

Carol Bowman has made a fascinating study of children's past lives. In her books *Children's Past Lives: How Past Life Memories Affect Your Child* and *Return from Heaven: Beloved Relatives Reincarnated within Your Family,* she details the stories she's collected for two decades from families who claim multilife recall—in other words, relatives who remember reincarnating into each other's lives as new relations. For instance, as she related during an interview, a beloved grandmother may return as a newborn child to the same family or a child who dies young may return to the same mother as a later child. Conscious recall by children of their former lives, how we choose our parents, and why we come back to the same families is beautifully documented in her books.

Usually children who recall past lives will begin talking about them between the ages of one and five. They are very matter of fact about their memories, which appear to be very vivid to them. Often they will describe what it was like "when I was big before," and frequently they remember how they died.

"It's usually the tone of voice that captures the parent's attention," Bowman said. "It differs from the lilting voice of when a child is making up a fantasy. The children are consistent with their stories. The story may unfold over a period of years." She tells of some parents who have followed up on their children's stories to validate the historical reality of the story's details. They looked for the towns they reportedly lived in and the names of people and families they were related to. Some even had the opportunity to reintroduce the reincarnated "soul/person" to their previous families, in the present.

But Bowman's book focuses on reincarnation within the same family, describing how behavior from one life can carry over into the next. She discusses how a mother who had died in her early fifties returned as the newborn daughter of her grown daughter Candy. Candy reported her new daughter Carrie, born three years after her mother's death, "was just like her grandmother, singing and dancing all of the time." Candy's mother had been a performer in the theater and this "two-year-old acted like her grandmother. One day Candy was driving in the car with her daughter Carrie and her own grandmother (Carrie's great-grandmother) when the three-year-old Carrie burst into song, singing all the verses to "Chattanooga Choo Choo," a song popular during the 1940s, which even Candy didn't know. Candy's grandmother explained that that had been her daughter's favorite song.

"Candy, who was open to reincarnation, did begin to suspect while watching her daughter's behavior over time that it was, in fact, her own mother reincarnated. As Carrie got older she would recognize things from her grandmother's life. She would specify belongings many times, saying, 'that's mine, that lipstick was mine.' This is reminiscent of Tibetan Buddhism when they look for the reincarnation of the Dalai Lama or other high lamas. One of the tests they will do with children is to give them items that belonged to the prior personality of a deceased lama" to see what they recognize.

Others in the community also seemed to recognize a presence in the small child. "As a two-year-old the child recognized a waitress in a restaurant which had been a favorite of her grandmother's. She recognized this elderly waitress and called her by her name. Even the mother didn't know who the waitress was. There was another incident when she was in a shopping cart and a little old lady came and pinched her cheek and said 'Oh isn't she adorable,' and Carrie got very excited and said 'Mommy, Mommy, there's my old friend.' Her mother then realized that this woman had been her grandmother's neighbor for thirty years. So in this instance, a two-year-old child recognized two people from her previous incarnation."

Bowman and I agreed that the importance lies not in whether one believes in reincarnation, but rather in the fact that these memories and traits help communities of people experience a continuity of the soul, deeper love for each other, and the world and God or creation. The immortal aspects of one's essential nature and beingness that continue from lifetime to lifetime demonstrate continuity over centuries, and perhaps give deeper meaning to the warning that the sins of the fathers are visited upon their children. What we do, think, and say in one life will indeed affect us in others. Relationships do not end at death, but rather continue into the next life, sometimes starting off where we left before.

When children claim to remember their former lives "when they were big," it can severely alter a family's belief system. Bowman tells of a little boy named James in Chicago who died at the age of two years and two months with a large tumor behind his left eye, which had caused blindness, and a tumor behind his left ear that had been biopsied as cancerous. After James died, his mother Cathy moved away, remarried, started a new family, and never mentioned her first child who had died. Twelve years later she gave birth to her fourth child Chad, who was born blind in his left eye and with a cyst in the same place James had the biopsied tumor. Most striking to the mother, however, was a birthmark on Chad's neck where an incision from the intravenous drip had left a scar on James's neck. Although raised a Baptist in the West, something came over Cathy immediately and she realized that her child had been reincarnated. The beloved child she had lost had returned.

"She was reluctant to talk about this with anyone," said Bowman. "She tried to share this with her husband, but he told her she was crazy and that she had lost her mind. So she learned to keep quiet. But when Chad turned four he started talking about his life as James. He wanted to go back to their other house. He described the apartment they had lived in when he was James. He asked for specific toys that had belonged to him as James, which the present family did not have. So at that point she realized that he knew, as well, that he had lived before with her as her son named James and had come back to her again as Chad."

Bowman came to the field of children's past-life recall as a result of her own experience with her five-year-old son Chase. When he suddenly developed a fear of loud sounds, like the firecrackers on the Fourth of July, she looked for ways to help him. "He had become hysterical," she said. "There was nothing we could do to console him. It was really out of character for him to be afraid of anything." When a hypnotherapist friend came for a visit she told him of Chase's phobia of loud noises. "He told Chase to sit on my lap and tell him what he saw when he heard these loud noises that frightened him. Immediately he began to describe how he was once an adult male soldier carrying a long rifle with a sword at the end. . . . As he was saying this, the hair on my arm stood on end. Chase had only been allowed to watch Sesame Street, but he began to describe himself in the first person as an adult male in the heat of battle. He described how he was scared, confused, and missed his wife and children and at that point he went on for about fifteen minutes. He went on in great detail describing how he was shot in the right wrist and taken to what he described as a hospital, a military tent. 'They bandaged my wrist,'" Bowman recalled him saying, "'and ordered me back into battle. I don't want to be there, I don't want to fight.' He described a cannon on a wagon being pulled by horses," even talking about the chickens on the road as he walked down it before he was put behind the cannon. "He finished his story, hopped off my lap, and went off to play."

The location on his wrist where Chase had described being shot in a previous life was a spot troubled by eczema in this life. As Bowman noted, "physical evidence is an important clue to understanding reincarnational patterns." Dr. Brian Weiss, author of *Mirrors of Time: Using Regression for Physical, Emotional, and Spiritual Healing* and many other books including *Through Time into Healing,* has specialized in this field and has shown how our physical bodies of one incarnation carry the scars and memories from others, especially when an injury has resulted in a traumatic death.

After Chase recalled and verbalized the injury to his wrist in a previous life, the eczema that had not responded to almost five years of treatment completely vanished. Bowman elaborated on the phenomenal work of Dr. Ian Stevenson (1918–2007) at the University of Virginia Medical School. "Over the past forty years, almost single-handedly, Dr. Ian Stevenson has amassed about 26,000 case studies of children from around the world who spontaneously recall their past lives. A lot of his cases are from Asia, as that is where people are more likely to appreciate this kind of recall. In 1997 he published a huge, two volume set called *Reincarnation and Biology.* This is a study of 220 children with birth defects and birth marks that correspond to the injuries, fatal wounds, diseases, or death circumstances that the children recall from a previous life."

It seems clear that the cellular memory of the body impacts the memory stored within the soul—a sort of emotional snapshot of an incarnation that, according to some traditions, is carried with us from life to life. It is what is sometimes called the *permanent monad,* or that part of the soul that accumulates experience and wisdom from life to life and, in some cases, is a reminder of the prior life's unresolved challenges.

This echoes the findings of the previously mentioned field of biogenealogy, which Patrick Obissier writes about. We are imprinted in each lifetime by our own past lives and the past lives of the parents who create us biologically. This is why it is accurate to say that we are each a composite of influences from the past, the present, and the future.

At the age of six, I had eye surgery to my left eye to remove an eyelash that had imbedded itself there. Since that otherworldly experience of screaming through tears at the surgeon and nurses, "Why are you trying to kill me?" I have carried a little slice of paradise in my eye. I had a past-life experience during the surgery and wrote it down when I woke up, even though my writing was then imperfect. In the past life that I saw, I had been a nun caring for the animals in a wildlife sanctuary centuries ago. In it I met a giraffe, an elephant, and thousands of cranes. They expressed the environment of my soul and it is the same environment I have manifested in my life as an animal lover and advocate for the emancipation and protection of the animal kingdom. I share this only as a personal example of the way in which the transcendent experience can shape our lives.

THE LIFE OF THE WORLD TO COME

The way in which we live our lives seems to have everything to do with the type of death experience we will have. In fact, most sacred traditions teach that one's death is a more important moment than one's birth. After reading Raymond Moody's early works, researcher Carol Zaleski, Ph.D., became curious to find out if near-death experience testimonies could be found in older religious writings and, if so, how they compared to modern accounts. She says that not only did she find an abundance of such testimonies, but that it didn't take her long to find them.

Her first book, *Otherworld Journeys: Accounts of Near-Death Experience in Medieval and Modern Times,* examined medieval Christian accounts of people who had apparently died and returned from death and described their journey to the next world. "By looking at testimonies from across time," Zaleski explained on one of my broadcasts, we can see "unanimity among the accounts in the first flush of near-death tellings. We were getting positive, wonderful stories of people leaving their bodies and being transported effortlessly to another realm with no sense of any period of judgment or final recognizing of deeds." I wonder if this does not delineate, in some ways, the threshold at which perhaps there can be no return. In her book, Zaleski has cited accounts of our passing over a bridge into the other world and on that bridge one meets a maiden who is either a beautiful maiden or an ugly hag. She is the embodiment of your thoughts, words, and deeds." Zaleski's book *The Life of the World to Come: Near-Death Experience and Christian Hope* looks at the conceptions of the afterlife in multiple world religions, finding that the thoughts we have of the afterlife while we are alive definitely influence our experiences after life as well. Heaven and hell may be in part projections from our own fears and hopes as well as our religious, personal, and/or cultural programming.

PERCEIVING OUR OWN IMMORTALITY

Those who work in therapy with past-life memories are not trying to convince anyone of anything. Rather, their goal is to find how these experiences have impacted our lives and how we are changed by them. We are still learning in what ways nonlocality, immortality, and between-life memories affect our physical bodies in the physical realm, but it appears that we are growing distinctly conscious of the fact that all life is one and that we are all sparks of the Godhead.

Memories of God and Creation: Remembering from the Subconscious

Mind is a helpful book written by Shakuntala Modi, M.D. It is a collection of first person accounts of the afterlife experience (ALE), or what some have called the *between-life* experience. Modi is a board-certified psychiatrist who has used hypnotherapy successfully in her practice for over twenty-five years [at the time we spoke], but nothing had prepared her for a patient who came to her in the 1980s.

This woman had come to Modi's office troubled by severe phobias and panic attacks. As the doctor recounted on radio, "I asked her, when was the last time that she had claustrophobia? She started gasping for breath and said 'Doctor, I am having an attack right now.' So I asked her to close her eyes and concentrate on her feelings and let those feelings take her wherever they did. All of a sudden she said 'Doctor, I am in another time, another life. I am a young girl but it is a different body. I am in an office and people think I am dead, but I am still alive and I am afraid I am going to die.' I was surprised and wasn't quite sure what to do as she was still experiencing her shortness of breath." Modi described leading her through calming breathing exercises while she was having this recall, slowly bringing her patient's attention to the present moment they were sharing. "But at her next session, she announced that her almost life-long claustrophobia was totally gone."

Modi's book is especially good at listing the common traits described by those who have experienced past-life recall or the near-death experience. "Sometimes, when my clients go back to the source of their problems or just before there was a problem, they will recount the experience of being one with God and then at incarnation feeling rejected by and separated from God." Another example of commonality between those who have before-life or afterlife recall is their references to the Akashic Record, or the library of records that store all life events. "They describe these huge, huge libraries," Modi related, "as a cosmic library or God's history of the world. Looking like our universities with different departments, they say all our books, the books of our lives, are there and make it possible to tap into our beginning lives and the whole cosmic knowledge." And it is not just adults who report these libraries, but children as well. "What I am seeing now is that we can tap into any knowledge we please.

What was previously given to only a few individuals is now available to everyone who seeks it," Modi said. She discovered what Ingo Swann and others worldwide have discovered as well.

Why do we choose the families that we do? How do we select the time and place of our births? Why do we come back at all? I asked Modi to summarize the descriptions given by her patient population that would address these questions. "We come back again and again because we need to evolve and grow," she answered. "No one described a violent God. Everyone described his beingness as peace, love, and mercy with no negative feelings. They described God as being one huge ball of light and in that light of consciousness there were small balls of light of different sizes and powers. And God created us so that we all get a chance to grow. We choose our parents, husbands, wives, other people, and gifts we will bring. We choose the time, the exact time, of the birth because that has a great deal of impact on our way of being. We choose even the time of our death and how we are going to die."

According to Dr. Modi's research, not only do we choose our parents and time of birth and death, but we also choose groups of people with whom to reincarnate. Her patients recount that there are groups in heaven that have been working together from the beginning of time and the main goal is the evolvement of humanity and beings of other planets as well. There are smaller groups who incarnate together over and over, like families, and there are scientific groups and spiritual groups who have specific talents for specific purposes. Some of these souls may be incarnate and others in spirit form. Of the ones on Earth, they may be placed all over the world and never meet. I have often felt this closeness to people I interview and to each of the people whose work is profiled in this book; I believe that we are a group of souls who have worked together over many incarnations to elevate humanity.

FUTURE INCARNATIONS

So where do we go when we die and how do we prepare for our next incarnation? Michael Newton, Ph.D., has made a specialty of examining the time/space between lives. He holds a doctorate in counseling psychology, is a certified master hypnotherapist, and is a member of the American Counseling Association. His clients' testimony suggests that it is possible to review our life between lives, recall it, make use of the information, and be positively changed by the memory. In the accounts he offers up there are numerous descriptions of our souls being light bodies, which is similar to the teachings of Judaic Kabbalah and numerous traditions worldwide throughout time.

It seems that the Eastern and Western or perennial wisdom teachings are becoming more and more validated. Memory is not stored inside our minds, but all around us; making our past lives and future lives a product of everyone's soul awareness. We grow as a group, whether we want to or not. We are not just our brother's and sister's keepers, we are our brothers and our sisters and they are us. While differentiated, we form a union that exists inherently in life.

In his book *Journey of Souls: Case Studies of Life between Lives,* Newton explains that he began his clinical practice as a traditional psychotherapist working for many years, like Dr. Modi, with hypnotherapy to uncover childhood trauma issues. "Occasionally," he explained, "someone would call and ask if I would do past-life regression. Of course, it wasn't the sort of thing I did or was interested in. But a man came to me for a problem and through hypnotherapy he took me to the source of his pain and we were back on the battlefields of World War I. With that, I realized that this was something I should look at more closely. It was a long time, though, before I came to find a client who could take me into the spiritual world. This was new ground and for years I didn't discuss this work with my colleagues. I just kept deep records and journals and notes. And I was a skeptic. But the underlying thing of all of it was the consistency of the reports. That is what got me."

Newton explained that it took many years to learn how to guide someone into the spirit world. "Clients need to be able to go very deeply. They can detail the act of crossing over, tell you who comes to meet them, what stations they went to, what kinds of souls they have in their soul groups, what kind of superior guides they meet, and with whom they review their life. Regardless of whether they were religious or not during life, what happens when we first enter the spirit realms is that the average client feels a tremendous release. It is suddenly like they are set free and allowed to go home. They are going home, mentally, to our permanent home. Earth is a temporary home and our bodies are temporary stations. Some clients don't want to return to their present lives after their exposure to the afterlife is felt."

He corrected a common misperception that the afterlife is a place of punishment. "Many people have the view that they will come back to the spirit world and be punished or reprimanded or denigrated and as far as I can tell it never happens. Instead we review our life with the guidance of others who encourage our further development. We actively role-play with our soul mates and soul companions. We have loosely bonded partners who, between lives, see if we could have done better with the same bodies, et cetera, and in this way there is an afterlife school of groups."

The clustering of humans, or group reincarnations, was categorized in three different ways according to Newton's findings. Primary soul mates are those to whom we have been bonded for many, many lives. They will not always be a spouse, but maybe a friend or a sister or brother. Some people have even reported meeting similar souls in meditation in the immaterial realm, yet never meeting on Earth. We are associated with another category called *companion souls* on very different levels. And then there are affiliated groups, which are made up of primary soul mates, our primary soul groups, and our affiliated soul groups. It makes for a tremendously large cluster that enables all sorts of dynamics in our lives. Just because souls are in the same group does not mean to say that they are all alike.

"Yes, we were all brought together," Newton explained, "and no new souls are added to our groups, but the souls in our group are very different. You have brave souls, souls that are quiet, risk takers, souls that are analytics, and so forth. Often I am asked whether, if we are connected to all these souls, but if we do not have a close relationship with a primary soul mate, will we have an unfulfilled life? Many people want to know why they are not close [in this lifetime] to that closely bonded soul mate.

. . . There may be a very good reason why a soul is intended to be with others and not a primary soul mate. I recently had a case of woman who had a past life in the South in the last century where she had a sixty-year, closely bonded marriage with her soul mate. They had a cyclic life experience. They were given a relaxing life after very difficult ones. Now they are back in lives that are difficult, and the reason they are not together is that they leaned too much on each other and needed to learn more independence."

A separate category altogether is one of the guide. Newton learned that guides are assigned to us for our mortal makeup. "They are often assigned to us to help us cultivate new traits and strengths," he said. "Some of my clients who have re-created near-death experiences in the office go on to detail what would have happened had they not come back to life. They can also describe who this shadow figure or guide or guides are that they are affiliated with. . . . They learned early on that our guides are our intermediaries in the spiritual world. They are loving and wise beings who have been assigned to us to help us through the long trials of incarnation and, ultimately, when we no longer have to reincarnate." Often when his patients first realize they are with their guide they will start crying or laughing joyfully. "It is very emotional," he says. "It's a very profound moment because these teachers have been with them from the very beginning."

One of the important tasks of these guides is to help us in our learning between lives and in our career choices later, which seems to be a key part of the between-life cycle. In other words, we prepare ourselves for the next incarnation. One of the activities described by Newton's clients as an afterlife process was a training in the supernal realms: learning how to manifest plant life or small suns or looking at protoplasm inserted with energy. They were working with the molding energy and called them the creation classes. "What became clear," Newton said, "is that not every human was at the same level of capacity or had the same talents. Some might be better working with children or exploring new worlds. . . . People were pointing to an endless cycle of preparing before life for incarnation. During life, while living present to each moment, we are also preparing for death and union in the afterlife, and then preparing once again to reincarnate."

THE IMMORTAL HUMAN SPACE AGE

The researchers in this chapter are attempting to show through human testimony, or anecdotal case studies, that the soul doesn't die with the physical body and consciousness exists outside the physical body. As Rabbi Simon Jacobson, founder of the Meaningful Life Center in New York City, said during one of our many discussions, "It seems as though the universe insists that the soul reincarnates and the soul is happy to do so as it gives it more completion and reflection" of divine perfection. Or as Gregg Braden, author of *The Isaiah Effect: Decoding the Lost Science of Prayer and Prophecy,* said during an interview, "When we are in our bodies, we are in the temple, in a place of worship where something miraculous is going on. We are not biological machines. We are, rather, shimmering particles of energy embedded in a constant flux of patterns of energy. . . . When outside the constraints of our body, time and space have no meaning."

Physicist Frank Tipler, Ph.D, author of the *The Physics of Immortality: Modern Cosmology, God, and the Resurrection of the Dead,* told me that he began his research as an atheist, or at least an agnostic, but found after studying quantum physics that he realized human beings are immortal and that our bodies will resurrect "at the end of time." This is a professor of mathematical physics at Tulane University who says that resurrection is inevitable, though what kind of bodies we may have is up for discussion. Maybe they will be our eternal light bodies we will cocreate with conscious intention.

The afterlife experience and the recollection of it is part of our treasure house of being. From it we learn that what we do in this life is important not just to the now, but forever. Everything we think, say, and do ripples out into the world and becomes the world. In this, we are the creators of the world outside ourselves, as much as we are discoverers of the world within ourselves. We are the archaeologists of our own souls and the space explorers of our shared human destiny. When our bodies are cast off of the Earth for circulation as carbon molecules, imagine that we are each, then, used by the stars for their own formation. From atom to star, from Adam and Eve to creator source, we find out that we and the cosmos are one. We are light in varying states of vibration, composed of the light of creative force, which like breath sustains beingness in its potential. As we travel to our inner space and take our bodies into outer space, will we take the best of our capacities as immortal, human, god-like beings? Are we asking ourselves all the right questions? Who are we? How do we relate to other travelers of the stars? What is our intention as we move off planet to become conscious co-creators and sustainers of the universe?

10

TRAVELING OFF PLANET

I was born in 1954, born into the space age. Growing up with rockets and spacemen was as much a part of our culture as science fiction stories about Mars and Venus. We even dressed up as Martians one year as part of our school's annual May Day festivities. We had hula hoops sewn into circular red fabric, with a hole for our heads on which we wore antennae made of pipe cleaners covered in tinfoil. It was a delicious combination of scientific development and imaginative wonder. Over the past few decades, however, the question of extraterrestrial intelligence has been both open and veiled: an amalgamation of propaganda and commercial enterprise with fact-finding revelations about contact with other types of humanoid beings.

One of the most fascinating and comprehensive overviews of this subject that I've seen, a virtual who's who of research on the subject of UFOs, is *The Encyclopedia of Extraterrestrial Encounters: A Definitive, Illustrated, A–Z Guide to All Things Alien* edited by Ronald D. Story. Not only does this compendium detail the variety of crafts witnessed, such as cigar-shaped craft, dome-shaped craft, and boomerang-shaped craft, but also the various types of alien species reported; blonde, Nordic types that are over 7 feet tall; humanoid-looking types called hybrids, a cross between humans and greys; greys, which are small with big eyes and long thin limbs; reptiloids or reptilians, which are large scaly beings; and insectlike species and others. In addition, Story frames thought-provoking questions like the relationship between science fiction, politics, religion, science, and technology and much more.

It is with deep love for the future of our planet and humanity that the last chapter of this book looks candidly at off-planet civilizations (OPC) and space travel. I believe that the way in which we address our intergalactic existence will determine the degree to which Earth life will flourish or diminish for centuries to come. While the government of the United States continues to shroud the subject in secrecy and denial, the civilian public has relentlessly investigated these phenomena enough to demonstrate, beyond the shadow of a doubt to me, that we are both contacting and being contacted by other life intelligences. One fascinating account that involved U.S. military intelligence in the United Kingdom is *Left at East Gate: A First-Hand Account of the Rendlesham Forest UFO Incident, Its Cover-up and Investigation*, authored by Larry Warren and Peter Robbins. Many South American countries, the nation of France, the former Soviet Republics, China, and others are very candid about their numerous sightings and reports of abductions, contacts, and what humans are being told about these visitations and bodily experiments reportedly taking place on board alien craft where humans are temporarily held captive. Among the many common themes reported worldwide is that certain families have been tracked for generations for both genetic and environmental reasons, as have sentient animals like cattle whose tissue is sampled to determine the degree to which Earth's support system has been destroyed. They seem to have a particular interest in nuclear plants, which they have been able to shut down, and nuclear radiation on Earth. The contacts may be coming from life-forms from off-planet civilizations or they may be some sort of multidimensional reality or both. That we on Earth are having telepathic and physical engagement including informative conversations with these aliens is quite clear. It's no longer science fiction and perhaps it never was if we use ancient accounts as a historical record.

As we venture into outer space, what values and intentions do we take with us? As with any relationship, how it begins has a lot of effect on what it will become and now is the time to ask these questions. Have there been other civilizations who have already taken these evolving journeys in their own development? What evidence is there for life on other planets? Might life on Earth reflect some type of hybridization that took place long ago between our own species and others?

ARE WE FROM THE STARS?

A theory gaining more support in this country since the mid-1970s has taken on even more new life with the breakthroughs in genetic engineering of the late 1990s. This theory is known as the ancient astronaut theory and it was originally popularized by Charles H. Fort (1874–1932) and Erich von Däniken among others. It posits that ancient astronauts, or "god men," came to Earth, genetically engineered our species, and then assisted in the development of human civilization. Today's findings in archaeology and off-planet exploration give humanity a better understanding of the clues left in ancient mythologies that point not only to visitations by ETs (extraterrestrials) in prehistory, but to their genetic intervention in the evolution of the Homo sapiens species or at least their interaction with us. Does this theory, if true, represent a missing link in our development?

The late Zecharia Sitchin (1920–2010), language expert and Sumerian scholar who authored thirteen books on the origins of mankind, has presented a translation of Sumerian creation texts full of tales of ETs and genetic manipulation. According to both Sitchin's translations and our numerous radio discussions on the subject, a space-voyaging civilization called the Anunnaki came to Earth in order to extract gold several hundred thousand years ago. Their own crewmen mutinied and the leaders, Enki and Enlil, embarked upon a genetic engineering task to make a humanoid that could mine for gold using the Homo erectus inhabitants native to Earth for this purpose.

The books that Sitchin wrote after 1976 further elaborate upon and detail this subject. One of these books is *The Lost Book of Enki: Memoirs and Prophecies of an Extraterrestrial God*. Against the specter of today's experiments in genetic engineering, robotics, and artificial intelligence, this author's work begs the question, is our future already a part of the past? In one of our shared broadcasts, Sitchin theorized that modern science is retracing steps taken millennia ago. For example, he says that Sumerian records show that the Anunnaki—knowing that Mars had lakes, oceans, and atmosphere—used the planet as a way station, a purpose we may use it for in the future.

The Sumerian story, if true, could be interpreted as a genetic engineering of *Homo erectus.* Sitchin says, "there was not one single once-and-for-all genetic engineering. . . . Throughout the centuries there was a continuous mixing of the genes." I have often wondered what a study of our blood types might reveal about some sort of progressive genetic enhancement. Perhaps over the centuries there has been a deliberate alteration of our physiological traits, which modern abductions are a part of.

Author of *The Aliens and the Scalpel,* Roger Leir, D.P.M., is a podiatrist delving into an examination of the alleged implants that various UFO abductees report as having been inserted into their bodies, just under the skin. He has also made a study of the so-called millennial children whose traits he says show evidence of some sort of evolutionary development. As one example, it has been observed that human babies are sitting up and crawling at earlier ages and showing a marked change in the speed of their development. Others have noted the numerous children who have developed extrasensory talents, giving rise to popular television shows about psychic kids or genius children who make enormous contributions to the world of science while still quite young. It's easier today than even ten years ago to discuss this subject, although considering human beings as ancient hybrids really upsets status quo thinking both in science and religion. But what if some human beings are, in part, the laboratory adaptation of another civilization of humanoids or other space beings? This does not discount the creation stories of the Blessed Creator, but it does raise the specter of genetic tampering along the way, at least to some parts of the human race.

To me, this possibility is important to consider, especially as we embark on such an odyssey ourselves with our genetic scientists altering our seed bank, attempting to alter disease patterns in humans, and hoping to produce people with specific attributes. As a race we are already capable of manufacturing the manner by which the life force can express itself in newly created ways, like the glow-in-the-dark bunny rabbit specially "designed" and commissioned by an artist in France. (Geneticists took matter from a fluorescent jellyfish and mixed it with the DNA of a rabbit.)

Speaking of ancient advanced civilizations, the conversations on the *Zoh Show, Future Talk,* and *21st Century Radio* inevitably turn to life on Mars, where the evidence of a prior civilization appears widespread. One year before NASA trumpeted the find of evidence of life there—on July 11, 1995, I broke the story on carbonaceous meteorites from Mars with Vince DiPietro, for whom the D&M Pyramid on Mars is named (the *M* stands for his codiscoverer, Greg Molenaar). Both have been guests of mine well over a dozen times discussing this and other evidence of life on Mars. The Cydonian hypothesis advanced by DiPietro, Molenaar, and John Brandenburg, Ph.D., a plasma physicist, in 1979, states that Mars was once a home to a great civilization. The hypothesis is based on the careful examination of Viking photos of the surface of Mars, particularly the region called Cydonia.

The fact is that we have known for decades there was life on Mars, due to the evidence that water exists there now and Martian meteorites show evidence of life-forms. Recent identification of the ability of meteorites to carry life-forms throughout the galaxy (panspermia) without getting so hot in their interior that any life would perish has been added to the discoveries that bacteria have lived for millions of years in salt crystals and at the hottest center of the Earth. This evidence collectively confronts us with the reality that life can flourish in ways we don't fully appreciate. It also confirms that cosmic waters are an integral part of our water cycle on Earth, which Rudolph Steiner, Christopher Bird, Terry Ross, and William Marks Waterway promote.

As a broadcaster I feel obligated to address the cover-up of information about life on Mars that continues to this day. Just as we have seen how the suppression of cold fusion has inhibited our departure from the carbon-based fossil fuel empire, and that the suppression of our biomind superpowers affects our evolution, the interference with our practical understanding of prior civilizations in our solar system and beyond does as well. We are not alone—and we need to accept that fact. It's been the topic of science fiction for decades, but now there is proof of the existence of water and life-forms and, as I and many others believe, evidence of a prior humanoid-like civilization apparent on the surface of Mars, where artifacts resembling a face and pyramids mirror structures on Earth. Nikola Tesla (1856–1943), a Serbian-American electrical engineer, mechanical engineer, physicist, futurist, and arguably the greatest inventor of the twentieth century, claimed that his knowledge came in part from Martians. Of course he was ridiculed, but now it is easier to appreciate this possible reality that he was pointing to.

Why is this space-related information kept from the public, or sensationalized and denied? For what reason is the entire UFO and alien contact issue kept in the ridicule corner or entertainment sector of our society when, throughout human history, human cultures through their stories, paintings, and sacred precepts and rituals have pointed to an ongoing collaboration with off-planet intelligence as part of our own survival and evolution? Why would our own space program deliberately mislead the public about evidence like the face and pyramid on Mars when these Martian geological artifacts show that we on Earth are not alone in our solar system and never have been? Is it in the end an issue of control—control of the human population by the current power structure of government in the United States, which funds and promotes a lot of false science?

THOMAS VAN FLANDERN AND THE MARS ENIGMAS

In celebration of the launching of Atlantis on September 8, 2000, on its way to help prepare the permanent International Space Station for its future occupants, I called on astronomer Thomas Van Flandern, Ph.D., to review the issue of potential extraterrestrial civilizations. Given that we are now a space-voyaging society with colonization in the works, I thought the occasion a good time to address the question of whether there is, or has been, life on other planets. Of greatest significance when considering extraterrestrial ruins, which the monuments on Mars are conjectured to be, is what happened to the civilizations that built them? Was a catastrophe part of their planetary history? Could we learn something about our own problems on this planet by examining theirs?

Thomas Van Flandern is a world-renowned astronomer and author of *Dark Matter, Missing Planets, and New Comets: Paradoxes Resolved, Origins Illuminated*. He has been a consultant to the Jet Propulsion Laboratory (JPL) and is a former director of the Celestial Mechanics Branch of the Nautical Almanac Office of the U.S. Naval Observatory. On that historical day in 2000 when the Atlantis was launched, he addressed the serious consequences of scientific manipulation of data concerning images from the surface of Mars. "Discovering evidence of life on other planets is supposed to be one of the top priorities of our space program," Van Flandern began, "but for some reason, those in control of the data collected on the most recent Mars missions are deliberately preventing the scientific community from seeing the best. The last time we sent cameras to Mars in the late 1970s, certain areas like the Cydonia region appeared to contain evidence of a prior civilization on Mars. And yet, over two decades [now three] later when we finally send new cameras, getting new photos of this region was almost impossible and the photos that were eventually released suffered from deliberate tampering."

He went on to explain the difference between the two organizations at fault for this debacle: the JPL and NASA. "The Jet Propulsion Laboratory is an independent contractor for NASA that is owned and operated by the California Institute of Technology. JPL and NASA had some disputes over some important issues with regard to the Mars missions. NASA takes the credit when things go right and tends to get the blame when they go wrong," he added with a chuckle, suggesting familiarity with the issue and the players. Referring to the resistance faced by independent scientists like himself interested in updated photos of the Martian anomalies he asserted that, "The problems, I think, can be attributed directly to the Jet Propulsion Laboratory rather than to NASA itself. The JPL was asked to get additional photographs and, at first, refused. When 'bribed' with money and personnel, they took some pictures and then disclaimed them on the grounds that they were a waste of public funds and a slap at the integrity of the scientists."

There are hundreds of scientists in this country requesting access to data that is garnered from these publicly financed space missions. I asked Van Flandern to give us a few examples of how JPL and those who work for them have, according to some researchers, been involved in scientific fraud. "I would personally stop short of using a word like fraud," he said. "Let's just explain what happened with the picture that they released to the press. The Society for Planetary SETI Research (SPSR) is a group of independent scientists who have donated some of their professional time to research the issue of anomalies on Mars and the possibility of artifacts, such as the famous face on Mars. In the fall of 1997 they approached NASA with enough evidence to justify giving priority to taking high-resolution pictures of the Cydonia region of Mars. NASA agreed, offered to do that, and asked the Jet Propulsion Laboratory to get these pictures. After the aforementioned incident where they first refused, they finally took the first of those pictures on April 5, 1998. In a press conference on the afternoon that the pictures were released, instead of releasing the actual image that came down from the spacecraft, the JPL Public Information Office released one that had been passed through a high-pass filter.

"The purpose of a high-pass filter is to suppress detail in an image. It is used, ordinarily, only with line art or [when] you need to sharpen up borders or something that is in black and white, but not gray scale. We know of no appropriate reason for its use in connection with this image, but it is documented on their website that that is, indeed, how they obtained the image that they released to the press. Many people in the world saw *only* that image and everyone looking at that image would agree that it doesn't show much more than a pile of rocks or anything that someone could imagine was artificial." This means that a public contractor deliberately tampered with scientific evidence.

So what would the image have looked like had they not purposefully filtered it? Van Flandern and several others set to work to find out. "The unfiltered image," he explained, "gives a very different impression. Now that we have been able to bring advanced computer processing techniques to bear on it, to reconstruct the view as it would have been if it had been photographed from overhead and with proper lighting, we see that the actual object looks remarkably like a humanoid face. There are some things about it that have enabled us to prove that, indeed, they are artificial rather than of natural origin."

These were compelling statements, all right, but I wanted more proof. What evidence does a scientist look for to support the possibility of a prior civilization on Mars? Van Flandern explained how they set out to test the Cydonian hypothesis. "It's important to realize," he said, "that if you just look at something and it looks very much like a face, that is not proof. There are things that look like faces in clouds, mountainside profiles, and other natural settings. All kinds of regular shapes can occur. In science there is a distinction between the kind of statistics that you cannot trust and the kind that you can. The kind that you can is distinguished by making a prediction before the data is in and not altering it afterwards according to what you see."

Van Flandern explained that the baseline data for the research on this subject are the Viking I and II pictures of the 1970s. These images have been subjected to all the latest enhancement techniques that were developed over the past quarter of a century. From them, Van Flandern and others were able to make precisely defined scientific predictions of what would be seen when a camera with better resolution returned to Mars. "The Viking pictures of 1976 showed us something that looked like a face on Mars and we were impressed to see that it was an actual three-dimensional face and not a profile. [It was] not a light and shadow thing. We were impressed to see that it was symmetric [giving] the impression of a face in those low-resolution photos; an eye, a nose, and a mouth. We made a prediction then that if this was intended to be built as an artificial object there would be secondary facial features. Whereas, if it was a natural object, when seen in high resolution it would look much less like a face," he said.

Just the opposite turned out to be so. "When we got the high resolution photos," he explained, "every single secondary facial feature you would expect to see is actually present in the mesa. So there is an eyebrow over the eye socket, an iris inside the eye socket, and a symmetric eye on the

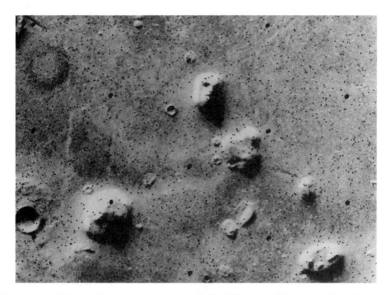

Fig. 10.1. Viking Orbiter *1 image of the "Face on Mars," taken July 25, 1976, from an altitude of 1,873 kilometers. Image courtesy of NASA/JPL.*

other side with an eyebrow. The mouth consists of parted lips, the nose has nostrils at the end tapered towards the forehead, and so on. In other words, when you look at this in high resolution there is just no question that it was actually built to portray a humanoid face. All of these additional features, the eyebrow, the irises, nostrils, and so on could surely not have arisen by chance in a natural feature when they were predicted in advance."

There's the proof I was looking for, but Van Flandern didn't stop there! "At a statistical level," he added, the chances for this formation to have occurred naturally are, "definitely at a thousand billion billion to one against chance." Sounds like winning odds to me! This is not a natural phenomenon on the surface of Mars.

But what about other regions on Mars? Is there anything other than the famous face that suggests a prior civilization? Van Flandern thinks so and has cataloged these images at his website and in the *Meta Research Bulletin,* the periodical he edits which I urge every reader to subscribe to. "Now that we have the strong evidence in one case of artifacts, we are looking at anomalies all over Mars," he said. "None of the other cases have such a compelling interpretation at that level of significance, but there are things that if any of us saw in a photograph on Earth we would immediately assume they were the product of the activity of man. We have dozens of photographs of things of that caliber on Mars that are unquestionably associated, in our minds, with intelligence. But without an on-site inspection we can't quite prove that they are artificial as opposed to accidents of nature."

He indicated that of the fifty thousand–plus images he and his colleagues have worked with, about 67 of them point to even greater evidence of organized activity on the surface of Mars. "We have seven categories of images," he told us. "There are images that if seen on this planet we would call trees, others like art of fishes [and] horses. All sorts of animals are in pictographic form. [There are] 'glass tubes' or things that could best be described in that fashion." He presented these stunning images to an astonished, but rather silent media in the summer and fall of 2001 at two press conferences in Washington, D.C., and New York City.

The impact of JPL's actions regarding the filtered face photo were far-reaching from a scientific perspective. "We face the risk that it could be another generation before we learn the truth about the matter," said Van Flandern. "Just as it's been that long since we've had astronauts fly to the moon." This serves as a grim reminder as to how the decisions of just a few men can impact billions of peoples' lives. Though the Mars Global Surveyor [MGS] continued to orbit the planet taking high-resolution photographs, in the remainder of the spacecraft's lifetime it could only photograph less than 1 percent of the total surface of Mars. "So we relied on a combination of good luck and scientific goodwill on the part of the Jet Propulsion Laboratory and the team that operates the camera to point at these interesting objects and photograph them during the remaining part of the mission. Even though other missions to Mars followed the MGS they did not have cameras capable of taking the necessary high resolution images," concluded Van Flandern.

As a space-traveling civilization, other things can impact our evolution and it seems to me that the issue of catastrophism may have been directly connected to JPL's cover-up of information about Mars. If Earth people were shown the evidence of an extraterrestrial civilization that was wiped out, perhaps by meteor storms or galactic explosions, we would have to accept this possibility as a scenario in our own future. Not a real crowd pleaser, especially for those in charge, for those who hold dominating power. If there was a filter deliberately applied to this scenario so that it wasn't clear for the world to see, one has to think that there is a reason beyond personal hubris.

It is very disconcerting to think someone, be it JPL or NASA, may not want us discussing this possibility. Could it be because it might have a destabilizing effect on Earth-based authority systems and their structures? Does the Martian hypothesis upend the dominating exploitation story on Earth? In simple terms, are there prior civilizations in our solar system that were wiped out by harsh weather and planetary changes?

As science fiction this might be entertaining to some, but as science fact it calls out the need for higher thinking and broader consideration to be brought to life's challenges worldwide. This is done most quickly by a conditioned field, as Bill Tiller proved. The more humans use their expansive and nonjudgmental awareness, the more the field is conditioned for others to access theirs. Sheldrake's morphic resonance added to Goswami's quantum action tells us that some of the greatest changes we can make in the world are in our own thinking. Imagine humanity being awake to their capacity as conscious co-creators who can see and participate anywhere in the cosmos.

Another scenario that is suppressed due to fear of public discussion and panic is the very real threat to the Earth posed by near-Earth objects (NEOs). This is a subject that Van Flandern has also been studying for years, but just in the past decade has it been deemed worthy of investigation. Only now is the space community saying, "Yes, this Van Flandern is right. Maybe we should monitor comets and things that could cause considerable damage on our planet." I wonder how long it will be before they come to appreciate his ability to refute the big bang theory.

"There is a tendency in science," Van Flandern explained, "to always prefer noncatastrophic explanations over catastrophic ones. But gradually we are learning that catastrophe is a real part of both nature and history. Scientists need to overcome that bias. For the explanation about why [JPL released the filtered picture], I am not as convinced that there is a conspiracy to keep us from knowing, as it's more of a reaction to being accused of being conspirators. That happened before these recent pictures were taken and it so angered and upset the scientists involved that I think they went into taking these pictures with the view that they were finally going to put this nonsense off the table. When the initial pictures didn't seem as though they were going to end the controversy, they let their good judgment slip away from them and released a filtered version of the picture that they hoped would kill the controversy in the media. They were very successful at doing that. I think [their motivation] was more because they were insulted by being accused of being conspirators than there was any intent to keep us from knowing."

Whatever their motivation, however, I still find their actions reprehensible, especially in light of the fact that they are beneficiaries of the public trust and the public treasury. But in addition, it is a safe assumption that everyone at NASA has also seen these powerful images suggestive of vegetation and water and glasslike tubes on Mars. JPL's effort to discourage a careful examination of the evidence is therefore hampering the evolution of our species. Humanity has important decisions to make about our shared natural resources on our home planet, and before we become a space-inhabiting society as well, we must know who we are relative to the space we now plan to inhabit off planet. Some of us wonder if, based on current power structures and economies, humanity on Earth is mature enough to inhabit space safely?

NEAR-EARTH OBJECTS

During the past decade the threat to Earth from a potential comet or meteorite impact has finally become an audible part of the dialogue in astronomical and national security communities. This is probably explained, for the most part, by the concern that a meteorite could be mistaken for a nuclear warhead and accidentally instigate a nuclear conflict. The creation of a centralized, global meteorite and space watch is becoming increasingly inevitable. Expressing frustration over the lack of aggressive thinking about NEOs, Lord Sainsbury, while he was science minister in the United Kingdom, established a panel in 1999–2000 to study the problem. This issue is not academic, it is essential and it compels us to ask fundamental questions about humanity's survival on Earth.

Looking at the arid landscape of Mars, a planet that was once rich with water and possibly cityscapes, coupled with the evidence that high civilizations on Earth have been decimated by encounters with NEOs, it would seem more appropriate to me to take a more aggressive interest in something we know could eliminate 99.9 percent of life on our planet today. We need a concentrated effort like the Manhattan Project. Only this time, instead of working together to manufacture a weapon of mass destruction, wouldn't it be nice to come together to create a project to protect Earth from an approaching meteorite or some other annihilating force?

The study of NEOs should be a fundamental issue for a planet that is, literally, hurtling through space. One currently accepted theory of what led to the extinction of the dinosaurs puts the blame on a meteorite impact in Mexico. Other planetwide extinctions are also well known and blamed on NEOs. A meteorite no larger than three to seven miles across struck the Earth 250 million years ago, eliminating 90 percent of all marine species and 70 percent of land vertebrates. According to a research team led by Luann Becker of the University of Washington in Seattle, the extinction continued over 8,000 to 100,000 years. Could it happen to us?

EARTH IN SPACE

William Burrows, a writer on the subject of space exploration and author of *The Infinite Journey: Eyewitness Accounts of NASA and the Age of Space,* expressed my own concerns when he stated on my radio show that our survival depends on our ability to move into outer space if need be. He presented a checklist of possible factors that could make life on Earth nearly or completely uninhabitable: nuclear war, nuclear accident, meteorite strikes, weather changes, plagues, and chemical and biological terrorism. "There may come a time," he said, "when our hope for survival will be to live elsewhere—on Mars or the moon." While it may be difficult for all of us to imagine this scenario when we don't even have a decent train system operating in America, technological advances are on a very steep curve as Moravec pointed out earlier in this book (see chapter 7) and that astronaut Joe Allen can show is so just during his own life span. If the advances in space travel are any indication of our rapid advancement in technology, asking the right questions, as we learned from dowser Terry Ross, is essential.

Joseph P. Allen, Ph.D., is a NASA astronaut featured in Burrows' book *Infinite Journey*. Allen served with NASA as an astronaut, flying once aboard *Columbia* and once aboard *Discovery*. Before that he was a mission controller for three Apollo and Space Shuttle flights and was also the director of astronaut training in the early 1980s. Upon leaving NASA, he served as director and chairman of the board of Veridian, a company dedicated to intelligence, surveillance and reconnaissance, and systems engineering services, until his retirement in 2004. He joined me to speak about the generation of children who have grown up with space travel, noting the critical juncture in time that we find ourselves at right now. Remarking that in his own lifetime he went from living in a small town with a party line phone to being the astronaut in charge of communication with the Apollo 7 crew while in orbit, he said, "The speed of change is only increasing exponentially. Human beings like to build things. We are good at making things and solving problems. I have a lot of faith in us, that we can do it right and in the right way."

Paula Berinstein interviewed dozens of leaders of the private space venture sector and concluded that the current general direction in private space ventures is modeled very much on the current economic model of ownership, extraction, and property rights. She joined me to review her book, *Making Space Happen: Private Space Ventures and the Visionaries behind Them* and revealed that the primary arguments made for space development are economic. In other words, it will be good business for Earth beings. It will be wonderful for tourism. Entrepreneurs are the ones pushing the envelope, and they are forming organizations to explore developing habitats on the moon, Mars, and elsewhere. "They're asking questions about the rights of individuals, corporations, or even nations to claim entitlement to an asteroid, a portion of the moon, or any other space body near or far."

It is disconcerting to me to see this model exported off planet, as it has led to unethical competition, division, war on Earth, and increasing scarcity of resources, suggesting a similar outcome elsewhere. Some of the visionaries Berinstein wrote about are on the same track apparently. There are vocal proponents of the Antarctica model, which would mean we treat space much like we do the continent of Antarctica—shared between the nations, a universal commons. Perhaps making space a shared and cogoverned resource will be the eventual direction in which we go. Many who argue for vigorous off-planet development say that, most importantly, it may just save humanity from extinction sometime in the future.

The practicality of becoming a space-traveling race presents a list of refreshing challenges. Not the least of these are air supply, sustainable resources at the host planet, the development of requisite technology and the financial resources to develop it, and the impacts of living in space on the human biosystem, some of which we have been studying already. All of these can be mastered as long as we attend to them with an ethical vision. This brings us to the complex issue of the militarization of space, or as one visionary—Carol Rosin—prefers to identify the problem: the weaponization of space.

In an attempt to forge a peace-in-space-based paradigm, Rosin created her "space development initiative" in contrast to the other SDI, the strategic defense initiative, which is all about putting weapons in space. Her work began with a children's letter-writing campaign to world leaders in 1976 describing what they thought it would be like to live in space. Although not opposed to military uses of space for monitoring activities or communications, Rosin believes the development of space should not begin another arms race and began looking for ways to reorient this approach into a peace-in-space-based agenda.

In 2003 she described for us how she was first introduced to the idea by one of the world's foremost rocket engineers and a leading authority on space travel, Werner von Braun (1912–1977). In their conversation, which took place shortly before his death, he told her to work on preventing the weaponization of space because, as she says, "von Braun really saw the capacity of space technology for information services. He believed space could provide for protecting human and other animal species in preserving our environment, making it cleaner and safer. But he also saw, having worked in the Hitlerian war machine, that the direction being taken was always in the war industry to get the high ground, in this case space superiority."

At the time of our interview, Congressman Dennis Kucinich of Ohio, co-chair then of the U.S. House of Representatives Aviation and Space Caucus, was planning to introduce a Space Preservation Act that would create a global agreement to monitor space activities and ban weapons from space. Rosin believed that this initiative "would not interfere with our thousands of satellites and the things we're already doing, but it would assure that the future research and development, and our entire way of viewing space, would be based on the positive, life-supporting efforts the entire world could benefit by."

Rosin made clear that she was not anti-corporation or anti-profit or even opposing the militarization (which is not the same as weaponization) of space—in fact, she said, "We are like an aikido [master] here. We are going in another direction, in a nonconfrontational, beneficial way. [Our plan] will stimulate the economy and create a new security system. We have outlined a new space-age paradigm to get us out of this Earth bound one. It doesn't work. We know we are all in great danger. . . . What we see [already] as we evolve off of the planet is that for instance the satellites we already have in space can assist in enhancing communication between all the nations of the world. We are talking about a vision in outer space that will bring real peace and economic stimulation, more than any hot or cold war time, including for those in the 'industrial-military-university-lab-intelligence complex.' We have to shift consciousness. We have to decide that exploitation is not acceptable. Instead what is acceptable is going right for the new paradigm available to us.

"What we are seeing now is that we are at a critical point of decision making. We aren't going to be able to stop wars by calling for a stop to them. . . . What we are going to be able to do is to show what a positive vision is." Rosin wants nothing less than a world treaty that establishes the premise of peace in space before weaponization occurs.

She is not alone in her thinking that our only option to preserve Earth is to move into space peacefully. I have spoken to many so-called contactees during my decades on the air and while many listeners still prefer to believe this to be the stuff of science fiction, for me and countless others who have attended to it with unbiased consideration, it is a story of our reality. In 2003 I interviewed Phillip Krapf, a twenty-five-year veteran reporter of the *Los Angeles Times,* who braved the general mainstream ridicule of his story when he published his accounts of personal contact with a space-voyaging civilization called the Verdants. In his book *The Challenge of Contact: A Mainstream Journalist's Report on Interplanetary Diplomacy,* he makes it clear from the perspective of the "Intergalactic Federation" that weapons are not allowed in space. "I know it's strange," he admits, "but I also know what I experienced." This statement echoes the sentiments of thousands of conscious contactees and abductees around the planet including children worldwide, who report meeting unusual aliens whom through their eyes communicate the danger that Earth's environment is in.

As both Krapf and Rosin made clear, each with their individual desire for peace on Earth and Earth's initiation into our next phase of beingness in the universe, we are at a critical juncture in our evolution. We are conscious of our inventive talents and more capable technologically to manifest them. Will we choose selfless service to each other and the cosmos, or will we continue to be controlled by destructive forces both within ourselves and around us? Will we replace the death economy with a life economy that values the enhancement of life?

UFOS ARE REAL

Although the practical businessmen in NASA may not like to talk about it, UFOs are real, they are here, and they have been all along. I have interviewed a wonderful global community of individuals from the military, scientific sector, and lay public over the past quarter century and feel confident in reporting to you that something enormously significant is going on. The two biggest developments impacting our future now are that human beings are interacting with other forms of intelligence and our own self-realization of who we are may be the greatest of all the wild cards. When we manifest our innate divine potential, what will it mean for humanity? And what will it mean for the rest of the universe of intelligent life?

As we venture off planet, what kind of aptitudes and intentions do we take with us? What kind of humanity from planet Earth will the galactic communities meet? That we are journeying forth is a fact. Perhaps space exploration will deepen our awareness of the universe and our connection to systems larger than our own. Some suggest that our spiritual tendencies will unfold with the journey of space travel and that as we venture into the cosmos the cosmic aspect of ourselves will be better understood. It is a hopeful way to look at our space exploration.

HYBRIDIZATION

Some researchers theorize that the interactions between humans and off-planet civilizations are intended to save the endangered species of human beings on Earth. Are we not doing the same for other life-forms on Earth today? Who is to say that there is not already an on- or off-planet project by other space voyaging civilizations working to preserve the human gene bank or to make use of it for other purposes? Is it really likely that the thousands of people all over the Earth who are reporting alien abductions and alien hybridization programs are perhaps lying, delusional, or part of a disinformation effort? And how many thousands more are too afraid to speak of their experiences for fear of ridicule or worse: imprisonment in psychiatric wards (as has occurred in the past).

Possible reasons for a hybridization or breeding program may be to continue another species or our own. Or maybe hybridization is necessary for us to become space-living beings in physical bodies in the coming centuries? Perhaps it is the natural progression toward a time that many traditions say will be one of a thousand years of peace and

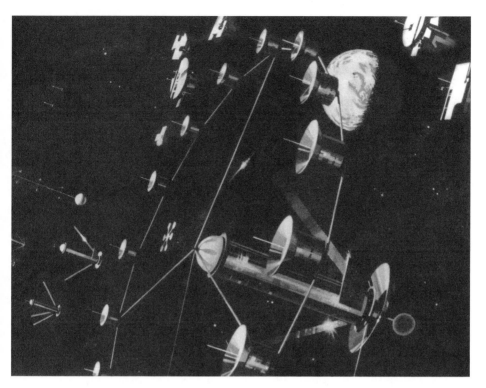

Fig. 10.2. Future space colony. Image courtesy of NASA.

bounty on Earth before we begin our journey back to our immaterial natures. Perhaps one day we will have no need of physical bodies at all, as Hans Moravec said in chapter 7, and as the Kabbalistic tradition and the teachings of other sacred societies assert. Our immortal consciousness will be our natural state without the need to incarnate. Our consciousness will operate the Earth—our planet itself being a spaceship on which we exist and travel in the universe.

As we explore all of these questions and the likelihood of these future scenarios, it is worth considering that we may be the last of the human purebreds from a particular epoch of humankind. For the truth is, if we ourselves are embarking on genetic engineering and interbreeding with other host carriers, we become no longer purebred. What we sometimes call the "preservation" of an endangered or extinct species is done by inserting their DNA into a substitute host animal. This is the creation of a new species because, although we may be saving genetic material for the gene pool, we are engineering not the birth of purebreds, but hybrids.

Maybe there is a cosmic cycle of evolution, revealing our natural role in a space-voyaging community of intelligent life in the universe. Perhaps we are an example of a humanoid civilization coming to terms with their scientific prowess, ethical makeup, and spiritual origins. The question of how a civilization flourishes or perishes is always both personal and collective at the same time. There is personal, natural, and cosmic selection.

The Future of Human Experience has demonstrated that we are multidimensional beings. Evolution is a cyclic process—not linear like we used to think. We are now becoming a space-voyaging civilization whose home planet is experiencing greater and greater bodily duress. Perhaps we are being shown aspects of our own past (or an off-planet civilization's past, as on Mars) in order to inform us of the significance of the choices we are now making on Earth. We are divine beings whose minds and souls are far more than localized phenomena in a single body. In fact, whether we are Earth beings or from some other planet, it does not change the fact that consciousness is universal and perennial. It operates through patterns and is capable of creating and reflecting the perfect model of love and unity on Earth and in the cosmos.

Perhaps Earth is the place where souls are given the opportunity to individualize their wills—already having a model of perfection in their being—which is reflected in our minds and souls. We are "human becomings," an expression I first heard from mime artist and Kabbalist Samuel Avital decades ago. Each and every step we take together toward unity precipitates the conditions for paradise! May it be our blessing and merit to be a part of this eventuality. We are changing and will be compelled to continue doing so as a result of collective and personal transformation. With divine grace and by our efforts and awareness may we effectively deal with any environmental or extraplanetary events beyond our control. What is clear from global disasters in general is that people help people worldwide. This is our nature, to help each other.

This reality of dependant co-arising should be the basis of business

Fig. 10.3. International Space Station. Image courtesy of NASA.

and government: to prosper the world and to declare the workings of a life economy whose goals are to manifest a more just and sustainable Earth. Hopefully, it will be the foundation of our hearts and minds, our conscious will, as we work together to preserve our home planet and as we venture off Earth as well.

Let us ask ourselves: What talents will we cultivate among ourselves? What powers in each person will be nurtured? What values will we hold as sacred and precious, and what values will we use to guide our actions collectively? What kind of space-voyaging society will we become? What kind of humanity are we capable of becoming and being together, now and in the future?

CREATING THE GOOD EARTH SOCIETY NOW!

So what, then, is the future going to be like? If the future holds the potential of paradise, the archetype which gives Earth a meaningful pattern for humanity, how do we create and experience this state of being? Just how does one go about creating the Good Earth Society now, or at the very least sustaining the Earth and all that lives here? From inner space to outer space, the medium that connects our will with that of the universe or Creator is through our consciousness and through our selflessness toward others, which springs from a natural state of reverence.

It should be obvious by now that how we envision the future has a great deal to do with what the future will be like. By the sheer act of focusing our attention and asking appropriate, intentional questions we will be given descriptive scenarios and possible outcomes. All traditions remind us that any change made by any one of us at any moment in time, indeed, changes the entire universe.

Imagine seeing a cloud of dust particles in a sunlit window floating in the air. Blow a puff of air on them and there is a tremendous reshaping of their pattern. In the same way, when any of us use our free will to choose to do or not do something, we affect the entire world of atoms that we are all a part of.

Our consciousness reveals that wisdom can be cultivated through the use of interpretive arts. Consciousness is integrated through patterns. The relationships between our individual lives and the world demonstrate the interconnectedness between us all in the manifest realm. This interconnectedness is demonstrated in the ancient systems of the I Ching, Kabbalah's Tree of Life, or astrology as easily as it is in the more modern models dealing with harmonic ratios and GPS coordinates. Ask the universe a question and it will answer in a natural design. Pray to the universal creative presence and praise the great beauty or power of light, and that light comes back through events, ideas, insight, grace, and miracles. Just like when we see the smaller matter of dust stirred by a breath in the sunlight, prayer affects the universe. Like shouting into a cave, our words and deeds echo back.

In the same way that our thoughts and actions make an impact, our consciousness is in the driver's seat of the manifest world. With the divine blueprint present in our body, mind, and soul and our mindful recollection of who we are as divine reflectors, we are able to draw from the historic past while also pulling to us an ethical and elevated future. Consciousness is the translator of the spirit or light waves that are expanding and contracting all of the time. With the ability of consciousness to connect with absolutely anything, anywhere in the universe, it seems we use the same talents, the same capacities, the same innate skills whether we are looking for our lost car keys or a lost sense of balance or perspective.

It seems too easy to think the universe operates in such a simplistic fashion, but in my opinion it is indeed that simple. It has taken a whole book to show, from all different fields and perspectives, that what we think has a whole lot to do with what will be or, put another way, what we see in the imaginal realm, in our mind's eye, will be more able to manifest if we have nurtured it first within ourselves. The difficulty and the blessing for the human race lie in our possession of free will. We have not just the right, but the obligation to choose what to do and how to do it, where and when to do it, whatever *it* is. We are constantly challenged to overcome our selfish natures for choices reflecting the higher good of all, born of love and a desire for unity. The future can be brought to a state of union only through our own desire to achieve it, our own burning passion to manifest it within ourselves and in the world. Our own peace within will generate a world peace without.

How can I be so optimistic for a peaceful world future and at the same time acknowledge the cyclic nature of planetary catastrophe as an undeniable wild card that we necessarily should be preparing for? I see it as a part of the whole: catastrophe reminds us that there is a divine force that runs an immaculate universe. Sometimes cleaning up the shop is necessary for new and more conscious life to recreate itself. We experience catastrophe and paradise within ourselves, and we hold the capacity for the annihilation of self and world together with the existence of a balanced state of the world, which is our full potential. As we have seen, catastrophe is the end of a material cycle. This is also the story of individual life and its eventual triumph in holiness and immortality.

Every minute of every day, we are asked, each one of us, to go about transforming the ego of materialism away from a selfish orientation to an open state of awareness of all. We are asked to create the conditions for a world within and without that enables the natural state of unity and harmony to unfold. If we look at the cyclical nature of civilizations, we find that many of the age-old anxieties are being experienced today. The knowledge that humanity has arisen from these catastrophes again and again to renew civilization gives us hope. Catastrophe asks the imagination to hold both dissolution and resurrection in a single glance, to hold within the heart the ability to elevate consciousness and then to selflessly rebuild the world and to help each other day by day.

We are not without tools or guidance in this process. In fact, we, like ancient civilizations, are coming to accept that the Earth's very makeup and our own are united through our awareness and that a reverent disposition allows us to experience being on Earth in a beneficial way. We already see that the tools we need are within us. It is taught in Judaism that each human being has two kinds of work to do on himself: one is that of agriculture—preparing the soil of self for the seed of Deity to flower in. The second is that of transformation—making our bodies and hearts clean parchment for sacred words to be written on. In essence, what connects us to divine right order is our effort to reflect divine laws and wisdom. We each have consciously sought incarnation on this Earth for a purpose and thus the Earth's destiny is as much under the influence of our presence as we are under hers. How we sustain our own lives impacts how we support the Earth's divine well-being. When we regard the living soil, the treasure of clean air, and the sanctity of the honeybee with the same enchantment as we hold divinity, we will be able to create a more just and sustainable future. We have everything we need to do so now.

How we feed ourselves, how we husband the animals, how we entreat nature to reveal her secrets must be directed by the awareness that the human Earth being is made of the same elements that compose life all around us. We must show the same regard for others and our planet as we do for the people we love. To do this is to treat the world as a sacred holy place, but it is not just the Earth's body we must tend to.

We can use technology either to enable a balanced world, or we can entrap our society by it, much in the way nuclear energy, oil, and gas technologies have. The choice is ours and it is a question of focus and will. What are we really seeking from the inventions that prolong human life, for instance? Are we seeking to use it for those truly in need or to sell it off to those with the biggest bank accounts and biggest egos? Whether we adapt artificial intelligence into organ systems or manufacture entire new body parts, the degree to which we ensoul material with spirit or the degree to which spirit is encased in material prisons of technology will be determined by the attitudes and goals we hold at the outset.

Our technology poses both a great advantage and an equal danger to our evolution. Technological evolution is intrinsic to our future, but the ethics we bring to these vast powers of transformation will determine whether they destroy life or support life. Clearly the choice is to enhance our lives while not forgetting our shared responsibilities. But it is equally clear that the economic incentives that usually drive research and development belie a consciousness of unity. Instead much technological enhancement is focused on exacting more control over natural systems and populations at the expense of the survival of that natural system or the people themselves.

What this book demonstrates over and over again is that what we intend from an action shapes the inherent nature of its outcome. What it becomes may not be in our control, but it is shaped by the response of every individual to each and every situation we encounter in the course of a day, a week, a year, a lifetime, or lifetimes after that. Our immortal souls carry the record of our actions from lifetime to lifetime. There is nothing that does not affect the whole. Each of us constitutes the world makeup. Each of us constitutes a portion of the world soul as it manifests in the Earth systems themselves. All of us are godly co-creators. The consciousness we bring to everything we do, to everything we think and say, is that which shapes its outcome and its potential future.

In Kabbalah this is described as an elevation of the sparks that are attached to all living matter. We are to return the light to its source by elevating atoms to realization through our consciousness. Human awareness is a pass-through of sorts, which actually instigates change in anything it focuses its attention on. This is why blessings are so important, in that we invest our consciousness in other matter—be it our food, a person, a place of worship, a distant planet. It is also why humans must act responsibly as well.

We are one civilization made of billions of people and wildlife and nature's gifts all having a life experience together. Our family is much larger than our parents and siblings and ancestors and children. The morphogenetic fields that we all influence, in turn influence everything, everywhere. Goswami is right—quantum activism happens when any one of us becomes awake to this reality of unity consciousness. In this the world is changed.

The fact that our souls are immortal makes it possible to appreciate even more the eternal nature of each other's presence. Consciousness is reflected in each one of us as differentiated experience. Who is to know which of us has victimized or loved another in some ancient time, or why things happen to us in this life that seem so unexplainable. But it is all connected in a seamless web of time and space. We are each prisms hanging in the light, connected by the same animating light and source of life. And so it is when any one of us moves from the physical to the immaterial realms after life our communication continues, our presence can be felt, sometimes seen, and known to our second senses. The value in appreciating our eternal or immortal nature is that we are always correcting ourselves, improving our conduct and natures, realizing that we are always human *becomings*. The universe responds exponentially to the forgiving and loving heart or the repaired attitude in such a way as to impart grace and what we call miracles.

From a quantum point of view one can see forgiveness as an interference wave that changes the ripples of the past as they impact the world. Forgiveness lessens a bad act's impact both for the individuals or communities involved and for the world, because the very frequency of the past is changed by the present letting go. All forgiveness, all repentance, is a sacred act of harmonizing the world.

OUR OUTER SPACE JOURNEY

As we take this divinity of reciprocality—of the reflexive universe—deeper into the body and soul of our awareness, we are asked to inhabit outer space in the same reverent manner as one explores inner space. What is our purpose in space? What allies will we make along the way? How will we engage other off-planet civilizations? What will Earth beings in space add to the universal conversation? From the simplest reaction to someone in the grocery store, to the way we address our children and grandchildren, our interactions either foster unity or disunity, either enhance life or diminish it.

I like the metaphor that our consciousness is part of the circulatory system of the Creator or cosmic body. Just like in the tiny microcosm of our own body where each limb is served by the circulation of blood, the unity of the divine God body is the source of the soul's vital life that makes us alive and makes us each holy vessels for the life spirit to animate. As we act to usher in sustainable technologies, economies, and social welfare systems; as we decide whether to augment our bodies or develop space-based colonies; we face severe challenges of conscience and ultimately of reverence. What do we hold sacred about ourselves as individuals and in each other? What is it about joyous laughter or holding the hand of a child that causes such delight? Joy is the natural outcome of unity and sustainability is the natural process of unity-driven designs.

Here we stand, on the precipice of the future. Whether it is one of heroic development or cataclysmic ruination, or perhaps both, is being determined right now by each and every one of us. While no one lives in their physical body forever (at least not yet), what we do live with forever is the role we play while incarnate. How we conduct our business, how we treat others, what we think about when imagining the future for others or ourselves actually matters to the whole world. That is why we should try to "envision ourselves richly and consider others' needs," which is how I closed my *Future Talk* radio broadcasts from which the majority of interviews profiled here were drawn. If in that quiet, shining moment of illumination we allow the heart to open and the mind to rest in the light of knowing that we and the cosmic order are one, there is peace. So, too, we can each then reflect this peace back out into the world by choosing rightly how we do what we do as individuals in the context of our surroundings, in our personal and shared communal lives. We invigorate the light in its circulatory return to its source, through our attention. Even more so, it is through witnessing life, which is not a passive action but a holy engagement, that the universe takes on its manifold physical forms. Our consciousness shapes what will be manifested. One day each of us will know that we have taken part in becoming a conscious, divine humanity awakened to the glory of our perfection.

The ability to stay open to the unknown with faithful attendance to its potentiality is what makes any of us remain connected to a more sacred way of being in the world. We become creative enablers of the future. Our minds, like the universal mind, can create something out of nothing. Our imagination can endow the world with solutions to our energy needs, our food supply, to creating just societies, cleaning up polluted waterways, earthen lands, and skies.

It's not enough to experience oneness. All of us need to take action with this awareness. May we all together know without doubt that we humans are born to care not just for ourselves, but for each other and the world. We help create peace and well-being every day by refining our own conduct. By this, the soil of the world soul is nurtured and the life that grows there is supported. In all our relations, may the world be blessed by the beauty of harmony, the endurance of good will, and the clarity of purposeful meaning and action—thereby improving the world and our planet's well-being with our presence.

This human goodness within each one of us is capable of shaping the future of human experience now.

BIBLIOGRAPHY

Allen, Jim. *Atlantis: The Andes Solution; The Discovery of South America as the Legendary Continent of Atlantis.* New York: St. Martin's Press, 1998.

———. *Decoding Ezekiel's Temple.* rev. ed. Cambridge, England: printed by author, 2010.

Avital, Samuel. *The Body Speak™ Manual.* Boulder, Colo.: Author House, 2001.

———. *The Invisible Stairway: Kabbalistic Meditations on the Hebrew Letters.* Boulder, Colo.: Kol-Emeth Publishers, 2003.

Bauval, Robert. *Secret Chamber: The Quest for the Hall of Records.* London: Century, 1999.

Bauval, Robert, and Adrian Gilbert. *The Orion Mystery.* New York: Random House, 1994.

Bauval, Robert, and Graham Hancock. *Talisman: Sacred Cities, Secret Faith.* London: Penguin Books, 2004.

Begich, Nick, and James Roderick. *Earth Rising: The Revolution; Toward a Thousand Years of Peace.* Anchorage, Alaska: Earthpulse Press, 2000.

Berinstein, Paula. *Making Space Happen: Private Space Ventures and the Visionaries behind Them.* Medford, N.J.: Plexus Publishing, 2002.

Bird, Christopher. *The Divining Hand: The 500-year-old History of Dowsing.* New York: E. P. Dutton, 1979.

Bird, Christopher, and Peter Tompkins. *Secrets of the Soil: A Fascinating Account of Recent Breakthrough—Scientific and Spiritual—That Can Save Your Garden or Farm.* New York: Harper & Row, 1989.

———. *Secrets of the Soil: New Solutions for Restoring Our Planet.* rev. ed. Anchorage, Alaska: Earthpulse Press, 1998.

Boone, J. Allen. *Kinship with All Life.* New York: Harper Collins, 1976.

Bowman, Carol. *Return from Heaven: Beloved Relatives Reincarnated within Your Family.* New York: Harper Collins, 2001.

Braden, Gregg. *The Isaiah Effect: Decoding the Lost Science of Prayer and Prophecy.* New York: Three Rivers Press, 2001.

———. *Secrets of the Lost Mode of Prayer: The Hidden Power of Beauty, Blessings, Wisdom and Hurt.* Carlsbad, Calif.: Hay House, 2006.

Bradshaw, Gay. *Elephants on the Edge: What Animals Teach Us about Humanity.* New Haven, Conn.: Yale University Press, 2010.

Brown, Lester R. *Full Planet, Empty Plates: The New Geopolitics of Food Scarcity.* New York: W.W. Norton & Company, 2012.

Burrows, William E. *The Infinite Journey: Eyewitness Accounts of NASA and the Age of Space.* New York: Discovery Books, 2000.

Callahan, Phillip S. *Paramagnetism: Rediscovering Nature's Secret Force of Growth.* Austin, Tex.: Acres U.S.A., 1995.

Calleman, Carl J. *The Purposeful Universe: How Quantum Theory and Mayan Cosmology Explain the Origin and Evolution of Life.* Rochester, Vt.: Bear & Company, 2009.

Celente, Gerald. *What Zizi Gave Honeyboy: A True Story about Love, Wisdom, and the Soul of America.* New York: William Morrow, 2002.

Childre, Doc Lew, Howard Martin, and Donna Beech. *The Heartmath Solution: The Institute of HeartMath's Revolutionary Program for Engaging the Power of the Heart's Intelligence.* New York: HarperCollins, 1999.

Chopra, Deepak, and David Simon. *Grow Younger, Live Longer: 10 Steps to Reverse Aging.* New York: Harmony Books, 2001.

Clow, Barbara Hand. *Awakening the Planetary Mind: Beyond the Trauma of the Past to a New Era of Creativity.* rev. ed. Rochester, Vt.: Bear & Company, 2011.

Cremo, Michael A., and Richard L. Thompson. *Forbidden Archeology: The Hidden History of the Human Race.* San Diego, Calif.: Bhaktivedanta Institute, 1993.

DeMeo, James. *Saharasia: The 4000 BCE Origins of Child Abuse, Sex Repression, Warfare, and Social Violence in the Deserts of the Old World.* Ashland, Ore.: Natural Energy Works, 1998.

DiPietro, Vincent, Gregory Molenaar, and John Brandenburg. *Unusual Martian Surface Features.* 4th ed. Glenn Dale, Md.: Mars Research, 1988.

Dossey, Larry. *Healing Words: The Power of Prayer and the Practice of Medicine.* San Francisco: Harper, 1994.

———. *Prayer is Good Medicine: How to Reap the Healing Benefits of Prayer.* San Francisco: Harper, 1996.

———. *Reinventing Medicine: Beyond Mind-Body to a New Era of Healing.* San Francisco: Harper, 1999.

Fox, Matthew. *The Pope's War: Why Ratzinger's Secret Crusade Has Imperiled the Church and How It Can Be Saved.* New York: Sterling Ethos, 2011.

Hamaker, John D., and Donald A. Weaver. *The Survival of Civilization Depends upon Our Solving Three Problems: Carbon Dioxide, Investment Money, and Population; Selected Papers of John D. Hamaker.* Woodside, Calif.: Hamaker-Weaver Publishers, 1982.

Hancock, Graham. *Fingerprints of the Gods: The Evidence of Earth's Lost Civilizations.* New York: Bantam Books, 1996.

———. *Underworld: The Mysterious Origins of Civilization.* New York: Crown, 2002.

Hartmann, Thom. *The Last Hours of Ancient Sunlight: The Fate of the World and What We Can Do before It's Too Late.* rev. ed. New York: Three Rivers Press, 2004.

Hauk, Gunther. *Toward Saving the Honeybee.* East Troy, Wis.: Biodynamic Farming and Gardening Association, 2003.

Herm, Eric. *Son of a Farmer, Child of the Earth: A Path to Agriculture's Higher Consciousness.* Brooklyn, N.Y.: Dreamriver Press, 2010.

Hieronimus, J. Zohara Meyerhoff. *Kabbalistic Teachings of the Female Prophets: The Seven Holy Women of Ancient Israel.* Rochester, Vt.: Inner Traditions, 2008.

———. *Sanctuary of the Divine Presence: Hebraic Teachings on Initiation and Illumination.* Rochester, Vt.: Inner Traditions, 2012.

Hieronimus, Robert R. *America's Secret Destiny: Spiritual Vision and the Founding of a Nation.* Rochester, Vt.: Destiny Books, 1989.

———. *The Founding Fathers, Secret Societies.* Rochester, Vt.: Destiny Books, 2005.

———. *United Symbolism of America.* Pompton, N.J.: New Page Books, 2008.

Jacobson, Simon. *Toward a Meaningful Life: The Wisdom of the Sages.* rev. ed. New York: William Morrow, 2002.

Jenkins, John Major. *Galactic Alignment: The Transformation of Consciousness according to the Mayan, Egyptian, and Vedic Traditions.* Rochester, Vt.: Bear & Company, 2002.

Kosko, Bart. *Heaven in a Chip: Fuzzy Visions of Society and Science in the Digital Age.* New York: Three Rivers Press, 2000.

Krapf, Phillip H. *The Challenge of Contact: A Mainstream Journalist's Report on Interplanetary Diplomacy.* rev. ed. Mt. Shasta, Calif.: Origin Press, 2003.

Kurzweil, Ray. *The Age of Spiritual Machines: When Computers Exceed HumanIntelligence.* New York: Viking, 1999.

———. *Are We Spiritual Machines: Ray Kurzweil vs. the Critics of Strong A.I.* Seattle, Wash.: Discovery Institute, 2001.

Laszlo, Ervin. *The Chaos Point: The World at the Crossroads.* San Francisco: Hampton Roads, 2006.

———. *Science and the Akashic Field: An Integral Theory of Everything.* 2nd ed. Rochester, Vt.: Inner Traditions, 2007.

LaViolette, Paul A. *Earth Under Fire: Humanity's Survival of the Apocalypse.* Alexandria, Va.: Starlane Publications, 1997.

———. *Earth under Fire: Understanding Mythology as the Science of the Past.* Broomfield, Colo.: Conscious Wave, 1999. Videocassette (VHS), 54 min.

———. *The Talk of the Galaxy: An ET Message for Us?* Alexandria, Va.: Starlane Publications, 2000.

Lavoie, Gilbert. *Resurrected: Tangible Evidence That Jesus Rose from the Dead.* Chicago, Ill.: Thomas Moore Publishing, 2000.

Leir, Roger. *The Aliens and the Scalpel: Scientific Proof of Extraterrestrial Implants in Humans.* Columbus, N.C.: Granite Publishing, 1998.

———. *Casebook: Alien Implants; Shocking Evidence That Alien Implants Are Real as Told by the Doctor Who Removed Them.* Edited and compiled by Whitley Strieber. New York: Dell, 2000.

Mallove, Eugene. *Fire from Ice: Searching for the Truth behind the Cold Fusion Furor.* New York: John Wiley & Sons, 1991.

Marks, William E. Waterway. *The Holy Order of Water: Healing Earth's Waters and Ourselves.* rev. ed. Great Barrington, Mass.: Bell Pond Books, 2001.

———. *Water Voices from around the World,* ed., Ashland, Ohio: Atlas Books, 2007.

Martin, James. *After the Internet: Alien Intelligence.* New York: Regnery, 2000.

McTaggart, Lynne. *The Field: The Quest for the Secret Force of the Universe.* New York: Harper Collins, 2002.

Metzner, Ralph. *Green Psychology: Transforming Our Relationship to the Earth.* Rochester, Vt.: Park Street Press, 1999.

Michell, John. *The Sacred Center: The Ancient Art of Locating Sanctuaries.* Rochester, Vt.: Inner Traditions, 2009.

Mini, John. *Day of Destiny.* Sausalito, Calif.: Trans-Hyperborean Institute of Science Publishing, 1998.

———. *The Aztec Virgin: The Secret Mystical Tradition of Our Lady of Guadalupe.* Sausalito, Calif.: Trans-Hyperborean Institute of Science Publishing, 2000.

Modi, Shakuntala. *Remarkable Healings: A Psychiatrist Discovers Unsuspected Roots of Mental and Physical Illness.* Charlottesville, Va.: Hampton Roads, 1998.

———. *Memories of God and Creation: Remembering from the Subconscious Mind.* Charlottesville, Va.: Hampton Roads, 2000.

Molnar, Michael R. *The Star of Bethlehem: The Legacy of the Magi.* Piscataway, N.J.: Rutgers University Press, 1999.

Moody, Raymond. *The Light Beyond: New Explorations.* New York: Bantam, 1988.

———. *The Last Laugh: A New Philosophy of Near-Death Experiences, Apparitions, and the Paranormal.* Charlottesville, Va.: Hampton Roads, 1999.

Moody, Raymond, and Diane Arcangel. *Life after Loss: Conquering Grief and Finding Hope*. New York: HarperCollins, 2001.

Moody, Raymond, and Paul Perry. *Reunions: Visionary Encounters with Departed Loved Ones*. New York: Villard Books, 1993.

Moore, Thomas. *Original Self: Living with Paradox and Originality*. New York: Harper Perennial, 2001.

Moravec, Hans. *Robot: Mere Machine to Transcendent Mind*. Oxford, U.K.: Oxford University Press, 1999.

Morse, Melvin L., and Paul Perry. *Closer to the Light: Learning from the Near-Death Experiences of Children*. New York: Villard, 1990.

———. *Transformed by the Light*. New York: Villard, 1992.

———. *Parting Visions: Uses and Meanings of Pre-Death, Psychic, and Spiritual Experiences*. New York: Villard, 1994.

Newland, Kathleen. *Climate Change and Migration Dynamics*. Washington, D.C.: Migration Policy Institute, 2011.

Newton, Michael. *Journey of Souls: Case Studies of Life between Lives*. St. Paul, Minn.: Llewellyn Publications, 1994.

———. *Destiny of Souls: New Case Studies of Life between Lives*. St. Paul, Minn.: Llewellyn Publications, 2000.

Obissier, Patrick. *Biogenealogy: Decoding the Psychic Roots of Illness; Freedom from the Ancestral Origins of Disease*. Translated by Jon E. Graham. Rochester, Vt.: Healing Arts Press, 2006.

Oslon, James. *The Whole-Brain Path to Peace: The Role of Left- and Right-Brain Dominance in the Polarization and Reunification of America*. San Rafael, Calif.: Origin Press, 2011.

Oz, Mehmet. *Healing from the Heart: A Leading Surgeon Combines Eastern and Western Traditions to Create the Medicine of the Future*. New York: Plume, 1999.

Pearce, Joseph Chilton. *Crack in the Cosmic Egg: Challenging Constructs of Mind and Reality*. New York: Pocket Books, 1973.

———. *The Biology of Transcendence: A Blueprint of the Human Spirit*. Rochester, Vt.: Park Street Press, 2002.

———. *Spiritual Initiation and the Breakthrough of Consciousness: The Bond of Power*. rev. ed. Rochester, Vt.: Park Street Press, 2003.

———. *The Death of Religion and the Rebirth of Spirit: A Return to the Intelligence of the Heart.* Rochester, Vt.: Park Street Press, 2007.

Perkins, John. *Confessions of an Economic Hit Man.* New York: Plume, 2005.

———. *Hoodwinked: An Economic Hit Man Reveals Why the Global Economy Imploded—and How to Fix It.* New York: Crown Business, 2011.

Pert, Candace. *Molecules of Emotion: Why You Feel the Way You Feel.* New York: Simon & Schuster, 1997.

Pesic, Peter. *Labyrinth: A Search for the Hidden Meaning of Science.* Cambridge, Mass.: MIT Press, 2001.

Petersen, John L. *Out of the Blue: Wild Cards and Other Big Future Surprises; How to Anticipate and Respond to Profound Change.* Arlington, Va.: Arlington Institute, 1997.

Robbins, John. *Diet for a New America: How Your Food Choices Affect Your Health, Happiness, and the Future of Life on Earth.* rev. ed. Tiburon, Calif.: H. J. Kramer, 1998.

———. *No Happy Cows: Dispatches from the Frontlines of the Food Revolution.* San Francisco: Conari Press, 2012.

Ross, T. Edward, and Richard D. Wright. *The Divining Mind: A Guide to Dowsing and Self-Awareness.* Rochester, Vt.: Destiny Books, 1990.

Sardello, Robert. *Love and the World: A Guide to Conscious Soul Practice.* Great Barrington, Mass.: Lindisfarne Press, 2001.

Schwartz, Stephan A. *Opening to the Infinite: The Art and Science of Non-Local Awareness.* Langley, Wash.: Nemoseen Media, 2007.

Schoch, Robert M., and Robert Aquinas McNally. *Voices of the Rocks: A Scientist Looks at Catastrophes and Ancient Civilizations.* New York: Harmony Books, 1999.

Shanor, Karen Nesbitt. *The Emerging Mind: New Research into the Meaning of Consciousness.* Based on the Smithsonian Institution Lecture Series. New York: St. Martin's Press, 2001.

Shanor, Karen Nesbitt, and Jagmeet Kanwal. *Bats Sing, Mice Giggle: The Surprising Science of Animals' Inner Lives.* London: Totem Books, 2009.

Sheldrake, Rupert. *Dogs That Know When Their Owners Are Coming Home: And Other Unexplained Powers of Animals*. New York: Three Rivers Press, 2000.

———. *Morphic Resonance: The Nature of Formative Causation*. 4th ed. Rochester, Vt.: Park Street Press, 2009.

Sitchin, Zecharia. *The Cosmic Code: The Incredible Truth about the Anunnaki Who Divulged Cosmic Secrets to Mankind*. Book 6 of the Earth Chronicles. New York: Avon, 1998.

———. *The Lost Book of Enki: Memoirs and Prophecies of an Extraterrestrial God*. Rochester, Vt.: Bear & Company, 2001.

Snow, Chet B., and Helen Wombach. *Mass Dreams of the Future*. New York: McGraw-Hill, 1989.

Stevenson, Ian. *Children Who Remember Previous Lives: A Question of Reincarnation*. rev. ed. Jefferson, N.C.: McFarland & Company, 2001.

Stock, Gregory. *Redesigning Humans: Our Inevitable Genetic Future*. New York: Houghton Mifflin, 2002.

Story, Ronald D., ed. *The Encyclopedia of Extraterrestrial Encounters: A Definitive, Illustrated, A–Z Guide to All Things Alien*. New York: New American Library, 2001.

Stover, Dawn. "The Big Melt." *Popular Science* 258, no.5 (May 2001): 54.

Swann, Ingo. *Penetration: The Question of Extraterrestrial and Human Telepathy*. Rapid City, S.Dak.: Ingo Swann Books, 1998.

———. *Secrets of Power, Vol. 1: Individual Empowerment versus the Societal Panorama of Power and Depowerment*. Rapid City, S.Dak.: Ingo Swann Books, 2000.

Sweet, William. *A Journey into Prayer: Pioneers of Prayer in the Laboratory; Agents of Science or Satan?* Bloomington, Ind.: Xlibris Publishing, 2007.

Talbott, David, and Wallace Thornhill. *Thunderbolts of the Gods*. Portland, Ore.: Mikamar Publishing, 2005.

Temple, Robert. *The Sirius Mystery: New Scientific Evidence of Alien Contact 5,000 Years Ago*. Rochester, Vt.: Destiny Books, 1998.

———. *Oracles of the Dead: Ancient Techniques for Predicting the Future*. Rochester, Vt.: Destiny Books, 2005.

Tiller, William. *Science and Human Transformation: Subtle Energies, Intentionality, and Consciousness*. Walnut Creek, Calif.: Pavior Publishing, 1997.

Tiller, William, Walter E. Dibble Jr., and Michael J. Kohane. *Conscious Acts of Creation: The Emergence of a New Physics*. Walnut Creek, Calif.: Pavior Publishing, 2001.

Tipler, Frank. *The Physics of Immortality: Modern Cosmology, God, and the Resurrection of the Dead*. New York: Anchor Books, 1997.

Toye, Lenard, and Lori Toye. *New World Atlas: Earth Changes Prophecies for Europe and Africa*. Payson, Ariz.: Seventh Ray Publishing, 1996.

Tunneshende, Merilyn. *Don Juan and the Art of Sexual Energy: The Rainbow Serpent of the Toltecs*. Rochester, Vt.: Bear & Company, 2001.

———. *Don Juan and the Power of Medicine Dreaming: A Nagual Woman's Journey of Healing*. Rochester, Vt.: Bear & Company, 2002.

Van Flandern, Thomas. *Dark Matter, Missing Planets, and New Comets: Paradoxes Resolved, Origins Illuminated*. Berkeley, Calif.: North Atlantic Books, 1993.

Wagar, W. Warren. *A Short History of the Future*. 3rd ed. Chicago, Ill.: University of Chicago Press, 1999.

Walker, Evan Harris. *The Physics of Consciousness: The Quantum Mind and the Meaning of Life*. New York: Perseus Books, 2000.

Walters, Charles. *Unforgiven: The American Economic System Sold for Debt and War*. 2nd ed. Austin, Tex.: Acres U.S.A., 2003.

Warren, Larry P. and Peter Robbins. *Left at East Gate: A First-Hand Account of the Rendlesham Forest UFO Incident, Its Cover-up and Investigation*. New York: Cosimo-ON-Demand, 1997.

Weidensaul, Scott. *The Ghost with Trembling Wings: Science, Wishful Thinking, and the Search for Lost Species*. New York: North Point Press, 2002.

Weiss, Brian L. *Through Time into Healing*. New York: Simon & Schuster, 1992.

———. *Mirrors of Time: Using Regression for Physical, Emotional, and Spiritual Healing*. Carlsbad, Calif.: Hay House, 2002.

Wells, Jonathan. *Icons of Evolution: Science or Myth? Why Much of What We Teach about Evolution Is Wrong*. Washington, D.C.: Regnery Publishing, 2000.

Whale, Jon. *The Catalyst of Power: The Assemblage Point of Man.* Findhorn, Scotland: Findhorn Press, 2001.

Wilhelm, Richard, and Cary F. Baynes, trans. *I Ching or Book of Changes,* 3rd. ed. Princeton, N.J.: Princeton University Press, 1967.

Wolf, Fred Alan. *The Dreaming Universe: A Mind-Expanding Journey into the Realm Where Psyche and Physics Meet.* New York: Touchstone, 1995.

———. *Mind into Matter: A New Alchemy of Science and Spirit.* Needham, Mass.: Moment Point Press, 2000.

Young, Arthur. *The Reflexive Universe: Evolution of Consciousness.* New York: Doubleday, 1976.

Zaleski, Carol. *The Life of the World to Come: Near-Death Experience and Christian Hope.* New York: Oxford University Press, 1996.

INDEX

Page numbers in *italics* refer to illustrations.

BOOKS OF RELATED INTEREST

Kabbalistic Teachings of the Female Prophets
The Seven Holy Women of Ancient Israel
by J. Zohara Meyerhoff Hieronimus, D.H.L.

Sanctuary of the Divine Presence
Hebraic Teachings on Initiation and Illumination
by J. Zohara Meyerhoff Hieronimus, D.H.L.

The New Science and Spirituality Reader
Edited by Ervin Laszlo and Kingsley L. Dennis

Dawn of the Akashic Age
New Consciousness, Quantum Resonance,
and the Future of the World
by Ervin Laszlo and Kingsley L. Dennis

New Consciousness for a New World
How to Thrive in Transitional Times and Participate
in the Coming Spiritual Renaissance
by Kingsley L. Dennis

Science and the Akashic Field
An Integral Theory of Everything
by Ervin Laszlo

Morphic Resonance
The Nature of Formative Causation
by Rupert Sheldrake

Lost Knowledge of the Ancients
A Graham Hancock Reader
Edited by Glenn Kreisberg

INNER TRADITIONS • BEAR & COMPANY
P.O. Box 388
Rochester, VT 05767
1-800-246-8648
www.InnerTraditions.com

Or contact your local bookseller